SEARCHING FOR
LONE STAR

SEARCHING FOR LONE STAR

A Tale of Two Brothers

By **Mike Farris**
and **Paul Heckmann**

TCU PRESS
Fort Worth, Texas

Library of Congress Cataloging-in-Publication Data

Names: Farris, Mike, 1955 June 30- author | Heckmann, Paul author
Title: Searching for Lone Star : a tale of two brothers / by Mike Farris and Paul Heckmann.
Description: Fort Worth, Texas : TCU Press, [2026] | Includes bibliographical references and index.
Identifiers: LCCN 2026025478 (print) | LCCN 2026025479 (ebook) | ISBN 9780875659862 paperback | ISBN 9780875659879 ebook
Subjects: LCSH: Kearns, John Wesley, III, 1942-1972 | Heckmann, Paul | United States. Central Intelligence Agency--Officials and employees | Vietnam War, 1961-1975--Secret service--United States | Vietnam War, 1961-1975--Campaigns--Laos | Tardive dyskinesia--Patients--Texas | Brothers--Texas | Adoptees--Family relationships--Texas | Adoptees--Identification | LCGFT: Biographies
Classification: LCC DS559.8.M44 F37 2026 (print) | LCC DS559.8.M44 (ebook) | DDC 959.704/38--dc23/eng/20260608
LC record available at https://lccn.loc.gov/2026025478
LC ebook record available at https://lccn.loc.gov/2026025479

TCU PRESS

TCU Box 298300
Fort Worth, Texas 76129
www.tcupress.com

This book is dedicated to all the orphans and those waiting to be adopted. Stay positive. God has a plan.

Paul Heckmann

To the unsung heroes of the "secret war."

Mike Farris

CONTENTS

PROLOGUE
The Wall

"Vietnam presumably taught us that the United States could not serve as the world's policeman; it should also have taught us the dangers of trying to be the world's midwife to democracy when the birth is scheduled to take place under conditions of guerrilla war."

Jeane Kirkpatrick

A white marble wall stands at the north end of the original headquarters building of the Central Intelligence Agency in Langley, Virginia. The Wall bears the inscription: IN HONOR OF THOSE MEMBERS OF THE CENTRAL INTELLIGENCE AGENCY WHO GAVE THEIR LIVES IN THE SERVICE OF THEIR COUNTRY. It is intended as a memorial to CIA employees who died in the line of duty—"a silent, simple memorial to those CIA officers who have made the ultimate sacrifice,"[1] officers whose sacrifices are noted by stars carved into the Wall. Many of them were Paramilitary Operations Officers of the CIA's Special Activities Center.

The Wall was commissioned in 1973 by the CIA Fine Arts Commission and was sculpted by Harold Vogel in 1974. At its inception, it contained thirty-one stars carved in rows above and below the inscription, but they continue to increase in number to the current total of 140. The six rows below the inscription are progressively longer as they descend: Row 1 has twenty stars, Row 2 has twenty-one, and so on until Row 6, which has twenty-five. There is another row of five stars above the inscription. Each star is two-and-a-quarter inches tall, two-and-a-half inches wide, and a half-inch deep. The rows are six inches apart. Likewise, the stars are six inches apart.

An American flag is mounted on the left side of the wall while a CIA flag is mounted on the right. Below the stars is a steel frame with a case that bears a book bound in black Moroccan goatskin. *The Book of Honor.* In it, the stars are arranged by date. Some include the name of the fallen represented by the star, but the names of more than thirty still remain shrouded in secrecy.

A stone carver from Virginia named Tim Johnston, who began his career as a mason by cutting bathroom tiles, creates the stars.[2] The official CIA website describes the process of adding stars this way:

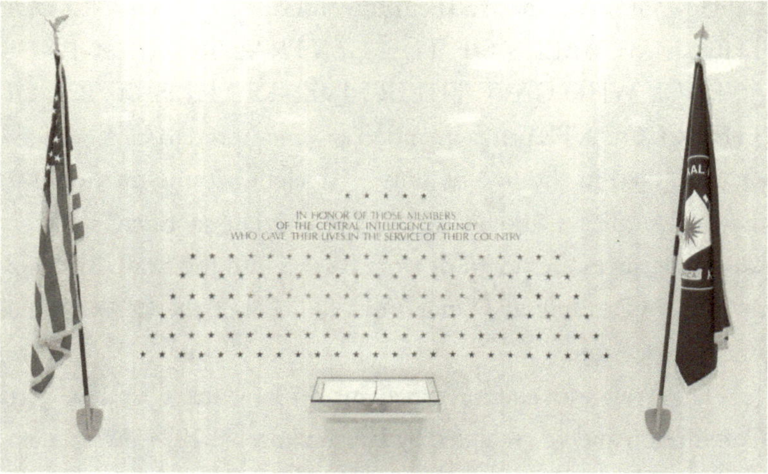

CIA Memorial Wall. *Public domain.*

> A stone carver creates a star by first tracing the new star on the wall using a template. . . . The stone carver uses both a pneumatic air hammer and a chisel to carve out the traced pattern. After carving the star, the stone carver cleans the dust and sprays the star black, which as the star ages, fades to gray.[3]

The Wall is considered sacred to the CIA and its officers. It's a memorial. A shrine. New CIA officers take their oath in front of the Wall, which looms over them as a reminder of the trust delegated to them. An annual memorial service is held in front of the Wall at which the names—at least those that have been disclosed—are read aloud. Sometimes, previously classified identities are revealed.

At the annual service on June 2, 2000, CIA Director George J. Tenet stood in front of the Wall and addressed a group that included past and present CIA employees, as well as some family members. In addition to honoring the sacrifice of those represented by the stars, which numbered seventy-seven at the time, he was there to lift the shroud of anonymity for some.

> To us, the men and women of CIA, they [the stars] are more than just inspiring symbols. They are fallen colleagues and cherished friends who profoundly touched the life of this Agency. And to you, their wives and husbands and fiancees, their mothers and fathers, sisters and brothers, children and grandchildren, nieces and nephews, they are loved ones forever lost, families forever fractured.
>
> Each of the seventy-seven irreplaceable individuals had places to go, goals to reach and people to love. None of

them would have wanted the distinction of being on this Wall of Honor. But now, they are eternally joined in quiet constellation.[4]

Among those whose names were revealed for the first time was a Texan named John W. Kearns III, a CIA special operations officer whose call sign was, fittingly, "Lone Star." Kearns was killed during the CIA's paramilitary operation in Laos during the Vietnam War, its so-called "secret war," though it was not really "secret." As former CIA Director Richard Helms wrote in his memoir, "The debate in the American press about the 'secret CIA war' in Laos comes down, as do many so-called secret things in Washington, to a question of whether or not the writer or his source knew the 'secret.'" Helms also wrote of the sacrifices made, especially by CIA personnel, during the action in Laos. "There are no bystanders in guerrilla warfare, and there are enough stars on the memorial wall in the Agency building to prove it."[5]

John "Lone Star" Kearns has been mentioned in passing in a few books,[6] including Richard Helms's memoir. But for the most part, his story has stayed pretty well unknown. He was shrouded in CIA secrecy for nearly three decades and then, even after the revelation of his name in 2000, mired in obscurity. Until now.

CHAPTER ONE

Who Am I?

"Knowing where you come from, good or bad, becomes more important the older you get."

Theodore "TC" Calvin, *Magnum, P.I.*

I guess I could have been a member of Baby Boomers Anonymous, if there were such an organization. I would introduce myself at meetings like this: "My name is Paul Heckmann and I am a baby boomer." But I am not your typical baby boomer. Oh, sure, I fit the birth date criteria. Most (but not all) historians, sociologists, and commentators define it as the period between the end of World War II in 1945 and 1964. According to the *Oxford English Dictionary*, that cutoff date was chosen because of the mass introduction in 1964 of the birth control pill, which had been approved by the FDA in 1960.[1]

Professor Leslie J. Nason of the University of Southern California is generally credited with first using the term "baby boomer" in a 1963 article in the *Daily Press*. The title of the article was "Baby Boomers, Grown Up, Storm Ivy-Covered Walls." He warned that colleges and universities were on the verge of being overwhelmed by a "flood of students who will be without the Federal Aid provided for the GI's" who entered college following World War II, doubling enrollments.[2]

One of the most famous explanations for why the boom happened was the Easterlin hypothesis, named for its champion, economist Richard Easterlin at University of Southern California (USC). He attributed it to a period of sustained economic prosperity that followed the end of the war. He hypothesized that a positive correlation existed between income and fertility when couples had more income and a higher standard of living relative to when they grew up, which he called "relative status." Following the Great Depression and the economic hardships of the war, young couples had more income and higher standards of living and, accordingly, were more amenable to, and financially capable of, raising families. Thus, the boom in babies.[3]

I fit squarely in the middle of that time range—born July 9, 1954. But my entry into the world was atypical and didn't fit with the Easterlin hypothesis. My birth mother, Frances Kearns, was in the midst of a separation from her husband, who was stationed in Germany in the army. Following an affair with a Fort Worth police officer named Bobby Joe Reynolds, she became pregnant with me. Out of work, struggling to support four children she already had—two boys and two girls—and unable to support a fifth, she did the only thing she could under the circumstances: she gave me up for adoption. Her sister-in-law drove her to the Volunteers of America, which we now know as the Salvation Army, in Fort Worth, where she gave birth. A Waco couple named Fred and Joyce Heckmann adopted me a few months later. They had adopted a little girl, Kathi, from the same place two years prior, and that was the family in which I grew up.

In my late twenties, I began experiencing occasional episodes of uncontrollable anger that manifested in road rage and physical fighting. That followed me into my forties. Once, in the early 1990s,

I dealt with a tailgater with my fists. Or at least with my fist. I was living in Carrollton, a Dallas suburb, at the time, driving my nearly new Mustang convertible, when I noticed him in my rearview mirror. Each time I changed lanes, he followed suit. Finally I pulled into a turn lane and stopped, to see what he would do. He pulled in right behind me and got out of his car. I did the same. When he rushed me, I dropped him with one punch. Fortunately, police officers had observed the entire incident, including the fact that this guy had been tailgating me and provoked the altercation. A judge cut me loose, and I never found out what had upset my antagonist.

Because of my anger issues, I began seeing a psychiatrist, who diagnosed me as bipolar/manic depressive. I didn't know a lot about bipolar disorder at the time; though I've become quite an expert since then. It traces its roots back to the ancient Greeks, when Hippocrates, the "father of medicine" and namesake of the Hippocratic Oath, first documented mania and depression, or melancholia. Bipolar disorder manifests itself in wild mood swings as well as energy swings. It's more than just ups and downs, which is the popular perception. It's a study in extremes. The highs can result in mania, and the lows can dip deep into depression. These episodes can last for hours, days, or even weeks. Those suffering from it often find themselves overwhelmed by the minutiae of daily living.

The psychiatrist prescribed a drug I had never heard of at the time, called Seroquel. I would later come to know plenty about Seroquel, none of it good. But then he asked me a question that really surprised me: "Are you adopted?" At first it seemed as if the question came out of left field, but it made sense when he explained that family history might help determine whether my bipolar disorder was genetic. I don't ever recall a time when I *didn't* know I was adopted, but I had never really had a reason to search for my birth family. After all, as far as I was concerned, my mom and dad were always Fred and Joyce Heckmann, and I always had a big sister named Kathi. It never seemed that important to me to know who my *other* family was.

As I contemplated why the psychiatrist asked that question, I began, for the first time, to consider whether it might be beneficial, at least medically, to find my birth mother. My life path had been uneven, at best. As a youngster, I'd had run-ins with the police. During my high school years, those run-ins became more frequent. I began smoking pot and drinking heavily. I experimented, albeit only briefly, with LSD and other drugs. In college, I walked on to the football team at Texas A&I University. With the popular acceptance that came with that, and the social pressures that accompanied it, I drank more beer, smoked more pot, and even made the occasional trip to the desert to find peyote. As I grew into adulthood, I was still drinking and smoking pot, but I added a new drug into the mix: cocaine. The results were devastating. Drug addiction had a drastic psychological effect on me both physically and emotionally, but I went into rehab and got sober. Still, addiction exacted a toll that I have paid for most of my life since.

In my adult years, I learned of the possibility, if not probability, that I was dyslexic. With that possibility in mind, a lot of things fell into place that explained my difficulties in school as a kid, and even in college. I also learned that I might have a place on the autism spectrum, which would also explain some things, particularly as related to my "working memory," which was poor, at best. If autism had adversely affected it, that would explain why I could remember things from many years prior but couldn't memorize a simple phone number.

I also learned that all of those problems, whether officially diagnosed or not—drug addiction and alcohol abuse, dyslexia, autism, and bipolar disorder—can be hereditary. I began to wonder if maybe it was time for a little self-discovery. I knew how I had been raised, but I always seemed to have a bit of a rebel in me. There were times when my conduct was not a reflection of the values that Fred and Joyce Heckmann instilled in me. I had heard the arguments about how and what shapes our lives—nature versus nurture, and all that. I couldn't help but wonder if nature, of which I was totally ignorant, was controlling me. On the other hand, had I simply rebelled against nurture? That raised a corollary question: If I had been nurtured differently, raised in another family—my biological family—would I have turned out differently? Would I have been sitting in a psychiatrist's office wondering what the hell was wrong with me?

I decided to look for some answers. That meant searching for my birth family, which triggered, really for the first time, my curiosity on specific questions. Who was my birth mother? Who was my birth father? I considered Joyce to be my "real mother" and Fred to be my "real father," because they had raised me. But what were my birth parents like? Did I look like either of them? Did I act like either of them?

There was another family question. My sister Kathi was my "real sister," not in the sense that she was my biological sister, though she was the only sister I had ever known. But she, too, was adopted. Did I have any flesh and blood siblings? What difference might it have made in my life if I did and if I had been raised with them? These thoughts and questions all swirled around in my dyslexic, autistic, bipolar, drug-and-alcohol-addled brain. Maybe it was time to find some answers.

I didn't have much to go on other than a "birth certificate." I put "birth certificate" in quotation marks because, when I was born in 1954, adoptions in Texas courts were closed. A supplementary certificate would be issued that identified the adoptive parents, but not the birth parents, and the original birth certificate was sealed. The Internet wasn't as pervasive in the 1990s as it is today. Just some little E-groups that were really not all that widely used. But I figured a little help was better than no help, so I latched on to a group that focused on finding birth families. Much to my surprise, in response to my posting, a woman contacted me. She said she had read about my journey and that she thought she could help me. I readily agreed. I didn't have my hopes up, but within a few months, she called and said she had found my birth family. Specifically, she had found my birth mother, a woman named Frances Kearns.

We set up a phone call to talk to her. I acted like a lawyer working to prepare for a deposition, writing down questions and random thoughts about all the things I wanted to learn from her. Who was I? Why did she give me up? Who was my father? Why didn't they keep me? Did I have any brothers and sisters? I had so many questions, yet at the same time I was apprehensive about the possible answers. My nerves were a jumbled wreck.

First time Paul met his birth mother, Frances Kearns, in Hillsboro, Texas. *Photo courtesy of Paul Heckmann.*

When I finally, after forty years, connected with my birth mother by telephone and heard her voice for the first time, emotion overwhelmed me. I had barely introduced myself when she cut me off in mid-sentence with "I've been waiting for this call all my life!"

And so began my introduction to my birth family.

But my birth father, Bobby Joe Reynolds, who was living in California and whom we also located a little later, was not nearly so gracious as Frances. One day I got up my nerve and called him. "Is this the Bobby Joe Reynolds who was a Fort Worth Police officer in late 1953?" I asked when he answered.

"Yes," he said, but his tone was wary. I, however, was really excited!

"My name is Paul Heckmann. Frances Kearns is my mother, and you are my father."

There was a brief pause, then, "I don't know who you are. Leave me alone." *Click.*

Well, at least I tried. I later sent a letter with some photos of him with Frances and her kids, just to point out that, even if he denied being my father, I indeed knew Frances—or how else would I have gotten the photos? After several months, he initiated a call to me. He said, "If I'm your dad, I need to tell you that all the men in our family die early from heart disease."

How uplifting. As if I didn't already have enough physical problems to worry about, now I would have to add cardiac issues to the list. Our conversation went on for a while longer, and he finally opened up. A bit. He told me about meeting Frances. He said that, when she told him she was pregnant, he asked her to marry him. I had to give him credit for doing the honorable thing. Or at least offering to. But she turned him down. He told me that he worked at a dog track in California and suggested that I come out to see him. I told him I would.

I never did. He passed away a few years ago without my ever meeting him in person. I guess you could say that my entire relationship with my biological father consisted of two telephone calls.

I had other conversations with Frances, though, and actually met her in person in 1995. I learned that I had two half-brothers, John and Ron, and two half-sisters, Sandy and Sharon, all older than I. But I also found out that one of those brothers was no longer alive. In fact, he had been killed in Laos in 1972 during the Vietnam War. I had been eighteen at the time, dreading the possibility of being drafted and sent to Vietnam while he was dying over there. As I am a curious person by nature (or is it by nurture? I'm not sure), I started doing my homework to find out more about that half-brother I would never meet. And asking questions of my newfound half-sisters. They loved to talk about their brother. Johnny, they called him. *Was I anything like Johnny?* I wondered.

Johnny, as it turned out, was a bona fide American hero. He had been a soldier in the US Army during the Vietnam War, but then came the kicker: After returning from Vietnam and getting a college degree, he had been recruited by the CIA as a paramilitary operator in Laos. That little bit of information really intrigued me, so I began to investigate in earnest to learn about my hero half-brother. A hero who died halfway around the world while I was still struggling with drugs and alcohol, still struggling to become a high school graduate, still struggling to grow up, and still without the remotest clue that I even had a brother.

The search helped provide me with a sense of meaning to my life, particularly in light of the physical calamities, beyond addiction, that had befallen me—and that would befall me in the future. With the assistance of Texas Senator John Cornyn, my investigation involved Freedom of Information Act requests and declassification of previously secret government documents on US involvement in Laos during the Vietnam War. I learned that my half-brother had, indeed, been a hero. And that he had been awarded the CIA Intelligence Star "in recognition of his courageous performance under hazardous conditions."[4]

What follows is a cautionary tale. At the same time, it is ultimately an inspirational tale of heroism, of personal discovery, and of overcoming adversity. It is a story of two half-brothers who never knew each other, yet one inspired the other.

It is a story of sacrifice, of love, of loss, and ultimately, of family.

CHAPTER TWO

1954—It Was a Very Good Year

"One day I'll remember. Remember everything that happened: the good, the bad, those who survived . . . and those that did not."

Bilbo Baggins in *The Hobbit*

As 1954 dawned, few could predict exactly how event-filled it would be, including a lot of "firsts." On New Year's Day, NBC broadcast the first coast-to-coast color television program, featuring the Tournament of Roses parade. Other notable events that followed included:

The first mass polio vaccination of children took place in Pittsburgh, Pennsylvania.

The first hydrogen bomb was tested in the Bikini Atoll in the Pacific.

Sun Records released Elvis Presley's first single, "That's All Right."

Roger Bannister ran the first sub-four-minute mile.

Sports Illustrated published its first issue.

Texas Instruments announced the world's first transistor radio.

Burger King opened its first store, in Miami, Florida.

Not quite a first, but Marilyn Monroe married her second husband, the "Yankee Clipper," Joe DiMaggio.

In other news from 1954, President Dwight Eisenhower authorized the creation of the Air Force Academy.

Bill Haley and the Comets released "Rock Around the Clock."

From Here to Eternity won the Oscar for Best Picture, but William Holden, in *Stalag 17*, beat out Burt Lancaster for Best Actor; Audrey Hepburn won Best Actress for her role in *Roman Holiday*.

Brown v. Board of Education of Topeka struck down the "separate but equal" standard of *Plessy v. Ferguson* and began desegregation of public schools.

The New York Giants swept the Cleveland Indians in baseball's World Series, and the Giants' Willie Mays robbed Cleveland's Vic Wertz of extra bases with "the catch" in centerfield.

The Cleveland Browns bowled over the Detroit Lions 55-10 to win the National Football League championship.

The Minneapolis Lakers, led by bespectacled George Mikan, a future Hall of Famer, bested the Syracuse Nationals to win the National Basketball Association championship.

President Eisenhower signed a bill adding the words "under God" to the Pledge of Allegiance.

Halfway around the world, a series of events was taking place that led to the first steps of an ultimate morass for the United States. In February, President Eisenhower warned against US intervention in Vietnam.

In April, President Eisenhower gave his "domino theory" speech.

In May, the French colonial rulers of Vietnam suffered a devastating defeat at Dien Bien Phu.

In July, the Geneva Accords were signed, which, among other

things, split Vietnam into two halves, North and South, at the seventeenth parallel. They also guaranteed the neutrality of Laos.

In September, the Southeast Asia Treaty Organization (SEATO) was formed to block the spread of communism in Southeast Asia.

In October, the communist Viet Minh took control of North Vietnam. Two weeks later, President Eisenhower pledged US support to South Vietnam.

In Texas, on May 8, John Wesley Kearns III turned twelve years old. Two months later, on July 9, John's mother, Frances Kearns, gave birth to another boy at the Volunteers of America orphanage in Fort Worth. The baby was adopted by Fred and Joyce Heckmann of Waco and named Paul.

CHAPTER THREE

Agreement on the Cessation of Hostilities—1954 Geneva Accords

"You have a row of dominoes set up, you knock over the first one, and what will happen to the last one is the certainty that it will go over very quickly."

Dwight D. Eisenhower

Some might wonder what the CIA was doing in Laos in the first place, fighting a so-called "secret" war as an adjunct to the larger, and certainly better-known, Vietnam War—even though war in Vietnam was never officially declared by the US Congress. How and why does a country fight a war that no one knows about? It's probably impossible to do in today's technologically advanced world, but it was quite possible in the days of only three major television networks and a tight lid kept on media, both print and visual.

Former CIA director Richard Helms said that the country of Laos first came to his attention in 1962 when he was appointed Deputy Director of Plans. That position was renamed in 1973 as Deputy Director for Operations and then, in 2005, was given its current name of Director of the National Clandestine Service.

Helms held the position from February 17, 1962, until April 28, 1965. In his memoir, Helms wrote,

> Until then, I had known the kingdom only as a small former French colony in a remote region—a hotchpotch of jungle and mountains squeezed between Thailand on the west, Vietnam on the north and east, China on the north, and Cambodia on the south, and plagued with conflicting ethnic and regional interests, feuding clans, and local warlords. Few areas in Southeast Asia are ridden with a more complex history or a more complicated tangle of political interests than this "accidental country."[1]

The United States feared that if Laos fell to communism, communism would then spread west. This had already become known as the infamous "domino theory," which President Eisenhower expressed at a news conference on April 7, 1954. Asked by Robert Richards of Copley Press to comment on the "strategic importance of Indochina to the free world," Eisenhower said,

> . . . you have broader considerations that might follow what you would call the "falling domino" principle. You have a row of dominoes set up, you knock over the first one, and what will happen to the last one is the certainty that it will go over very quickly. So you could have a beginning of a disintegration that would have the most profound influences.
>
> . . . .
>
> But when we come to the possible sequence of events, the loss of Indochina, of Burma, of Thailand, of the Peninsula, and

> Indonesia following, now you begin to talk about areas that not only multiply the disadvantages that you would suffer through loss of materials, sources of materials, but now you are talking really about millions and millions and millions of people.
>
> Finally, the geographical position achieved thereby does many things. It turns the so-called island defensive chain of Japan, Formosa, of the Philippines and to the southward; it moves in to threaten Australia and New Zealand.
>
> It takes away, in its economic aspects, that region that Japan must have as a trading area or Japan, in turn, will have only one place in the world to go—that is, toward the Communist areas in order to live.[2]

Pulling out another metaphor, Eisenhower referred to Laos as the "cork in the bottle. If Laos fell, then Thailand, the Philippines and of course Chaing Kai-Shek would go."[3] In other words, the "cork" was the first "domino."

But why Laos? Why Helms's "hotchpotch"? In order to understand the secret war and how the United States became involved in Laos, one needs at least a cursory understanding of the origins of the Vietnam War, specifically, and the history of the geopolitics of Southeast Asia, generally.

America's ultimate involvement in that part of the world actually started through a chain of events that commenced with the French. Under a pretext of responding to the persecution of French missionaries, but, in reality, primarily to reach overseas markets and expand French colonial power, Napoleon III launched an invasion of Vietnam in July of 1857. The result was a nearly thirty-year war in which France ultimately prevailed and acquired the modern-day countries of Vietnam, Laos, and Cambodia, which it made part of the French empire as the territory of French Indochina.

One of the downsides for a colonial power occupying territory across an ocean is an upsurge among the native population to regain sovereignty. The United States is still witnessing that today, though less violently, with the Hawaiian sovereignty movement. French Indochina was no different. Nationalistic parties formed, inspired by the desire to throw off colonial rule, particularly in the southern region of Vietnam known as Cochinchina. Local officials in the region sometimes refused to cooperate with the occupying French, and guerrilla groups launched attacks on French outposts. In the twentieth century, a man named Phan Boi Chau led an unsuccessful rebellion against France. He ended up in China with a government-in-exile, though he was ultimately arrested at the insistence of the French and died under house arrest.

The most successful nationalist movement in Vietnam was led by a man named Nguyen Ai Quoc, better known as Ho Chi Minh. He formed a Vietnamese version of the Communist Party in 1930 and endeavored to return rule in Vietnam to the Vietnamese people.

With the fall of France to the Germans in 1940 in the infancy of World War II, French Indochina became a protectorate of Japan. That Axis country permitted the colonial French leaders to appear, at least nominally, to still be in control of Vietnam, but the country was actually ruled by the Japanese military. In 1941, Ho Chi Minh organized anticolonial resistance into the Viet Minh, whose goal was the expulsion of both the Japanese and the French. After the Japanese surrender in August of 1945, the Viet Minh took control of the government and, on September 2, proclaimed it the

Democratic Republic of Vietnam. Just a few weeks later, however, the French reasserted themselves, seizing control of Cochinchina. This effectively, though not officially, divided Vietnam into two halves, communist in the north and noncommunist in the south. The battle lines were drawn.

Perhaps seizing on his knowledge of history and the desire of the American colonies to achieve independence from England, or maybe even the American Civil War fought to bring the wayward Confederacy back into the fold, Ho Chi Minh believed that the United States might be an ally, or at least sympathetic, to his struggle for reunification and independence for Vietnam. On January 18, 1946, he wrote a three-page letter to US President Harry Truman soliciting American help in attaining, once and for all, protection for Vietnam from the French.

> On September 23, 1945, while the New Vietnam Democratic Republic was making strenuous efforts to carry out her reconstruction program, the French launched a night attack on the innocent population of Saigon, which was followed up by a systematically destructive and murderous warfare. Facts of looting, assassination of civilians, violence, indiscriminate bombing of non-strategical places by war planes, are reported everyday [sic]. Their intention is to invade the whole country and to reestablish their domination.

He then made his plea: "I respectfully request you to interfere for an immediate solution of the Vietnamese issue. The people of Vietnam earnestly hope that the great American Republic would help us to conquer full independence and support us in our reconstruction work."[4]

When Truman failed to respond, Ho Chi Minh tried again. On February 16, 1946, he wrote to Truman and reminded him that the Vietnamese people "stood by the Allies' side and fought against the Japanese and their associates, the French colonialists." Citing French violence against the Vietnamese people ("a murderous and pitiless war in order to reestablish their domination"), and Vietnam's desire "to achieve internal prosperity and welfare, and later to bring its small contribution to world-reconstruction," he concluded,

> These securities and freedoms can only be guaranteed by our independence from any colonial power, and our free cooperation with all other powers. It is with this firm conviction that we request of the United States as guardians and champions of World Justice to take a decisive step in support of our independence.[5]

Still no response from Truman, so one final appeal, via telegram on February 28:

> ON BEHALF OF VIETNAM GOVERNMENT AND PEOPLE I BEG TO INFORM YOU THAT IN COURSE OF CONVERSATIONS BETWEEN VIETNAM GOVERNMENT AND FRENCH REPRESENTATIVES THE LATTER REQUIRE THE SECESSION OF COCHINCHINA AND THE RETURN OF FRENCH TROOPS IN HANOI STOP MEANWHILE FRENCH POPULATION AND TROOPS ARE MAKING ACTIVE PREPARATIONS FOR A COUP DE MAIN[6] IN HANOI AND FOR MILLTARY [sic] AGGRESSION STOP I THEREFORE MOST EARNESTLY APPEAL TO YOU PERSONALLY AND TO THE AMERICAN PEOPLE TO INTERFERE

URGENTLY IN SUPPORT OF OUR INDEPENDENCE AND HELP MAKING THE NEGOTIATIONS MORE IN KEEPING WITH THE PRINCIPLES OF THE ATLANTIC AND SAN FRANCISCO CHARTERS.[7]

Greeted with silence from the United States, Ho Chi Minh negotiated an agreement with the French in March to allow Vietnam to exercise freedom within the French Union. Then he consolidated control over other nationalist groups and brought them into the fold of the Viet Minh. Things went well for a few months, until the French had an epiphany. There was an insurmountable difference between them and Ho's followers: The Viet Minh wanted total independence while France wanted its colony back.

So France decided to act militarily. In November of 1946, the French navy bombarded Haiphong, setting off an eight-year war. The Viet Minh sought, and gained, backing from the Chinese. The war ended with a devastating French defeat in a two-month battle at Dien Bien Phu, which lasted from March 13 until May 7, 1954. Thirty-seven American pilots, serving as civilian employees of Civil Air Transport,[8] participated in the battle, dropping supplies to French soldiers in the valley of Dien Bien Phu. Pilot James B. McGovern Jr. and his copilot, Wallace A. Buford, were killed in action. On February 24, 2005, McGovern, Buford, and seven pilots who had survived were awarded the French Legion of Honor.

In 1954, a conference was held in Geneva in an effort to restore peace to the area and to resolve the Indochina issue. Attendees came from Cambodia, Laos, the People's Republic of China, France, the United Kingdom, the United States, the Soviet Union, North Vietnam (represented by the Viet Minh), and South Vietnam. The attendees entered into agreements making up the Geneva Accords of 1954, which called for a cease-fire in Indochina. The Accords included an "Agreement on Cessation of the Hostilities in Viet-Nam [sic]," which drew a provisional military demarcation line and demilitarized zone. In layman's terms, it officially split Vietnam in half, dividing the "forces of the People's Army of Viet-Nam to the north of the line and the forces of the French Union to the south" at the seventeenth parallel. The demilitarized zone extended east and west across Vietnam. The zone had a width of no more than five kilometers, or roughly three miles, on either side of the demarcation line "to act as a buffer zone and avoid any incidents which might result in the resumption of hostilities." The agreement also prohibited "the introduction into Viet-Nam of any troop reinforcements and additional military personnel."

The Accords provided that the parties to it were responsible for the execution, or carrying out, of its terms, but an international commission of neutral countries was established to "ensure the control and supervision of this execution." That commission was to be comprised of representatives of Canada, India, and Poland, with India as the presiding member.

A separate "annex" was made to the Agreement on the Cessation of Hostilities in Viet-Nam, with further provisions on the demarcation line and demilitarized zone. An "Agreement on the Cessation of Hostilities in Cambodia" was also made, to be enforced by the "Commanders of the Armed Forces" of the warring parties. Likewise, because fighting had spilled over into Laos, there was an "Agreement on the Cessation of Hostilities in Laos." Both agreements were under the supervision and control of Canada, India, and Poland and presided over by India.[9]

But then came the capper on the agreements, the "Final Declaration of the Geneva Conference on the Problem of Restoring

Peace in Indo-china [sic]," dated July 21, 1954. Parties to it were Cambodia, the Democratic Republic of Viet-Nam (which would later be recognized as North Vietnam), France, Laos, the People's Republic of China, the State of Viet-Nam (which would later be recognized as South Vietnam), the Union of Soviet Socialist Republics, the United Kingdom, and the United States of America. The Final Declaration recognized the preceding "agreements ending hostilities in Cambodia, Laos and Viet-Nam and organizing international control and the supervision of the execution of the provisions of these agreements." The goal was a peaceful transition to independence of the countries making up Indochina.

Paragraph 2 of the Final Declaration provided:

> The Conference expresses satisfaction at the ending of hostilities in Cambodia, Laos and Viet-Nam; the Conference expresses its conviction that the execution of the provisions set out in the present declaration and in the agreements on the cessation of hostilities will permit Cambodia, Laos and Viet-Nam henceforth to play their part, in full independence and sovereignty, in the peaceful community of nations.

The Final Declaration, in paragraph 4, also noted that clauses in the agreement ending hostilities in Vietnam "prohibit[ed] the introduction into Viet-Nam of foreign troops and military personnel as well as of all kinds of arms and munitions." It didn't take long for this prohibition to fall by the wayside.

While Laos and Cambodia took a bit of a back seat in the Final Declaration, those countries agreed, in paragraph 4, "not to request foreign aid, whether in war material, in personnel or in instructors except for the purpose of the effective defence [sic] of their territory and, in the case of Laos, to the extent defined by the agreements on the cessation of hostilities in Laos." In Article 8 of the Agreement on the Cessation of Hostilities in Laos, Laos had agreed that "the introduction into Laos of armaments, munitions and military equipment of all kinds is prohibited, with the exception of a specified quantity of armaments in categories specified as necessary for the defence [sic] of Laos."

In paragraph 5 of the Declaration, Cambodia and Laos agreed not to join

> [i]n any agreement with other States if this agreement includes the obligation to participate in a military alliance not in conformity with the principles of the Charter of the United Nations or, in the case of Laos, with the principles of the agreement on the cessation of hostilities in Laos or, so long as their security is not threatened, the obligation to establish bases on Cambodian or Laotian territory for the military forces of foreign Powers.

The other parties to the Declaration vowed:

> In their relations with Cambodia, Laos and Viet-Nam, each member of the Geneva Conference undertakes to respect the sovereignty, the independence, the unity and the territorial integrity of the above-mentioned states, and to refrain from any interference in their internal affairs.[10]

So, all was taken care of and everyone was happy. What could possibly go wrong?

CHAPTER FOUR
Deep in the Heart of Texas

"Belonging to a family is a natural and vital component of life, and every child deserves to be a member of a loving and nurturing family."

Ronald Reagan

When you're a baby, things are out of your control. You don't get to choose your family and your family doesn't get to choose you. The exception to the latter is adoption. Singer/songwriter Sheryl Crow, an adoptive mother, reportedly said, "Little souls find their way to you whether they're from your womb or someone else's."[1] Another aphorism goes something like this: "I was chosen, I was wanted, I was cherished, I grew in their hearts, I was the missing piece, I was loved, I was adopted." I don't know who first said that, but I second the motion.

Others who might agree are fellow adoptees like Steve Jobs, John Lennon, Nelson Mandela, and Eric Clapton. Actor Jamie Foxx, whose real name is Eric Bishop, was adopted and raised by his mother's adoptive parents at seven months. A fellow Texan, from the small town of Terrell, about thirty miles east of Dallas, he credits his adoptive grandmother's influence as being at the center of his success. "That's not actually my biological grandmother," he said. "That's somebody who said, 'I see something in that little boy that's very special.'"[2]

I'm in good company.

My adoptive father, Frederick Arthur Heckmann, who went by Fred, was born in Queens, New York City. He was a very intelligent man, one of the smartest I've ever known. After graduating early from high school, he went to City College of New York. My memory is hazy on the progression of his professional life after graduation, but I believe that he first worked for now-defunct Braniff Airways before eventually joining the Army Air Corps, which became the United States Army Air Forces in 1941. Promoted to the rank of second lieutenant, he trained in Waco, Texas, as a navigator for service on a B-24 Liberator bomber during World War II. Maybe more significant about that stint in Waco, though, was that he met Bertha Joyce Nelson at a USO club there. They married just prior to his going overseas, where he flew thirty-two missions out of England, including two on D-Day, the second as a volunteer.

Upon his return, he and Joyce moved around a bit before settling back in Waco, where they had support from Joyce's family. Dad had the opportunity to purchase a small paint and prep store, so they took it. He grew it into one of the strongest in Central Texas. He also set up an equipment rental business, owned a Gulf station, and served as an officer of the Texas Rental Association. He once told me he wanted to run for president of the Association but didn't because he stayed busy getting me out of trouble. He was big on assigning blame, and it often fell on me, rightly or not.

Dad expected my sister Kathi and me to be brilliant like he was. High expectations often lead to disappointment, as it did for him with me. I wasn't cut out for the public schools of the 1960s. The mantra from teachers and administrators was that I was either

The Heckmann family at 1202 N. 22nd Street in Waco, Texas; Dad, Mom, Paul, and Kathi. *Photo courtesy of Paul Heckmann.*

stupid or lazy. It turns out I was neither. Years later, I was making small talk with a girl I was dating, and I told her that, when I was a kid, I spelled my name "PO9." She immediately asked if I was dyslexic. She explained how dyslexia worked and the problems it can cause, particularly for school-age kids just learning to read and write.

Dyslexia was not a new condition when I was in school, having been studied and named by German physicians in the late nineteenth century, but it was certainly little recognized, and even lesser understood, in the 1960s. Stupid and lazy, on the other hand, were easy diagnoses that everyone could understand. But all that did was create a stigma that was nearly impossible to overcome. The temptation for an accused student was simply to lean in to the false assessments and be stupid and lazy.

When I began grappling, as an adult, with psychological, emotional, physical, and addiction issues, in addition to considering any genetic influence of my birth family—the nature—I also had to look back at the nurture, including my relationship with Dad. He was really good at hiding his emotions. I don't think it was uncommon for fathers of that time to be stoic, the family disciplinarians, and he was right there with the stereotype. For some of my friends, dinnertime was a pleasant family event, with chatter about various topics. It was different in the Heckmann household. Dinner seemed more like a chore to be accomplished rather than an event to be enjoyed. It was not a time for joking and sharing our days, nor for development of our social skills. There was very little conversation at dinner, other than maybe about church. We were good Lutherans in the Heckmann family, attending First Lutheran Church of Waco. My forefathers, at least through the Heckmann line, came over from Norway and helped found the church in the 1800s. We were there whenever the doors were open, at least twice a week and more during Lent. That might have been good for the soul, but it didn't really make for scintillating dinnertime conversation. Dinner was just shut up and eat, then leave the table. Ozzie Nelson or Ward Cleaver, Dad was not.

He was given to fits of uncontrollable anger—something I thought about when I was having my own fits of rage in the 1990s. Obviously that was not something I inherited genetically, but I understand, through my research and experience, that adopted children can nevertheless inherit traits from their adoptive parents by virtue of environmental conditioning. Dad would whip both my sister and me for just about anything we did wrong, or that he perceived to be wrong. We knew we had pushed things too far when he would issue this command: "Go get my belt and grab the throne (the toilet)." Then he would begin to deliver licks. If we tried to defend ourselves . . . well, that would be a mistake. The result was usually more licks, harder licks, and huge welts on our legs and arms. By today's standards, it would probably be classified as child abuse, but back then, it was just good ol' plain discipline. Call it a spanking or a whupping or whatever you like. Spare the rod and all that.

It wasn't until 1977, in the case of *Ingraham v. Wright*, that the United States Supreme Court weighed in on the issue of corporal punishment in schools.[3] The court found that, while it might be distasteful, corporal punishment in schools didn't violate the Eight Amendment's prohibition on cruel and unusual punishment. Since then, a lot of states have outlawed it, but that's in schools, not the home. Home discipline gets to be a tricky issue today, but in the 1960s? Well, it was every family for itself.

Not only was Dad quick with the Biblical rod, he was loath to dole out physical displays of affection. Even in moments of kindness and tenderness, he was not a hugger. Mom was, but not Dad. That carried on even into my adulthood. I remember once, later in life, when I tried to give him a hug and he backed off quickly. That's not to say that he didn't love us. He just had some strange ways of showing it. One of the few times I remember him being proud of me was when I brought the family on one of the cruise ships where I worked as an adult. It was probably in 1987 or 1988, on board the *Stardancer* for Admiral Cruise Lines, which later became Royal Caribbean Cruise Lines. I got Dad up to the bridge when we were leaving Los Angeles Harbor, also known as San Pedro Harbor. He was hard of hearing but didn't want to admit it, so he kept yelling at me, telling me how great this was. At one point, the captain looked over to see what the ruckus was. I just pointed to my ear, which he picked up on, grinned, and went back to his business.

Dad passed on August 13, 1999—Friday the 13th. He always seemed to have a purpose for everything he did. I have often wondered whether, at the end of his life, he held on until that mystical date so that I would always remember it. Probably not, but whether he did or did not, I do.

My mother, Bertha Joyce (Nelson) Heckmann, went by Joyce. She was probably the most Christian woman you will ever meet. A true believer. She was born and raised in Waco, where she graduated from high school at the age of sixteen and attended the local business college to become proficient in shorthand and other secretarial/office skills. She was a very smart woman. As a boy, I remember her work ethic, doing the books and accounting for the small store the family ran, taxiing my sister and me to school and then, after the school day ended, to whatever lessons we had been signed up for. Mine was piano. I actually trained in classical piano for about five years and got pretty good at it. But then I started playing football and didn't have time for it anymore. Besides, that might seem kinda sissy for a football player. (I should point out that I was very insecure at that age.)

Unlike Dad, she wasn't physical with us kids when it came to punishment. But if we misbehaved, she was always ready with the famous mother's line: "Wait until your father comes home." I don't know how she felt about his not sparing the rod, or the apparent brutality of it. At least, that was how Kathi and I viewed it as kids. Maybe to Mom, it was just a father delivering a spanking, like all good fathers did. She always deferred to him. I think that was pretty much the norm in those days, before the age of women's lib and rebellion against the submissive wife model. When Dad died, she kinda came out of this shell that she appeared to be in when he was alive. She became a lot friendlier and more approachable as far as her kids went. Sometimes I wonder what the effect might have been on me if she had always been that way.

Kathi was also adopted from the Volunteers of America Orphanage in Fort Worth. She was street smart. Like me, though, she had a tough time in a lot of her school years. However, she did excel in the band. She played the flute at first, then picked up the saxophone. Sometimes in my sleep, I can still hear the dreadful sounds of that sax when she was first learning.

★ ★ ★ ★ ★

A family friend in Waco named Eddie Fadal regularly commuted the hundred miles to Dallas where he was a disc jockey at KRLD. He also did a lot of promotions for the station and, in the late '50s, met this handsome young kid who fancied himself a singer. Once, when Eddie was working on his house, he grabbed this young guy, who happened to be in town, to help out. They needed a floor sander so they drove over to my family's equipment rental place to pick one up. This young guy saw me, a chubby four-year-old, so he grabbed me and started tossing me in the air while Eddie rented the sander. Being thrown like that scared me, so I did what any kid would do: I started screaming.

Eddie looked over and laughed. He said, "Elvis, put Paul down." My first brush with greatness.

★ ★ ★ ★ ★

In 1958, we moved to the small town of Woodway, about ten miles southwest of Waco, just east of what would become Lake Waco. I loved growing up "in the country," because that was what it seemed like. According to the *Texas Almanac*, Waco had a population of 97,808 in 1960, while Woodway was at 1,244.[4] Our address was on a "Rural Route" and the streets were dirt. Quintessential country. However, Woodway would ultimately grow into a suburb (population 9,383 in 2020) and lose much of that rural charm. You will see a lot of it on the Chip and Joanna Gaines *Fixer Upper* TV show. But it didn't look anything like that when I grew up there.

I went to first grade at Midway Elementary School in 1960. I had the same teacher for second and third grades, Mrs. Tebeaux, and Mrs. Pirkle for fourth and fifth. Mom said that Mrs. Tebeaux must have spoiled me because I couldn't get away with the same things under Mrs. Pirkle that I did under her. Mrs. Pirkle's paddle flew relentlessly during my years with her, with my rear end as its target. I took to wearing multiple pairs of underwear to school—just in case. Sometimes those paddlings were for innocent things, at least as I saw them. Like forgetting homework assignments. What kid never forgot a homework assignment? And even when I did my homework or studied, my memory problems and undiagnosed dyslexia created hardships. I got an occasional eighty on a test or two, but sixties or seventies were more my speed.

When I was in the fifth grade, Dad's mom, my grandmother from New York, came for a summer visit. Central Texas can be semi-arid in the summers, with lots of dry brush and grassy fields, and county officials sent out a fire warning. In my eleven-year-old brain, a warning like that really didn't mean anything. Or maybe I simply interpreted it as a challenge. In any event, a couple of buddies and I traipsed up the road to shoot off bottle rockets. Not the smartest thing we could have done in the dry conditions. Sometimes boys simply do stupid things, even if they are not inherently stupid.

Everything was fine at first. But then a bottle rocket erupted in an array of sparks. Sparks that landed in dry grass. Sparks that started a small fire. As boys will do, our first reaction was to laugh. We followed that with a half-hearted effort to stomp out the flames. Then it got bigger. And bigger. Pretty soon we were afraid to try to stomp it for fear of catching on fire ourselves. We had no choice but to run to a neighbor's house, where we called the appropriate authorities. We may have neglected, though, to say that we were responsible for the fire.

Later, a knock sounded on the front door at home. My grandma opened it and there stood the Chief of Police, a man with whom I would have a rocky relationship in the future. He asked me about the fire. I lied at first and denied having anything to do with it. Then he told me that one of my buddies—he didn't say which one—had already admitted to it and had named me as one of his accomplices. There was nothing left for me to do but to confess and repent in sackcloth and ashes. Or the mid-twentieth century equivalent.

That small fire turned out not to be so small after all. My memory is hazy in my old age, but I seem to remember that the fire burned up the abandoned wooden city water tower, along with about 26 acres. I spent a full afternoon of anxiety waiting for Dad to get home and order me to fetch his favorite belt. There seems to be something perverse, now that I think about it, in making a kid bring the instrument of torture to the torturer.

But there was still more penance to pay. Sometimes I worked at the family store for my spending money, but Dad made me work for free, at least for a while. He sent my pay to the appropriate authorities to cover some of the damages. I'm sure it barely put a dent in the overall bill, but I learned a valuable lesson: Don't surround myself with accomplices who confessed too quickly and easily and who lacked loyalty. Of course, there might have been other lessons that *should* have come to mind.

By the time I was in the seventh grade, I had been getting into a lot of trouble around the area. Nothing major, at least from my perspective, but we received more and more visits from the Chief of Police. Finally, Dad had had enough. He called me into his study and told me that he was going to send me to military school. The Marine Military Academy in Harlingen, as I recall. I have come to understand that a military school stint there was a fairly common threat made to mischievous, or incorrigible, youth in Texas at the time. Opened in 1965, its website states, "We apply the U.S. Marine Corps concepts of leadership and self-discipline to youth development and our college preparatory curriculum."[5] I'm guessing there would have been more than just "self-discipline" administered. What red-blooded American teenager wouldn't want to go there?

Well, me, for one. Somehow I begged my way out of it. I probably should have gone, to be honest. I wonder how my life would have turned out if I had.

★ ★ ★ ★ ★

Lake Waco, west of the City of Waco, sits on the Bosque River, which is a tributary of the Brazos River. In 1928–1929, the city built a dam on the Bosque to create a lake for water supply and also for flood control and recreational purposes. Over the next decade and a half, sediment accumulated that greatly reduced the lake's water capacity. At the same time, folks realized that the lake, with the existing dam, posed a flood threat to Waco as well as downstream portions of the Brazos. The fix was going to be a new dam and new lake, which was authorized in 1954, though construction wasn't started until nearly four years later. In 1964, the dam created a "detention basin," which is an area that has been excavated to catch, or "detain," water as a means of flood control. The beginning of "deliberate" water impoundment for permanent creation of the lake didn't occur until February of 1965.[6] As an example of impoundment, one simply has to read the novel, or watch the movie, *Deliverance*, in which the fictitious Cahulawassee River was to be dammed to create a lake. The novel was inspired by the damming of the Coosawattee River in Georgia to build Carters Lake. The parallels end there, as I'm not aware of any malevolent mountain men who ever lurked around Lake Waco.

When I was ten or eleven years old, my buddy Steven Southwell and his dad decided to take advantage of the "impoundment" of water on an old pecan orchard, and they invited me along for some fishing in Mr. Southwell's little eleven-foot jon boat that fit the three of us comfortably, if a bit snugly. We put in along the old Estates Road that had become a boat ramp with the flooding, and we set out on the water, fishing along the shore. I don't remember whether we were after any particular type of fish. There are plenty in Texas: bass—whether striped or largemouth—bream, crappie, catfish. We weren't particular. We were after whatever would bite. We Heckmanns typically used cane rods, but Mr. Southwell probably provided me a casting rod.

After a while, Mr. Southwell brought the boat alongside the bank and tied off to a tree with a chain, using a wire that he wrapped through the links to hold the chain together. It was a great day on the water, just the three of us fishermen. I don't remember if we had caught any fish up to that point, but I do have a vivid memory of what happened next. I was fishing along, minding my own business, when I heard a thump and felt a slight vibration on the bottom of the boat, as if something had fallen in. I looked down and, sure enough, something had indeed fallen in: a cottonmouth! Or, as some call them, a water moccasin.

There are four varieties of poisonous snakes in Texas: rattlesnakes, coral snakes, copperheads, and cottonmouths. And there lay one just a few feet away from me. Cottonmouths may not be the biggest snakes in the world, typically growing to between two and four feet long, but it's not how long they are that matters. It's what the business end of that two-to-four feet can do. I had no real avenue of escape other than into the water. Not a good choice. Particularly not in light of what I saw next.

I looked up into the tree and saw a whole mess of snakes. They had apparently slithered up into the pecan trees to avoid the floodwaters, which probably meant the water around the boat was infested with snakes, too. Remember that scene in *Lonesome Dove* (or chapter, for book readers) where a horde of cottonmouths attack a rider on horseback crossing a river? Of course, I hadn't seen or read *Lonesome Dove* at the time (nor would it even be written by Larry McMurtry for another twenty years), but my little imagination was still fertile.

And these were not just cottonmouths in the trees. There were some rattlesnakes, too. I know, because I recognized their rattlers. It looked as if someone had decided to toilet paper the tree but used snakes instead.

"Stay calm!"

I'm sure Mr. Southwell meant . . . well. But how could you possibly expect ten-year-old boys to stay calm while grim death hovered just above their heads, in the boat with them, and in the surrounding water?

Somehow he managed to get the chain undone without jostling any more vipers into our boat. He took something heavy—it could have been a hammer or simply his metal tacklebox—to the head of the cottonmouth in the boat, beat it to death, and tossed the carcass overboard. Then we made our getaway. And lived to tell about it.

We all probably had to change our pants as soon as we got home.

★ ★ ★ ★ ★

In the '60s, my "uncle" Conrad sold Nimrod travel trailers. I called him "uncle" but he was actually my cousin. My mom's oldest sister was three decades older than she was, so her son was more like an uncle to my sister and me than a cousin. Nimrods were nifty little trailers that included a tent structure when you "unfolded" them. A man named Ashley Ward Jr. created the trailer. He had filed his first patent application for a windproof pipe-lighter that he called the Nimrod after separating from the US Air Force at the age of twenty-three. The lighter was perfect for hunters and outdoorsmen. Legend had it that he derived the name from a descendent of Noah in the Book of Genesis in the Bible. Nimrod, according to Genesis 10:9, was a "mighty hunter before the Lord."

Ward later hit on the idea of a pop-up trailer as recreational camping was taking off in the mid-to-late '50s in the United States. In 1957, he started the Nimrod Equipment Company, which later was a division of Ward Manufacturing, Inc., and created two lines of camping trailers—one called the Wayfarer and the other called the Nimrod. Uncle Conrad sold the latter.

I should also mention that Conrad lived much of his life in the Dallas area. Besides selling Nimrods, he was a professor at Southern Methodist University, and he had been director of franchising for Southland Corporation—the 7-Eleven folks. He was a brilliant man with brilliant kids. A couple of them were lawyers. A little intimidating.

Anyway, my folks bought a Nimrod and, when I was twelve, our family decided to go camping in the Lincoln National Forest in south central New Mexico. I planned to do some fishing—previous experience with snakes in trees notwithstanding—and bought some worms for the endeavor, which I kept outside the tent on a nearby picnic table. I was really excited when I went to bed, anxious for a big day ahead of fishing. I needed to pee in the middle of the night, so I quietly unzipped the tent, stepped out, and headed for a large tree nearby.

The first thing I saw was some black shadows—large black shadows—moving around in the night. As my eyes adjusted, I could make out what they were. Bears! Probably black bears, since that was the only kind of bear found in that part of New Mexico. There were at least a couple of them, digging around in my stockpile of worms. I froze for a few seconds. Then the bears spotted me and started heading my way.

I did what any scared-to-death little boy would do: I screamed. Dad came out with a flashlight, hollered, and scared them away. My hero.

I have always thought those bears saw me as nothing more than a chubby twelve-year-old morsel. But, just like that day in the jon boat, I had cheated death and lived to tell about it.

Probably had to change my pants, too.

★ ★ ★ ★ ★

When I was about thirteen, my dad bought in to the exercise craze that started in the '50s but carried into the '60s, revolving around a vibrating machine that would allow you to passively reduce weight. You strapped a belt attached to a motor around your waist and leaned back. Then, with the mere flip of a switch to turn on the motor, it vibrated and jiggled away your fat. The machines had been around for decades. In 1927, John Harvey Kellogg introduced one, called the Battle Creek Health Builder, at his Battle Creek Sanitarium in Michigan. Lucille Ball used one in an episode of *I Love Lucy* in the '50s and Fred Flintstone experimented with a prehistoric version. I don't think Fred's was real, though.

Dad decided that he would include, as one of the pieces of equipment he would rent in the family store, the Walton Belt Vibrator that was manufactured in the '60s by the Walton Manufacturing Company in Dallas. And you needed to advertise, right? How else would potential customers know of the life-giving, health-sustaining, magic vibrating machine that they could rent and use in the privacy of their own homes? So Dad had the bright idea to make a commercial promoting the store, and the vibrating machine, to air on local television, and he wanted my help. Maybe that was a precursor to my later years as a model or television stand-in and movie background work, but back then I didn't know any better. And I certainly wasn't going to disobey Dad. If he told me I was going to be the star of the commercial, I would be the star of the commercial. I would save disobedience for my more rebellious teen years. So I let him strap me into that machine and flip the switch.

And he turned on the video camera.

I was pretty chubby at that age and had plenty of fat to jiggle around. And jiggle around, it did. He made the commercial, with me as its unintentional comical star, and it aired all over McLennan County. That near-death experience didn't involve snakes or bears, but I nearly died of shame. We now know that those machines were worthless as far as weight reduction went, so I can't even say I traded in my dignity for a worthwhile endeavor.

And with all that jiggling, I probably had to change my pants then, too.

★ ★ ★ ★ ★

Those Walton Belt Vibrators provided me with my first experience as an entrepreneur. When I was in my early teens, Dad loaned me $50 to buy one and put it with our stock at the store. Every time it rented, he applied some of the rental proceeds to my debt. When I paid off the $50, I saved up additional rental proceeds to buy a second machine. Then a third. I ended up with five or six of them. I made about $1,900 and put some money into stock in the Technicare Company. When I was about nineteen or so, I sold my stock and bought a Kawasaki 750 motorcycle to impress the girls. The school of thought was correct—the results were a disappointment.

I felt like I was living in tall cotton!

CHAPTER FIVE

1962—It Was Not Quite as Good a Year

"So we must presume that the worst, rather than the best, choice will be made. The sober and responsible elements will be defeated in the present clash."

Philip K. Dick, *The Man in the High Castle*

Like 1954, 1962 offered twists and turns of its own. Some events were political, some geopolitical, and some cultural. Some were simply interesting.

The year started with a coup and countercoup in the Dominican Republic, ousting and returning the old government in the space of three days.

The United States imposed a trade embargo on Cuba, completing an embargo trifecta that had begun with an arms embargo in 1958 and an energy and agricultural embargo in 1960.

U-2 pilot Francis Gary Powers, who had been shot down over the Soviet Union in 1960, was freed in a prisoner exchange that saw the United States release a Soviet spy named Rudolf Abel.

Carol Cox won in the Super Stock class at the National Hot Rod Association Winternationals. She was the first woman to race in an NHRA national event.

John Glenn orbited the earth three times in *Friendship 7*, becoming the first American and second human to do so. American Scott Carpenter would also orbit the earth three times later that year in *Aurora 7*.

Marvel Comics published *The Incredible Hulk #1*, introducing a new superhero. Later in the year, Marvel introduced Spider-Man.

West Side Story won the Academy Award for Best Picture. Other winners included Maximilian Schell for Best Actor in *Judgment at Nuremburg* and Sophia Loren for Best Actress in *Two Women*. William Inge won for Best Writing for Story and Screenplay Written Directly for the Screen for *Splendor in the Grass*, and Abby Mann won Best Writing for Screenplay Based on Material from Another Medium for *Judgment at Nuremberg*.

The New York Yankees beat the San Francisco Giants in seven games in the World Series. Yankee pitcher Ralph Terry was named the MVP. It marked the twentieth championship for the Yankees.

The Green Bay Packers defeated the New York Giants 16-7 in the NFL Championship Game, giving head coach Vince Lombardi his second NFL championship. The Packers' fullback Jim Taylor was the league's MVP in 1962, while his teammate, linebacker Ray Nitschke, was the championship game's MVP.

In the championship game for the fledgling American Football League, the Dallas Texans (who would later move north and become the Kansas City Chiefs) defeated the Houston Oilers (who would later move east and become the Tennessee Titans) in overtime, 20-17. Texans quarterback Len Dawson was selected as MVP. A famous faux pas occurred in that overtime. The Texans won the coin toss and intended to obtain favorable wind conditions. But captain Abner Haynes said, "We'll kick to the clock." The result was that the Texans kicked, giving first possession to the Oilers, but because Haynes had chosen to kick, the Oilers actually got to choose which end of the field to defend, giving them the wind advantage as well. No harm, no foul. The game went into a second overtime and the Texans prevailed.[1]

In basketball, the Boston Celtics defeated the Los Angeles Lakers in seven games to take the NBA championship. The Celtics' Bill Russell was the MVP.

In Cuba, a military tribunal returned convictions on nearly twelve hundred participants in the Bay of Pigs invasion.

The Rolling Stones opened for Long John Baldry at the Marquee Club in Oxford Street, London. It was the Stones' debut.

Marilyn Monroe overdosed on sleeping pills and died at the age of thirty-six. The official ruling was suicide, though conspiracy theorists dispute that even to this day.

The first color Godzilla and King Kong film was released in Japan.

An eighteen-year-old named Peter Fechter was killed by East German border guards as he tried to climb the Berlin Wall to escape to the West.

A former French Air Force officer named Jean-Marie Bastien-Thiry tried, and failed, to assassinate French president Charles de Gaulle. He was later executed by firing squad, the last person to be so executed in France. The failed attempt was depicted in Frederick Forsyth's novel *The Day of the Jackel.*

Heavyweight boxing challenger Sonny Liston knocked out champion Floyd Patterson to claim the title.

Johnny Carson became host of *The Tonight Show* on NBC.

The Cuban Missile Crisis riveted the world's attention.

Lawrence of Arabia opened in London, then six days later in the United States.

Paul Heckmann turned eight years old. His half-brother John Kearns enlisted in the US Army.

CHAPTER SIX

(Another) Agreement on the Cessation of Hostilities—1962 Geneva Accords

"All of the signers ignored the accords. The US government maintained the fiction of the accords, however. Washington opted instead for a covert war in Laos, the first such secret, CIA-run war in American history."

Joshua Kurlantzick, *A Great Place to Have a War*

Despite the terms of the Geneva Accords of 1954 that applied to Laos (or any of the other countries of French Indochina, for that matter), things did not go smoothly. The French may have been gone, but Laos lapsed into civil war in 1959. The belligerent forces were the Royal Lao Government and the indigenous Hmong, on the one hand, and the Pathet Lao, a communist force officially called the Lao People's Liberation Army, on the other, backed by the communist government of North Vietnam. The Pathet Lao were essentially the Laotian equivalent of the Viet Minh or the National Liberation Front, derogatorily known at the time as the Viet Cong, in Vietnam.

Notwithstanding prohibitions of the Geneva Accords of 1954, and before the ink had time to dry, Eisenhower committed significant financial aid to Laos and sent military advisors across its borders while the CIA increased its clandestine presence. It was that cork-in-the-bottle domino-principle thing. Christian Chapman, chief political officer at the US Embassy in Vientiane, Laos, between 1957 and 1959, and who served as Laos Desk Officer with the State Department from 1959 to 1961, said, "Already in 1958–59 their [the CIA's] operation was larger than the Foreign Service. And they were in touch with all the players." A new government was established in Laos represented by Phoui Sananikone, who replaced Souvanna Phouma, "courtesy, I suspect in part, of the CIA."[1]

In the transition following the 1960 presidential election in the United States, Eisenhower warned John Kennedy about the importance of Laos. Eisenhower had committed millions in financial aid and sent military advisors to Laos to prevent the Pathet Lao from taking over the Laotian government and toppling the first domino. Eisenhower cautioned that the US effort "was on the verge of failure and the US military might need to intervene."[2] One of Kennedy's first trips as president, in late January of 1961, was to Key West, Florida, to meet with British Prime Minister Harold MacMillan to discuss several issues. But, Chapman said, "the first big issue was Laos." Chapman himself "wrote some long papers" on the situation in Laos and made the trip to Key West along with Kennedy for the MacMillan meeting.[3]

Under the leadership of James William Lair, a veteran clandestine CIA operative in Southeast Asia for more than a decade, the United States launched Operation Momentum in Laos on January 17, 1961, three days before Kennedy assumed office. The purpose of the operation was to arm and train Hmong irregulars under the oversight of Laotian anticommunist military leader Vang Pao. Once in office, Kennedy expanded the operation,

President Kennedy at March 23, 1961, press conference with map denoting "Communist Rebel Areas" in Laos. *Public domain.*

which would continue for more than a decade, despite another agreement that was ironed out in Geneva in an attempt to settle the Laotian civil war.

It was a second shot at peace and independence in Southeast Asia.

It was a second failure.

"The Declaration on the Neutrality of Laos" was signed in Geneva on July 23, 1962—and was almost immediately breached by some of the signatories. Signed by, among others, Cambodia, China, Vietnam (both North and South), the USSR, and the United States, the 1962 Accords were premised upon the resolution of the Royal Government of Laos to "follow the path of peace and neutrality in conformity with the interests and aspirations of the Laotian people." The Laos government resolved, among other things:

- not to enter into any military alliance or agreement, whether military or otherwise, which is inconsistent with the neutrality of Laos
- not to allow establishment of any foreign military base in Laotian territory
- not to allow any foreign interference in its internal affairs
- to require (and this is key, although it contains a loophole that would make any lawyer proud) the withdrawal from Laos of all foreign troops and military personnel (this is the loophole), and not to allow any foreign troops or military personnel (still part of the loophole) to be introduced into Laos.

Laos then "appeals to the States participating in the International Conference on the Settlement of the Laotian Question" to, among other things:

- "recognise [sic] and will respect and observe in every way the sovereignty, independence, neutrality, unity and territorial integrity of the Kingdom of Laos"
- "not resort to the use or threat of force or any other measure which might impair the peace of the Kingdom of Laos"
- "refrain from all direct or indirect interference in the internal affairs of the Kingdom of Laos"
- "respect the wish of the Kingdom of Laos not to recognise [sic] the protection of any alliance or military coalition, including SEATO [Southeast Asia Treaty Organization]"
- "not introduce into the Kingdom of Laos foreign troops

or military personnel in any form whatsoever, nor will they in any way facilitate or connive at the introduction of any foreign troops or military personnel"

- "not establish nor will they in any way facilitate or connive at the establishment in the Kingdom of Laos of any foreign military base, foreign strong point or other foreign military installation of any kind."

Attached to the Declaration was a "Protocol" that ostensibly removed any ambiguities in the Declaration's language. For example, Article 1 defined the term "foreign military personnel" as including "members of foreign military missions, foreign military advisers, experts, instructors, consultants, technicians, observers and any other foreign military persons, including those serving in any armed forces in Laos, and foreign citizens connected with the supply, maintenance, storing or utilization of war materials."

If that weren't clear enough, Article 2 provided, unequivocally, that "[a]ll foreign and irregular troops, foreign para-military formations and foreign military personnel shall be withdrawn from Laos in the shortest time possible." Article 4 prohibited "[t]he introduction of foreign regular and irregular troops, foreign para-military formations and foreign military personnel," and Article 6 prohibited "[t]he introduction into Laos of armaments, munitions and war material generally, except such quantities of conventional armaments as the Royal Government of Laos may consider necessary for the national defence [sic] of Laos."[4]

And then, as historian Joshua Kurlantzick wrote, "all of the signers ignored the accords. The US government maintained the fiction of the accords, however. Washington opted instead for a covert war in Laos, the first such secret, CIA-run war in American history."[5]

★ ★ ★ ★ ★

US involvement in Vietnam started benignly enough, with "advisors" sent to "advise" the South Vietnamese in their armed struggle against the communist north. With the formation of SEATO in 1955, designed—at least in theory—to prevent the first domino of communist expansion from falling, President Eisenhower sent seven hundred personnel along with military and economic aid to South Vietnam. In May of 1961, President Kennedy sent an additional five hundred Special Forces personnel. To place that in chronological context, recall that the CIA had already launched Operation Momentum in Laos in January. The number of advisors increased over the next year and a half until, by the end of 1962, eleven thousand advisors were in South Vietnam, increased to sixteen thousand by the end of 1963.

Besides the rising number of advisors, 1962 was a significant year in another respect. During that year, fifty-three US military personnel were killed. It wasn't the first loss of American life in Vietnam for the US. On September 26, 1945, A. Peter Dewey, a member of the Office of Strategic Services (forerunner of the CIA), was killed by Viet Minh soldiers who mistakenly believed him to be a French officer, and two American pilots were killed in the battle of Dien Bien Phu. American lives, certainly, but neither incident was technically part of the Vietnam War involving the United States.

On December 22, 1961, Specialist Four James T. Davis, age twenty-five, became the first to die in ground combat action in Vietnam.[6] He was killed when the truck in which he was riding as part of a radio intercept team trying to confirm the location of an enemy radio transmitter was ambushed and a remotely detonated mine buried in the road disabled his vehicle. Though wounded, Davis sought to divert the enemy from the remainder of his team. Overtaken by the enemy, Davis was shot in the head, killing him. Nine other members of his team of South Vietnamese soldiers were also killed. Davis was a member of the Army Security Agency. Just a few weeks after Davis's death, the ASA renamed the Third Radio Research Unit station at Tan Son Nhut "Davis Station."[7]

John Kearns would later become a member of the ASA during his tour in Vietnam.

CHAPTER SEVEN
"We weren't there."

"Now we have a problem in making our power credible, and Vietnam is the place."

John F. Kennedy

John Wesley Kearns III was born on May 8, 1942, to Frances and John Kearns. He was the first of four children. Sister Sandy came in 1945, Sharon in 1948, and Ron in 1949. In 1954, at the age of twelve during a period of estrangement for his mom and dad, a second brother was born—one John would never know, but one who would later search for him.

John graduated from high school in Fort Worth in 1961, then enrolled at Texas Christian University, also in Fort Worth, in the fall. His father was the senior noncommissioned officer assigned to the Army ROTC unit at the university, so it seemed like a natural fit. But John grew restless after his freshman year. There was a war brewing on the other side of the world, a war very few people knew much about—and even fewer understood—with roots that went back into the prior century, to Napoleon III and the French. The communist world was seeking to expand its footprint in that part of the globe while the free nations, particularly the United States, were determined to stomp on those feet.

The Vietnam War draft wasn't implemented until 1964, although the US Selective Service System had administered peacetime conscription following the end of World War II. The Selective Service Act of 1948 required all males aged eighteen or over to register with the Selective Service, with those between the ages of eighteen and twenty-five eligible to be drafted. This was followed by the Universal Military Training and Service Act of 1951, spurred by the Korean War, which modified the system. In 1963, John Kennedy signed an executive order that granted exemptions for married men, which Lyndon Johnson later modified with another executive order that rescinded the exemption for married men without children.

The draft lottery came into existence with an amendment to the Military Selective Service Act of 1967, signed by Richard Nixon on November 26, 1969. Conscription would be based on random drawings of dates, with the first lottery held on December 1, 1969. There was hope of ultimately transitioning to an all-volunteer military, but at the height of the Vietnam War, the military needed fresh bodies every year. John Kearns's enlistment in 1962, perhaps fueled by Cold War patriotism instilled by his ROTC instructor father, was purely voluntary.

After enlisting, John completed his US Army basic training at Fort Jackson, South Carolina, on August 7. Because he scored high on his Military Occupational Specialty testing, John was selected for admission to the United States Army Security Agency (ASA). The ASA had been the signals intelligence branch of the army since it was established on September 15, 1945, at the end of World War II, and succeeded the army's Signals Intelligence Service, which had its origins during World War I. Although technically part of the army, the Director of the National Security Agency had operational control over the ASA, though that was later merged with the army's Military Intelligence branch to form the Army Intelligence and Security Command (INSCOM).

Signals intelligence refers to gathering intelligence by intercepting the transmission of data or signals. The US Army website describes the ASA, its establishment, and evolution this way:

John Kearns on Joint Civil Affairs team on Manomi Dieto Island, Japan, fall of 1964. *Photo courtesy of Malone family.*

> Signals Intelligence had been a part of the Army's warfighting toolkit since World War I, practiced by radio interceptors, code-makers and code-breakers. The first Army organization to take on the function was Signals Intelligence Service in 1930, led by William Friedman. This organization, which became the Signal Security Service in 1943, and later the Signal Security Agency (SSA), exploited the communications of both Germany and Japan during World War II. Control of communications intelligence collection assets were split between the SSA (under the Chief, Signal Corps), and the theater commanders. This arrangement created significant problems, since it proved impossible to neatly separate the tactical aspects of communications intelligence from the strategic ones.
>
> When the war ended, the SSA was removed from the Signal Corps and reorganized as the Army Security Agency (ASA) under the control of the Director of Military Intelligence. For the first time, Military Intelligence, through the organization

of ASA, assumed command of all signals intelligence and security establishments, units and personnel in the Army. The new agency inherited the mission, functions, and assets of the SSA, while adding the communications intelligence and security resources that had previously been at the disposal of theater commanders.[1]

In the Vietnam War, "in addition to listening for coded signals, two-member ASA units would move stealthily through the jungles using radio equipment to pick up enemy broadcasts. Once a signal was acquired, soldiers would move to a second location, then a third, until they could triangulate the signal and lock in on its origin. They would then call in bombers and missile strikes while retreating to safety."[2] Former army Sergeant Larry Matthews, an ASA veteran, was quoted as saying the agency had two mottos, one official and one unofficial. An ASA patch bore the motto: "We weren't there." The other, Matthews said, was "In God we trust. All others we monitor."[3]

Sent to Fort Devens, Massachusetts, John completed the High Speed Morse Intercept course and Radio Direction Finder course, then was assigned to the ASA Field Station at Torii Station in Sobe, Okinawa. In August of 1963, he requested a transfer, to the Four Hundredth ASA Special Operations Detachment (SOD), also on Okinawa, which was part of the First Special Forces Group. There, he completed the required basic airborne training, making him part of an "extraordinary" fighting force. According to the ASA website,

In the history of mankind, there are fleeting moments of time where, by fate or good judgement [sic] on the part of someone, a group of people are brought together at the most appropriate time and place or places to form extraordinary military units.

John Kearns monitoring First Special Forces communications, Taiwan, May 1963. *Photo courtesy of Malone family.*

One such fleeting moment of history, was the formation and life cycle of an extraordinary military unit called the United States Army Security Agency Special Operations Detachment, more commonly referred to as the ASASOD.

One may ask why the ASASODs were called extraordinary and not elite. There are many elite military organizations such as the Roman Legions, Merrill's Marauders, Rangers, Special Forces, SEALs, etc., however, there are few extraordiary [sic] units such as the ASASODs.

Why were the SODs extraordinary? Certainly, the timing was there and so were the places. But, the thing that really made the SOD an extraordinary unit was the people . . . good Special Forces soldiers . . . good technicians . . . loyal, dedicated, brave men . . . but, most of all, trusted and true friends.[4]

In September of 1963, John was transferred to the Four Hundredth Special Operations Detachment, where he completed the First Special Forces SCUBA course in August of 1964. The First Special Forces Group, also on Okinawa, played a key role during the Vietnam War. It also has the dubious distinction of having the first and last Special Forces soldiers killed in Viet Nam: Captain Harry Griffith Cramer Jr., who also had served in Korea, was killed on October 21, 1957. Although he represented the first special forces death, he was not killed in combat but actually died in a training accident when an explosive detonated prematurely. The last, Captain Richard Morgan Rees, was killed on December 15, 1973—a year after John Kearns was killed in Laos—and was awarded the Distinguished Service Cross and a Silver Star. According to an article in *The New York Times*, Rees was killed while attempting to surrender. "The operations officer of the United States search team that came under attack in an area southwest of Saigon this morning said that one American 'was murdered in cold blood' as he held up his hands in surrender."[5]

At the end of his enlistment in 1966, John returned to Texas to finish his bachelor's degree in Far East Studies. After graduating in 1968 from North Texas State University (now University of North Texas), in Denton, John soon found himself back in Southeast Asia, once again involved in the Vietnam War.

But this time it was in a more oblique manner.

John Kearns preparing for a parachute jump. *Public domain.*

CHAPTER EIGHT

Girls, Sports, Drugs, and Jail

He's in the jailhouse now.

Jimmie Rodgers and **Elise McWilliams**

I attended elementary school, junior high, and high school in Woodway, Texas. High school kinda changed me. Looking back, I see the summer between my sophomore and junior years as a transformational time, but not for the better. I would say it was a time of personal growth, but that might not be completely accurate. It was certainly a time of physical growth—a change from that pudgy kid jiggling in the Walton Belt Vibrator being advertised all over McLennan County. In hindsight, though, I see some foreshadowing of a future that brought personal tragedy and hardship. I was a lost soul. There were things happening on the other side of the world that I knew very little about, other than that I didn't want to go there. I didn't know then what I know now: I had a brother over there whose life was in almost constant danger and was ultimately snuffed out. Knowing that puts the travails of my high school years in a different perspective. I had it easy compared to what he went through.

I started the ninth grade, my freshman year, at Woodway's Midway High School in the fall of 1968, one of the most tumultuous years in modern American history. The Tet Offensive had started in Vietnam in January and antiwar sentiment rocketed sky high in the United States, particularly on college campuses. Martin Luther King Jr. was assassinated in the spring, and Robert F. Kennedy was killed in the summer before I started high school. For the adult world, it was a frightening time. For the not-quite-adult world, it wasn't as frightening, but the future was certainly uncertain. I turned fourteen that summer, still two years away from being legally able to drive and four years away from being eligible for the draft. Maybe the war would be over by then.

All my life, I had been shy and insecure. It took all my courage just to think about asking a girl on a date, much less actually broaching the topic. I had almost no ability to carry on a conversation with the opposite sex. But I tried. I even went to my Junior Prom with a girl I had known from church all my life. I wondered if she simply took pity on me. Maybe she did, but I'll take it.

I played football in high school. Although I liked football for its own sake, it wasn't lost on me that football players were typically among the most popular at school, particularly with girls. I worked hard to get myself into football shape, lifting weights and running. I became the strongest guy in school, bench pressing over three hundred pounds. Unfortunately, being the strongest guy in the school didn't translate into being the strongest guy on the varsity football team—you had to actually be on the team for that. My low grades and problems with the law, including smoking a little pot, got me demoted to the junior varsity. All my buddies I had grown up with were playing on the varsity and I couldn't even be on the team with them, much less on the field.

My junior year was particularly rough for me academically. I was borderline in most classes, but history was a different story. I loved history! I got history! Somehow, some way, for some reason, it resonated with me. The only problem I had with history was remembering exact dates—which can be quite a problem for a historian. I could tell you how and why some historical event happened, but I had a hard time putting a date to it. The possibility that I was an undiagnosed dyslexic would explain a lot of things, but I didn't know it at the time. In fact, my grades were so bad that I was on the verge of failing my junior year. Had it not been for a kind Latin teacher, Mr. Tom Baxley, who took pity on me and changed an F on a crucial test to a passing grade, I would have been doomed to repeat that year.

★ ★ ★ ★ ★

Lysergic acid diethylamide, or LSD, is a synthetic drug that was discovered in 1938 by a Swiss chemist named Albert Hofmann. LSD is a highly potent hallucinogen, known for its "psychedelic" effects, which Hofmann accidentally discovered when he ingested it unintentionally. Initially used by psychiatrists to treat schizophrenia and alcoholism, LSD, or "acid" as it was commonly called, was probably most associated, at least in popular culture, with the counterculture movement of the mid-1960s in places like London and San Francisco's Haight-Ashbury. Its usage spread across the country throughout the late '60s and into the '70s.

An experience with LSD, or a "trip," creates hallucinations for the user. There are other physiological effects, such as rapid heart rate, raised body temperature, and increased blood pressure. It can induce a distorted visual sense of shapes, sizes, and colors, alter sounds to the human ear, and induce anxiety and depression. One of its more well-known side effects is flashbacks, a term used to describe a sense of reliving the "trip" days, weeks, or even months later. LSD lent itself to jokes. For example, what do you get when you mix birth control and LSD? A trip without the kids. Or, why did the man on LSD cross the road? Because he thought he was a chicken.

Timothy Leary, a clinical psychologist at Harvard University, gained acclaim and condemnation in the '60s for advocating for psychedelic drugs like LSD. Sometimes called the "High Priest of LSD," he popularized the catchphrase "turn on, tune in, drop out." President Nixon called him "the most dangerous man in America." Biographer Bill Minutaglio, in an interview with NPR, said, "He's kind of, you know, a Mr. Magoo on acid, if you will. He's just tripping his way through life, and circumstances happen. He opens one door and then plummets nine stories but somehow or other lands on a trampoline and goes to another floor."[1]

In 1969, Leary announced his bid for governor of California against Ronald Reagan, with the campaign slogan "Come together, join the party." John Lennon wrote a campaign song for Leary called "Come Together," which was merely a chant of the slogan. Lennon later used it as the springboard for the Beatles' hit "Come Together" on their *Abbey Road* album.[2] Multiple run-ins with the law later, including prison, an escape from prison and recapture, becoming an FBI informant to shorten his prison sentence, release, and a stint in the Witness Protection Program, Leary died in 1996 of prostate cancer.

In a *Playboy* magazine interview in September of 1966, Leary said an acid trip creates "the experience of incredible acceleration and intensification of all senses and of all mental processes," that "[t]aste is intensified," "[t]ouch becomes electric as well as erotic," and that intensification of the sense of smell "is one of the most overwhelming aspects of an LSD experience. It seems as though for the first time you are breathing life, and you remember with amusement and distaste that plastic, odorless, artificial gas that you used to consider air." He also said that "sex under LSD becomes miraculously enhanced and intensified." He said that there are three "inevitable goals of the LSD session": "to discover and make love with God, to discover and make love with yourself, and to discover and make love with a woman."

It's easy to see that he was an effective, and controversial, spokesperson for the drug. One of the more outlandish claims he pressed in the interview was that "LSD is a specific *cure* for homosexuality" (emphasis in original). He explained, "we've had many cases of long-term homosexuals who, under LSD, discover that they are not only genitally but genetically male, that they are basically attracted to females," and that the same impact had been seen with lesbians.[3]

★ ★ ★ ★ ★

The summer of 1971 was experimental for me. It was also a time of making bad decisions. I had been smoking pot for a while, starting when I was a sophomore. I couldn't do it that often because I didn't have the money to buy it, but my friends always seemed to have some. I also tried LSD, which was "in vogue" (if I may use that term) at the time, as well as some other things, mostly pills. I didn't know much about Timothy Leary, much less paid attention to what he said, but I took LSD simply because . . . well, because it was the thing to do. There were all forms of LSD available at the time. There was a piece of paper with a blue dot on it that contained the drug in liquid form. There was Orange Barrel and Purple Haze and others. I remember one time taking LSD with a friend and then trying to drive home. Somehow I ended up lying on the ground in a cul-de-sac, with crickets all over the place.

Ultimately, LSD just didn't do it for me. Years later, though, after I moved to Dallas, I was introduced to another "in vogue" drug. In an almost unparalleled exercise of bad judgment, I invited it in for a visit. It overstayed its welcome and haunted me.

My other weakness was drinking. I wasn't really a beer drinker, but I drank it because that was what my peer group did. I was all about finding, and following, my peer group. Later, in the mid-1970s, while working at clubs in Waco, I became a clear liquor drinker. By the time I got to Dallas in the latter part of that decade, screwdrivers and gin-and-tonics were my problem areas.

Woodway was a very small town. When the bright lights of the big city were in Waco, sometimes you had to go a bit farther away. In what was maybe a precursor to my later years in Dallas, one weekend I took the family's 1965 Pontiac Catalina that my parents allowed me to use and, with some buddies, headed to Dallas's Lee Park. Dallas was less than a two-hour drive north and was known, at least among teenagers, for its party atmosphere. We were too young for the club scene, but Lee Park was different. You didn't need an ID card to prove your age.

Today called Turtle Creek Park, a 2017 name change that accompanied removal of a statue of Confederate General Robert E. Lee astride his horse Traveller, Lee Park was a popular hangout for so-called "hippies" back in my high school years. Local musicians often performed free concerts, and bands from other Texas cities showed up from time to time. It was also known for fighting. Apparently, a fun weekend activity for "rednecks"—avowed enemies of hippies often consisting of athletes, primarily football players, from local high schools—was to show up at Lee Park on weekends and terrorize the longhairs.

One of the most famous fracases (or would that be fracasae?), with "fracas" defined by *Merriam-Webster* as "a noisy quarrel: BRAWL,"[4] occurred on April 12, 1970. Known locally to posterity as the "Lee Park Massacre," a Sunday afternoon of fun and frolic for a group of about three thousand hippies who had gathered for a concert by local rock musicians turned into a riot (of sorts) when police descended on the park to arrest hippie swimmers and skinny-dippers in Turtle Creek. Journalist Kirby Warnock described the start of the "Massacre" this way:

> It was a warm spring day, with some of the first good weather in Dallas in a while. The crowd of young people was throwing Frisbees, smoking pot, dancing, and meeting up with the opposite sex. The bands had been playing for about an hour when a few people decided to take a swim in Turtle Creek. (Just the idea of swimming in that stagnant body of water should be enough to question their sanity.) The Dallas Police officers on hand for crowd control immediately arrested the swimmers, citing a Dallas city ordinance that forbade swimming in any inland bodies of water. As the cops were handcuffing the young offenders, the crowd didn't take too kindly to what they perceived as the police's rough treatment of their fellow hippies. Soon a few dozen of them surrounded the officers, shouting at them, while a few tossed bottles.[5]

Police arrested, and reportedly beat, a number of offenders. One of those beaten and arrested had simply been driving by the afternoon of the riot and was pulled from his car by police: a young attorney named Jim Mattox, who would later serve in the US House of Representatives and as Attorney General for the State of Texas. Warnock wrote, "Infuriated at his treatment, Mattox offered to defend several of the arrested youths at no charge."[6] Warnock also wrote that the Lee Park Massacre was one of the reasons why a number of Dallas musicians relocated to Austin, because they simply "wanted to get the hell out of Dallas." That included the Vaughan brothers, Jimmie and Stevie Ray; Doyle Bramhall, a blues singer, guitarist, and drummer, who later in his career would play with Eric Clapton; and Lou Ann Barton, a blues singer born in Fort Worth who later played with an Austin blues group called Triple Threat Revue, which included Stevie Ray Vaughan.[7]

Our trip to Lee Park was not quite as exciting as the weekend of the Massacre, but my buddies and I did manage to get ourselves arrested, though not beaten, with acid in our possession. The cops stuck us in what they thought was a secure room in a nearby structure of some sort and then headed back to arrest more kids. The room wasn't *that* secure, and we snuck out through an unlocked back window and disappeared. Unfortunately, the A-frame on the Catalina broke on the way home, so I had to take it to a nearby Texaco station, then hitchhike the rest of the way.

In my shortsighted view at the time, I thought that going back to school for my senior year wasn't a good idea. I no longer wanted to play football and I was a borderline student, at best. I had nearly flunked a grade, and I certainly didn't want to spend another year in high school and then flunk my senior year, but I didn't have any other plans. So, I started out the year in school, but not as a full-time student. I was part of a Home Economics program where I worked half a day at the local Dairy Queen, then went to school for the other half. That didn't last long. A few weeks into the semester, I got into a little fracas at school, the details of which shall remain secret, and was expelled. It was just as well, because I decided that I'd had enough.

Two guys I knew from school—who shall remain nameless—and I decided to take an impromptu road trip. Nobody had their own car, and I, because of various "infractions," had been forbidden by my father to drive the repaired Catalina. But "forbidden" doesn't mean "can't," it just means "not supposed to." So we took off in the Catalina. I didn't find out until later that, even though Dad knew it was me who had taken the car, he filed a stolen vehicle report with the police.

The three of us traded off driving so we each could rotate to the back seat and nap while someone else drove. We didn't have any destination in mind other than, I thought, going west, to California. But after waking from my first nap, I saw that the guy who was driving had changed direction. We were going northeast, toward Nashville. From there we went to Canton, Ohio, where he had friends. At one of our stops for gas, I opened the trunk and was shocked to see some things that our driver had stuck in there that I didn't know about, including tapes and a tape deck. I had no idea where he got them and didn't want to ask, but he was using them to barter for gas. I guess that was his form of a gas credit card.

It was September, so the weather was still hot in central Texas, but it was a different story up north in Canton. Average highs for that part of the country in September were in the mid-seventies and overnight lows were in the mid-fifties, compared to Waco's average September daytime highs in the low nineties and overnight lows in the upper sixties. Since the original plan was to go west, not north, none of us had brought winter clothes, and we weren't prepared for the cooler weather we faced in Ohio. If we couldn't afford to pay for gas, we certainly weren't prepared to buy sweaters and coats. We needed money.

One of my companions had a bright idea: Let's break into a few cars and see what we can find. Might be a jacket or two left inside, or maybe something we could sell. Maybe even some money. I wasn't too keen on that. I was mischievous, the kind of guy who fires off bottle rockets and accidentally sets fields on fire, and maybe was too eager to get drunk, drop acid, and smoke pot. But I wasn't a thief. At least I didn't consider myself one. Little did I know at the time that my family had already reported me as a car thief. So I reached a compromise with my principles. My partners in crime would go through cars parked on the street while I followed in the Catalina.

It wasn't long, though, before a report of car break-ins made its way to the local police, who showed up with sirens, red and blue lights, and Miranda warnings. My two companions made a clean getaway, leaving me alone in the Catalina with stolen goods inside. To top it off, one of them had brought all sorts of drug goodies with him, and that was in the car, too. So I got hit with multiple charges, both misdemeanors and felonies, from theft to drug charges.

They stuck me in a holding cell in the Stark County Jail. My "suite" was like all the others, with recessed lighting, recessed commodes, single window slits with bars and screens, concrete beds with a single one-inch mattress, and one pillow. My uniform, which they assigned me, consisted of blue jeans, a T-shirt with "Stark County" printed on it, and a pair of slippers. It actually wasn't all that bad, though—once you got past the notion that I was facing possible prison time. There were a couple of other guys already in there, both big African Americans. They turned out to be football players, good ones, at least to hear them tell it—All-Ohio—who had gotten into some kind of mischief and been busted. We spent most of our time talking football. Man, I sure did miss football.

A few weeks later, my parents arrived to take me back to Texas. Somehow, they managed to get the charges dropped. I figured it was probably because I was a minor, seventeen at the time, but later I learned there had been more to it. After Dad died, Mom showed me a letter from the Canton Police Chief that she held on to for all those years. In it, he had written Dad and told him how much he appreciated Dad's "contribution" to a local law enforcement fund. Putting two and two together in my adult years, I realized that he had bought my freedom. We were not a rich family by any means, so it meant something to me that Dad sacrificed to bring me home.

When I was first walked out the doors of the facility as a free man, I saw Dad standing outside. I immediately turned around to go back into the jail, but they wouldn't let me in. That might give you an idea of our relationship at the time. I didn't know then that he had paid to get me out. I still don't know how much it was.

Back home, I heard a knock on the door—one of those dreaded knocks—from the local Chief of Police. He wanted to talk about the stolen tapes and tape player. Turns out they belonged to my next-door neighbor's father, Thomas Golden, a man I really liked and respected. I had no idea that one of my companions had ripped him off and I felt really bad. We worked out a deal where I would pay him back for a new deck and tapes, and he didn't press criminal charges. He knew me well enough to know that I wouldn't have stolen those things from him. I was glad someone had a little faith in me, even after everything I had done.

But the whole affair created a dilemma for me. I was now less than a year away from eligibility for the draft and the war was still raging. I knew—the whole family knew—that if I was in school, or if I could *stay* in school, I could at least delay being drafted. Mom and Dad made the decision to move into Waco so I could enroll at Richfield High School in the spring of '72. A fresh start.

That semester went pretty well, and I actually had decent grades for the first time in my high school career. Not sure why. Maybe it was because I was away from my old friends and the temptations they brought. Or maybe it was the motivation to stay out of Vietnam. Spring turned into summer, when I turned eighteen—draft eligible—and summer turned into fall. Unable to play football because of the rule in Texas at the time that required transfers to sit out a year before being eligible to play at the new school, I fell into my old habits of smoking pot and drinking. Schoolwork didn't interest me, so I dropped out of Richfield. I briefly, *very* briefly, considered joining the Marines, ironic since I had gone back to school to avoid the military. But then I decided that, as much as I didn't want to go back to school, I even more didn't want to go to Vietnam. And that meant I needed to be a student. Somewhere.

I would start by getting my GED (General Educational Development) at Baylor University. After that, who knew?

CHAPTER NINE

1972—It Was a Very Bad Year

"I live in a rather special world. I know only one person who voted for Nixon. Where they are, I don't know. They're outside my ken. But sometimes when I'm in a theater I can feel them."

Pauline Kael

Like 1954 and 1962, 1972 had its highlights and lowlights. Clifford Irving was scheduled to publish a supposed autobiography of reclusive millionaire Howard Hughes, but in January, Hughes spoke by telephone to journalists and denounced Irving's book as a hoax. In March, Irving admitted to the "hoax" charge.

The *Godfather* movie, adapted from Mario Puzo's novel of the same name, premiered in New York City. It would go on to be nominated for seven Academy Awards and would win, among others, Best Picture and Best Adapted Screenplay. Marlon Brando won Best Actor but declined the award based on his objection to the depiction of Native Americans in film and television.

The Awards ceremony in 1972, for the previous year's films, honored *The French Connection* as Best Picture and its director William Friedkin as Best Director.

The television series *M*A*S*H* began its eleven-year run on CBS.

The Dallas Cowboys defeated the Miami Dolphins 24-3 in the Super Bowl. Roger Staubach was the game's MVP.

The Los Angeles Lakers defeated the New York Knicks to win the NBA championship. The Lakers' Wilt Chamberlin was the MVP.

The Oakland A's beat the Cincinnati Reds in the World Series, four games to three. The MVP was Oakland's Gene Tenace, who hit four home runs and drove in nine.

The Major League Baseball Players Association voted to strike, the first work stoppage in baseball history.

In a Cold War–esque match-up, American Bobby Fischer defeated Russian Boris Spassky in the World Chess Championship in Reykjavik, Iceland. Fischer was the first American chess champion.

On New Year's Eve, heading in to 1973, Roberto Clemente of the Pittsburgh Pirates was killed in a plane crash into the ocean while on a humanitarian mission to Nicaragua following an earthquake.

Arthur Bremer attempted to assassinate George Wallace, former governor of Alabama and presidential candidate.

President Richard Nixon ordered the development of a space shuttle program.

Five burglars were arrested for breaking into the Democratic National Committee's headquarters in the Watergate Hotel.

Richard Nixon defeated George McGovern for the presidency in a landslide, winning 520 electoral votes to McGovern's seventeen (McGovern won Massachusetts and the District of Columbia), and taking more than 60 percent of the popular vote.

Atari introduced the video game *Pong*.

HBO (Home Box Office) introduced paid television on cable.

The Dow Jones closed above 1,000 for the first time.

Apollo 17 conducted the final mission of NASA's Apollo program.

US National Security Advisor Henry Kissinger visited South Vietnam and said that "peace is at hand."

Negotiators for North Vietnam walked out of the Paris Peace talks in protest of U.S. bombing raids in the North.

The United States turned over Long Binh military base to South Vietnam.

The United States lost its first B-52 Stratofortress bomber in Vietnam, shot down by a surface-to-air missile near Vinh Moc, located north of the demilitarized zone on the border between North and South Vietnam.

On its way to the Gulf of Tonkin, a brawl between white and Black sailors broke out on the *USS Kitty Hawk*. It would become known as "The *USS Kitty Hawk* riot."

Operation Linebacker II, the "Christmas bombings," was ordered by President Nixon, dropping bombs on Hanoi and Haiphong in North Vietnam.

Paul Heckmann turned eighteen on July 9 and registered for the draft.

Shortly before Christmas, John Kearns lay mortally wounded on the floor of a helicopter. He died onboard while being evacuated from the site of a North Vietnamese mortar attack near Paksong, Laos.

CHAPTER TEN

The (Not-So-Secret) War

"Secrecy and a free, democratic government don't mix."

Harry Truman

For years after his death, John Kearns was just a nameless, faceless star on the CIA's Memorial Wall. It wasn't until the Annual Memorial Ceremony in the year 2000 that the anonymity could finally be peeled away, his name revealed and his heroism recognized. It's not clear why twenty-eight years had to pass before his contributions could be formally acknowledged, but one supposes that is just part of the "secrets" game, as CIA operatives so often operate under that cloak of secrecy. Such was the case for John Kearns's involvement in the covert war in Laos during the Vietnam War. And both of those "wars" require a bit of explanation.

Although it's common to refer to the Vietnam action as a "war," it was never a declared war—at least not constitutionally—any more than the "police action" in Korea was a war.[1] Article 1, Section 8 of the United States Constitution grants Congress the sole power to declare war. Although more than 3 million American military personnel had served in Vietnam by the end of official US involvement, peaking at nearly 550,000 in 1969, and although

58,318 names of service members killed in Vietnam are etched on the Vietnam Memorial in Washington, D.C., Congress never declared a war. Instead, following an alleged "series" of attacks on US ships in international waters by North Vietnamese patrol boats in August of 1964, Congress enacted the Gulf of Tonkin Resolution on August 7. That resolution authorized President Lyndon Johnson to "take all necessary measures to repel any armed attack against the forces of the United States and to prevent any further aggression." The Resolution was premised upon a contention that the Communist regime in Vietnam had "deliberately and *repeatedly* attacked United States naval vessels lawfully present in international waters." It called the "attacks" part of a "deliberate and *systematic* campaign of aggression" (emphasis added).[2]

The use of the terms "repeatedly" and "systematic" in the Gulf of Tonkin Resolution is questionable. There is some debate to this day whether there was more than one attack on US vessels. Documents declassified and released by the National Security Agency in 2005 and 2006 "reveal what historians could not prove: There was not a second attack on U.S. Navy ships in the Tonkin Gulf in early 1964. Furthermore, the evidence suggests a disturbing and deliberate attempt by Secretary of Defense McNamara to distort the evidence and mislead Congress."[3]

In January of 1971, the Gulf of Tonkin Resolution was repealed. In 1973, Congress passed the War Powers Resolution, which reimposed requirements upon the president to obtain congressional consent to commit the country to any armed conflict. In the meantime, though, those who fought in Vietnam had no doubt that they had been fighting a war, declared or not.

Whatever one chooses to call the armed conflict in Vietnam, coming up with a label for what transpired in Laos represented an even higher level of contortion. The 1962 Geneva Accords prohibited the Laotian government from entering into any alliance or agreement, whether military or otherwise, that would be inconsistent with the neutrality of Laos, or to allow any foreign interference in its internal affairs. The Accords then bound the other signing parties to refrain from "all direct or indirect interference" in Laos's internal affairs and not to introduce into Laos troops or military personnel "in any form whatsoever." The Accords defined "foreign military personnel" as including "advisers, experts, instructors, consultants, technicians, observers," and specifically forbade "foreign regular and irregular troops" and "foreign para-military formations."[4]

Many often refer to the CIA's paramilitary action in Laos as a "secret" or "covert" war. But that is likely a misnomer, particularly if you apply the common definition of those words. *Merriam-Webster* defines "secret" as "kept from knowledge or view," while the *American Heritage Dictionary* defines it as "kept hidden from knowledge or view; concealed."[5] Synonyms include hidden, concealed, unrevealed, and covert. *Merriam-Webster* defines "covert," in turn, as "not openly shown, engaged in, or avowed."[6] Boiled down to its essence, the terms mean something that is not generally known and is kept quiet or covered up. That's a little hard to comprehend in today's world of the Internet and twenty-four-hour news cycles. Five or six decades ago, secrecy was a little easier to maintain, but even then, it was never absolute.

By the time the 1962 Accords were signed, the United States had already been involved in Laos for some time and, Accords or not, wasn't about to back out. Part of the pretext for US involvement was that it was via the CIA, not the military, and thus, technically, not a violation of the Accords. By 1960, the CIA had established a station in Laos larger than the American embassy in Vientiane. Its private airline, which acted as a front, had already been operating in Laos and, in 1959, was reorganized as Air America. Operation Momentum had been inaugurated in 1961, which armed and trained the indigenous Hmong people, under the leadership of Laotian general Vang Pao, to fight against the Pathet Lao in the Laotian civil war.[7]

When Kennedy took office, he was surprised to learn that almost seven hundred US military personnel were already in Laos, almost half of whom were Special Forces.[8] He was determined not to commit to a ground war in Laos, notwithstand-

King of Laos with American personnel. *From right to left:* Theodore Shackley (CIA Station Chief), Bill Lair (CIA), Pat Landry (CIA), Tony Poe (CIA), Dr. Charles Weldon (USAID Public Health), and Howard Freeman (CIA). *Photo by Ernest Kuhn, courtesy of Ernest and Phaythoune Kuhn Image Collection, Southeast Asian Images & Texts Project, University of Wisconsin Digital Collections.*

ing Eisenhower's emphasis on the nation's importance, but he authorized the CIA to expand Operation Momentum. Bill Lair, a CIA paramilitary officer who had been in Laos since 1952—and a good Texan; though born in Oklahoma, he got to Texas as fast as he could, moving to Borger in the Texas panhandle when he was three and graduating from Texas A&M University, where the CIA recruited him—jumped on the leeway the authorization presumably provided. At his urging, the CIA approved new weapons shipments to the Hmong and permitted Vang Pao to send his forces to Thailand for training as pilots.

The United States justified violating the Accords on the basis that the North Vietnamese violated it first, maintaining a supply corridor from North Vietnam into South Vietnam along the Laotian border, but physically in Laos, called the Ho Chi Minh Trail. To maintain the fiction of compliance with the Accords, the CIA's work in Laos, as well as that of the US military acting in conjunction with the CIA's objectives, had to be carried out in the shadows. A group of air force pilots known as The Ravens participated in marking targets along the Ho Chi Minh Trail for air strikes. They called it the Steve Canyon Program after a comic strip "flyboy" created by Milton Caniff. British journalist Christopher Robbins, whose nonfiction book *Air America* was the basis for the film starring Mel Gibson, described it this way:

> As the war dragged on, so the myth grew. It started in the mid-1960s as a mix of gossip and bar talk among a battle-hardened elite who told stories that seemed fantastic to everyone who heard them. Apparently, there was another war even nastier than the one in Vietnam, and so secret that

Raven forward air controllers at Long Tieng, Laos, 1970. *Public domain.*

> the location of the country in which it was being fought was classified. The cognoscenti simply referred to it as "the Other Theater." The men who chose to fight in it were handpicked volunteers, and anyone accepted for a tour seemed to disappear as if from the face of the earth.[9]

"Disappeared" because they were subject to a process known as "sheep dipping," in which the pilots "resigned" (at least publicly) from the military, their official military records were shifted to Top Secret files, and they "flew into battle in civilian clothes—denim cutoffs, T-shirts, cowboy hats, and dark glasses."[10] Robbins writes that the phony resignations and transfers of records "posed extremely tricky problems when they were killed or captured. There would be all sorts of pension and insurance problems, which was one of the reasons the CIA found it necessary to set up its own insurance company."[11]

Joshua Kurlantzick called the action in Laos a "not-so-secret secret war," as a "small circle of people in Washington and Southeast Asia understood the growing operation but did nothing to publicize it to Americans."[12] There were suspicions. Journalists questioned how Vang Pao's army could be so well-equipped, although the CIA made sure they didn't see enough details to put the real story together.

Not everyone agreed that the action in Laos was secret, nor even that it was intended to be. Former CIA Director Richard Helms said it was only secret to those who didn't know about it. That may sound like a riddle, but it actually makes sense. It's one thing not to know about something because that something has been actively concealed. It's another to be ignorant of something that is available to be known. Helms admitted that the action in Laos was an "indisputable violation" of the 1962 Geneva Accords but argued that it was taken in direct response to North Vietnamese violations—the childhood playground "he started it" defense—and that "[a]ppropriate members of the Congress had full knowledge of Kennedy's action and were thoroughly briefed on CIA's responsibility for the paramilitary activity." In fact, Helms said, the "CIA's role was directed and monitored at every stage by the Special Action group formed by President Kennedy. In Laos, the paramilitary and associated activity was approved and directed by the U.S. ambassador in Vientiane."[13]

But what the president and ambassador knew, and even what "appropriate members" of Congress knew, did not correlate to what the press knew and, correspondingly, what the press would report to the American public. On January 26, 1968, *Time* magazine reported on US efforts to bomb the Ho Chi Minh Trail in a story entitled "Spillover into Laos." At that point, *Time* still believed the fiction of US adherence to the 1962 Accords, at least in terms of troops on the ground, and solely blamed the North Vietnamese for violations. They, like everyone else outside the "need to know" circle, had been kept in the dark on paramilitary activities in equipping and training both Laotian and Thai irregulars to battle the Pathet Lao. *Time* said,

> The neutralization and partition of the kingdom of Laos stipulated by the Geneva Accords of 1962 has served Hanoi's war against South Viet Nam admirably. Down the Ho Chi Minh Trail through the Communist-controlled portion of Laos have flowed the men and supplies enabling North Viet Nam to keep the war going, and Laotian rice has helped keep Ho's warriors fed. The U.S. regularly bombs the Trail to slow the flow. But unlike Hanoi, Washington has been unwilling to violate the ban on foreign troops in Laos and strike directly overland to interdict the enemy traffic southward.[14]

Technically, *Time* was correct—assuming one ignores the language in the Accords about "advisers, experts, instructors, consultants, technicians, observers" and "foreign and irregular troops" and "foreign para-military formations." It is more likely that *Time* was simply still largely ignorant of those American personnel in Laos.

Democratic Senator Stuart Symington of Missouri, the former (and first) Secretary of the Air Force, expressed his "surprise, shock and anger" in 1970 at his "recent discovery" of the CIA activity in Laos. Helms, in turn, expressed his own surprise at Symington's surprise. According to Helms, Symington "probably knew the most about CIA activity in Laos," going back at least to 1967, when he chaired Senate Armed Services Committee hearings on Laos and heard testimony from Ted Shackley, who had been the CIA station chief in Laos. Helms said that Symington "praised the program as a sensible way to fight a war" and noted that "CIA's annual budget in Laos was approximately what the U.S. military was spending per day in Vietnam." It wasn't just Symington who knew. Helms wrote that, between 1962 and 1970, approximately fifty U.S. senators had been briefed on the war in Laos.[15] One can almost hear echoes of Claude Rains's Captain Louis Renault in *Casablanca*: "I'm shocked! Shocked to find that gambling is going on in here."

Helms was not wrong, though. Government knowledge of the activity in Laos and violations of the predecessor 1954 Geneva Accords went back as far as the Eisenhower administration. Historian John Prados said that some of "President Eisenhower's decisions clearly indicate his concept of Laos as a secret war." Eisenhower specifically approved moving B-26 bombers to Thailand and T-6 strike aircraft to be flown, although without bombs, by Laotian pilots. In early 1961, he ordered a naval task force into position for possible intervention in Laos. Laos was a key topic of discussion between Eisenhower and Kennedy as part of the presidential transition. Eisenhower warned Nikita Khrushchev that he intended to ensure that the "legitimate government of Laos" remained in power. On December 30, 1960, he reportedly informed a gathering, which included CIA Director Allen Dulles and National Security Advisor Gordon Gray, that "[w]e must not allow Laos to fall to the Communists, even if it involves war."[16]

A Hmong armed company receives its final briefing before departing on a mission during the spring of 1961. *Public domain.*

In a different take on the issue, historian John Hart Ely considered the constitutionality of the CIA action in Laos and concluded that, although the main body of the war in Vietnam was, in fact, constitutional "under currently prevailing notions of congressional authorization," the "secret war" in Laos was not—even though it was not actually secret. Ely wrote that "a number of senators and congressmen knew more than they let on in 1969," making specific reference to Senator Symington. "At the very least they had been told enough to induce them, had they been inclined, to investigate further."[17] In legal circles, that is the "knew or should have known" standard, which charges someone with knowledge of facts that they would have known had they exercised reasonable diligence.

The wild card in the discussion was whether the American people were aware of the war in Laos. Did they know or should they have known? Or were they blocked from knowledge by government efforts to shield them from the goings-on in Laos? Unquestionably, the war in Laos was not widespread knowledge, at least not in the early to mid-1960s. But by 1969, the press was starting to latch onto it. It gushed into public view in a trifecta of news stories late that year, one in *Time* (October 17) titled "Laos: The Unseen Presence," one in *US News & World Report* (October 20) titled "More Aid to Laos: A Report on What the U.S. is Doing There," and one in *The New York Times* (October 26) titled "U.S. Runs a Secret Laotian Army."

The *Time* article complained of government efforts to maintain secrets about Laos. "It sometimes seems as if the U.S. Government would like to make the very existence of Laos classified information." In the capital city of Vientiane, "One sees few Americans, and none in uniforms. In a few bars one may find the freewheeling, CIA-paid Air America pilots, the Lord Jims of Laos. But the main accent is French." The article reported that the United States admitted that there were seventy-five military personnel serving as advisers in Vientiane and more than two hundred CIA agents. "The CIA men and the military advisers train, equip, support and transport the entire Royal Lao military effort. The Americans have been known to advise on tactics on the battalion level." So why was this all kept secret for so long? *Time* answered that unspoken question: "It is largely clandestine because, like the North Vietnamese presence, it violates the 1962 Geneva Accords, which supposedly neutralized Laos."[18]

The New York Times article reported, in its lede, "The United States maintains and largely controls an army of irregulars in Laos."

But even though the lid had been blown off of the secret war, at least to the public, certain aspects were still unknown. "The closest secrecy surrounds the presence of Americans and, other foreigners, including Thais, engaged by the Central Intelligence Agency for the secret force. Estimates range from 50 to several hundred, but few people know the total." Questions were raised about American deaths, but *The New York Times* was assured that "Americans are instructed not to expose themselves to combat operations in order to maintain the secrecy of their presence. However, the contention of American officials that no CIA agent had been killed by enemy bullets was contradicted by Laotians close to General Vang Pao."[19]

There had, in fact, been American deaths in Laos as part of the secret war—though maybe not as a result of "enemy bullets." Three CIA smokejumpers were killed when their Air America plane went down in 1961, two others were killed when their Air America helicopter crashed in 1965, and a CIA medical officer died in a plane crash along the Thai-Laos border in early 1969.

In March 1970, President Richard Nixon reiterated the party line, stating that "no American stationed in Laos has ever been killed in ground combat operations." Perhaps technically correct, with the reference to "ground combat operations." But the White House did confirm approximately four hundred casualties in the air in Laos. Two days later, on March 8, Nixon backtracked and acknowledged American deaths on the ground. His deputy press secretary, Gerald L. Warren, said that Nixon had been unaware, at the time of his statement, of the death of an American army advisor, Captain Joseph Bush, killed on February 10, 1969, in action against communist troops on the Plaine des Jarres, or Plain of Jars. Then the Nixon administration had to backtrack even further, acknowledging that not only Captain Bush but also twenty-six American civilians had been killed or listed as missing over the past six years.[20]

Within a few years, on December 15, 1972, John Kearns would also be killed in action on the ground in Laos, but technically his death was not one of military personnel since he was in the employ of the CIA. Tammy Arbuckle, writing in *The Washington Star*, complained that nonmilitary personnel were routinely excluded from death tallies in connection with the Vietnam War. "These unacknowledged deaths are of American civilians performing military duties normally carried out by U.S. Air Force or Army personnel." The article identified, specifically, Kearns.

> On Friday, Dec. 15, however, at a town on the South Laos' Bolovens Plateau called Paksong . . . John Kearns of Alvarado, Tex., was listed as killed by North Vietnamese mortar shells which hit the command post of the Lao irregular unit he was advising.
>
> **Killed at Saravane**
>
> An embassy spokesman described Kearns as "American contract personnel[21] attached to an irregular Lao unit." Irregular Lao units are handled by the Central Intelligence agency [sic]. Kearns was the third American advisor to irregulars killed in action since September.

The article further noted that roughly eight hundred Americans had been killed or were missing in Laos since May of 1964.[22] That was a far cry from Nixon's "no American" or even the number mentioned in the correction.

Legal scholar John Hart Ely argued that any excuses for keeping US involvement in Laos secret quickly collapsed and morphed into the defense that both Congress and the American public were actually aware of it. He concluded that attempts to hide information, particularly at the inception of US involvement in Laos, is what kept the general public from having that actual awareness at first. He provided six reasons: (1) the source of information for most Americans was the daily media, but the war in Laos wasn't covered; (2) when there was coverage of the war, Vietnam and, to a lesser extent, Cambodia dominated the news; (3) the war in Laos was on the other side of the world from the United States—out of sight, out of mind—though so were Vietnam and Cambodia; (4) what little reporting was done on the secret war was based on "rumor or allegation," and not personal observation; (5) those rumors and allegations were primarily generated by the communists, who were patently incredible; and (6) the US government denied those rumors and allegations and, surely, the government would not lie to its people. But, Ely concluded, "I do not see how our government can lie to us and then successfully claim as a defense that we were actually on notice as to the truth, because we should have known the government was lying."[23]

There is a distinction, though, between insufficient knowledge and secret, and between questions of constitutionality and questions of secrecy. Granted, the late 1960s were a different time than today, but it's fair to say that the term "secret war" was a misnomer. There was tension between governmental agencies as to whether to permit the war to go public or to maintain secrecy. In an April 1971 Staff Report prepared for the Senate Subcommittee on US Security Agreements and Commitments Abroad of the Committee on Foreign Relations, the staff noted that, from a military point of view, the situation in Laos "is growing steadily worse and the initiative seems clearly to be in the hands of the enemy." While the United States continued to train, arm, and feed the Laotian army under direction of the CIA, "there is an evident determination among U.S. officials in Laos to continue to prosecute the war with only gradually reduced secrecy." Besides, it was clear that the United States was violating the 1962 Accords and that, even though US violations were justified, going public with those violations while North Vietnam denied its own "would make it far more difficult, if not impossible, to reactivate the provisions of the 1962 agreements."[24]

In May of 1971, *The Washington Post* reported that two investigators who had just returned from Indochina "told a Senate Foreign Relations subcommittee in secret session yesterday that the CIA is covertly financing 4,800 Thai troops fighting in Northern Laos in support of the Laotian government." The expenditures, however, had "been kept secret from the public."[25] Even earlier, in February of 1971, the *Post* reported on Massachusetts Senator Edward Kennedy's charge that "nearly half of all American aid for war refugees is being supplied to guerrilla forces directed by the Central Intelligence Agency."[26]

Senator Symington continued his "I'm shocked" façade about the war. In a statement to the Subcommittee on Criminal Laws and Procedures on July 12, 1971, Symington addressed military operations in Laos and credited the press with bringing certain things to light. Referencing a July 7 article by Tammy Arbuckle in *The Washington Star*, reprinted in *The New York Times*, and one by D. E. Ronk in *The Washington Post* on July 8, he said, "Apparently this operation by Lao and Thai irregulars, whose costs are paid by U.S. funds appropriated by Congress has been under way since late

June; but we in the Congress, who have appropriated the funds, have had to learn about it in the press."[27]

Symington said the press reported that the irregulars are "being led by American military men in the employ of the Central Intelligence Agency and that top Lao military officers insist that the operation is being coordinated by the CIA." Discomfited by these revelations by the American press, of which he supposedly never had any knowledge otherwise, he expressed the "right to question the wisdom of this latest Laotian operation and to deplore the secrecy which surrounds it." He also asserted that Congress had the "right to resent the high-handedness of the executive branch in not consulting Congress before undertaking a major military operation with funds Congress appropriated."[28]

Ely noted Symington's outrage that much of Congress and the public may have been misled "seems to have skirted saying that he personally had been seriously misled, at least for very long." Ely concluded that Congress, including Symington, had, at the very least, "been told enough to induce them, had they been inclined, to investigate further. Admittedly this would have been an aggravating and politically unrewarding inquiry."[29]

In truth, Symington's knowledge of the secret war, despite his outrage, had been well documented. Christopher Robbins wrote that in October of 1967, Symington had been a houseguest of CIA station chief Ted Shackley in Laos, and he invited Shackley, who ran the CIA's Phoenix Program of political assassinations,[30] to testify before the Armed Services Committee about the actions in Laos. Senators on the committee who were present were John Stennis (D., Mississippi), Symington (D., Missouri), Henry M. Jackson (D., Washington), Howard W. Cannon (D., Nevada), Thomas J. McIntyre (D., New Hampshire), Harry F. Byrd (D.,

Virginia), Daniel B. Brewster (D., Maryland), James B. Pearson (R., Kansas), John G. Tower (R., Texas), Jack Miller (R., Iowa), and Peter H. Dominick (R., Colorado). Following Shackley's testimony, Symington stated his opinion that the CIA approach was to be congratulated.[31] After watching a film clip about CIA paramilitary operations in Laos, Symington commented that the United States was getting better results from money spent on Laos than "from all the money being put into Vietnam."[32]

On October 18, 1969, *The Washington Post* reported that Symington's Foreign Relations subcommittee on Overseas Commitments called CIA Director Helms to testify about the CIA's role in Laos. The article stated that US involvement was believed to be extensive, including B-52s flying as many as two hundred bombing sorties per day on the Ho Chi Minh Trail from bases in Thailand and South Vietnam, and concluded that US military aid to the Laotian government could have been $200 million per year.

In August of 1972, Symington authored an article in which he referred to the war in Laos as "characterized by a degree of secrecy never before true of a major American involvement abroad." He referred to it as a "perversion of the processes of government . . . a perversion to our democratic system and to the nation's future." But then he said,

> Who is responsible? The Constitution has been bypassed by a small group of men in various departments of the Executive Branch who, under the direction of four Presidents, initiated and carried out policies without any real Congressional knowledge and thus any true Congressional authorization. Needless to say, these policies were carried out without

> the knowledge and approval of the American people, on whose consent our government is supposed to rest.[33]

It's easy to understand how some might be skeptical of Symington's apparent memory loss of being briefed on the war in Laos. It's baffling, though, how he believed his faux outrage would not be noticed, at least by his colleagues and certainly by the architects of the secret war.

By 1972, the year of John Kearns's death, the government was starting to let down its defenses. In February, the CIA admitted it operated an airbase at Long Tieng (sometimes called Long Cheng) and even flew in a select group of journalists on an Air America plane to tour the base. Still, there were limits to how much the CIA was willing to admit. Ground rules were provided to those journalists, including a prohibition against filming, photographing, or otherwise identifying any US personnel either "by name or function." And the press was not given free reign, which triggered suspicions.

> The fact that all newsmen wanting to go to the Long Cheng area were made to go together on the same day picked well in advance, and that a single newsman is not allowed to go to the area on U.S. transport traveling consistently between Long Cheng and Vientiane, can only give rise to suspicion that the U.S. is sanitizing the area on specified days for the purpose of press junkets aimed at showing secrecy has stopped.[34]

Similar visits were allowed to other bases over the course of the year, including a base in Thailand at Camp Saritsena.[35] Secrecy was being lifted, slowly.

CHAPTER ELEVEN

Keep On Keepin' On

"Most people fail, not because of lack of desire, but because of lack of commitment."

Vince Lombardi

After obtaining my GED, I moved back into my parents' house in Waco. By this time, my dad had bought the Gulf station next door to his equipment rental store. I worked there part-time, pumping gas and changing oil, until Dad let the Gulf franchise go. We still kept the facility as a tool and maintenance shed for the rental store.

I also took classes at McLennan Community College. For the first time in my life, I had a 3.0 average. Books were really not my friends, unless they told something in such a way that I could paint a picture in my head. The better classes for me were things like history and geography, as long as tests didn't focus on dates or numbers. But math classes were a complete loss. Oddly enough, I enjoyed science—except trying to remember the periodic table. But I did what I had to do to stay in school and out of Vietnam. What I really missed was playing football. I don't know if it was the sport itself or if it was the feeling of being a member of a team. There was a real sense of camaraderie in being part of something bigger than yourself, particularly in a sport as brutal as football. Or maybe it was both. Whatever it was, I missed it.

Now that I was out of high school for good, if I was going to play football, that meant college. Not surprisingly, no schools had been banging down my door to offer me a scholarship, even before that troublesome road trip to Ohio. Getting kicked off the varsity and not playing my senior year was not appealing to college coaches. If I was going to play, I was going to have to walk on.

Walk-ons were those athletes who chose to play a sport in college without the benefit of a scholarship, usually in hopes that they would make a big enough impression on their coaches to be offered a scholarship for the next year. It was a long shot, but history tells us that there were notable players in the National Football League who got their starts as walk-on college football players. Among the most notable is Clay Matthews, who walked on at the University of Southern California, earned a scholarship, and was drafted in the first round by the Green Bay Packers. J. J. Watt left a scholarship at Central Michigan University to walk on at Wisconsin and earn a scholarship. From there, he was a first-round draft pick of the Houston Texans, where he was a multi-time All Pro, earned the AP NFL Defensive Player of the Year Award three times, and is likely headed for enshrinement in the NFL Hall of Fame. Neither of those guys had even been born when I got out of high school (Matthews was born in 1986 and Watt in 1989), but walking on was nevertheless a time-honored tradition, even in the 1970s.

Maybe it was just the exuberance of youth that made me think I could do it. Or maybe the arrogance, which sometimes went hand in hand with exuberance, or was mistaken for exuberance. It had been a couple of years since the last time I'd laced up my cleats, and I knew if I was going to play at any college, I had to get into shape. The best shape of my life. That meant I needed to start working out again and maybe lay off the dope and booze—at least for a while. I knew that I lacked the self-discipline to prepare for college football, so I needed someone to hold my feet to the fire. Fortunately, I found just such a trainer not too far from home: a guy named Allen who worked at a gym on Lake Air Boulevard in Waco. He was a hired hand at the time, but later he bought the place. He agreed to train me, so I joined the gym and threw myself into a workout program.

The guy was a bit of prick—arrogant and full of himself. He was curt with everyone he came in contact with, at least at the gym, and I was no exception. He was a big man, probably six-feet-four and weighed more than 250 pounds. All muscle, with very little body fat. Like an overgrown boot camp drill instructor. But prick or not, he knew what he was doing. Probably a good trait for a trainer. Knowing what you're doing, that is. I'm not so sure about the inherent value of prickdom.

All I had ever known as far as weight training had been run-of-the-mill pumping iron, but Allen had a full bag of tricks when it came to working out. He taught me some innovative methods I had never used, or even seen, before, like using a moving platform, in the form of a big medicine ball, to do dumbbell presses. This thing was made of stitched leather, almost like a giant baseball. Very heavy. Balancing on it was a delicate proposition. It was a struggle to keep the ball from rolling one way or the other, but you also had to concentrate on your lift. You couldn't rely on your back as a foundation, due to the movement of the ball, so it forced you to concentrate on, and isolate, the arm and shoulder action. Translate that to an actual bench press with a bar, with a steady foundation, and my numbers shot up dramatically.

I think one of the reasons he liked working with me was because I could move so much weight. My high school teammate Barry Joe Pledger called me the strongest kid in school when I was a junior. I considered that high praise coming from someone I considered "the guy" when it came to football. His nickname was "The Plug," because running into him was like running into a fireplug—you kinda bounced off and he never moved. Working with Allen, by the time I was ready to actually apply to colleges, I was bench pressing over 400 pounds with ease. I even pressed 450 once, though technically it would have been considered "cheating" since I arched my back off the bench. Details!

Another focal point was conditioning training. That meant running. Never my strong suit, although I wouldn't go so far as to say that I hated it. There was a track at the facility that we devoted hours to. I don't know how many miles I logged, but it would have put a marathoner to shame. One of the good things about football was that there was no real call to worry about distance training. After all, in your wildest dreams, the most you could be required to run was 110 yards, assuming you got the ball in the back of your own end zone and took it straight to the opposite goal line. Of course, you might have some weaving and direction changes along the way to add to it a bit, but you get my drift. Besides, I was a lineman and distance wasn't a particular concern of mine. But Allen had some different ideas about running, so I ran a lot of miles.

He quickly deduced that I had one leg longer than the other. It wasn't something that I had ever noticed, but he spotted it right away merely by watching me run. Because of the difference in length, slight though it was, I sprinted with my legs spread farther apart than necessary, which cut down on my speed. He worked with me to change my form, with legs closer together. I was never the fastest guy on a football field, though as a lineman I didn't have to be. For a lineman, quickness was actually better than speed, which was a bonus for a lineman. Working with Allen, I knocked a full second off my time in the forty-yard dash. That might not sound like a lot, but going from a 5.8 forty to a 4.8 forty represented nearly a 20 percent increase in my speed. And 4.8 was the kind of time you might expect from a running back, not a down-in-the-trenches lineman. I felt like a bird in flight. Maybe a portend of things to come.

I trained with Allen three times a week and ran every day, either on the track next to the gym or at Richfield High School's stadium across the street from my parents' house. At the stadium, I also ran the stands in addition to using the track. I kept this up for a full year until I was in prime shape.

I felt like I was ready for college football.

★ ★ ★ ★ ★

Just in case any reader is looking for a trainer in the Waco area and thinks Allen might be for you—sorry! He's still alive but you won't find him in Waco anymore. Robert Allen Stanford is his name, and he resides at the United States Penitentiary, Coleman II Unit, in Central Florida, where he is serving a 110-year sentence for conducting a seven billion–dollar Ponzi scheme.

Ponzi schemes are named after Charles Ponzi, an Italian immigrant who nearly perfected the fraud in 1920s Boston, creating an arbitrage scheme whereby he paid off early investors with money from later investors. His scheme collapsed and he served prison time before being deported. He wasn't the first, though. That was supposedly a scam run in the 1860s by Jacob Young, William Abrams, and Nancy Clem. Or at least so claims historian Wendy

Gamber in her book *The Notorious Mrs. Clem: Murder and Money in the Gilded Age.*[1] The most well-known, and possibly the largest, Ponzi scheme was perpetrated by Wall Street financier Bernie Madoff, accused of defrauding investors to the tune of nearly $65 billion dollars. My Waco trainer's scheme seems puny by comparison.

Stanford was born in Mexia, Texas, and graduated from Eastern Hills High School in Fort Worth before obtaining a finance degree from Baylor University. As good a trainer as he was for me, it turned out he wasn't such a good businessman. He was a pretty good con man, though. At least for a while. His gym in Waco, called Total Health Fitness of Temple, Inc., went belly up when he was hit with a default judgment for failing to pay back rent on the lease. That small failure led him to bigger and more spectacular failures, culminating decades later with the Ponzi scheme he carried out under the auspices of his Stanford Financial Group. When it collapsed—and Ponzi schemes always do—the Justice Department froze his assets. He was convicted of fraud in federal court, ordered to forfeit nearly six billion dollars, and relocated to Florida, with free room and board for the rest of his natural life. Prosecutors had sought a sentence of 230 years, but they had to settle for 110. Madoff got 150 years.

Although Stanford was a good trainer, he didn't provide me any financial advice or share any of his fiscal wizardry—probably just as well, given how things played out for him. That meant that, wherever I chose to attend college, it was either going to have to be cheap or it would have to provide a scholarship after I walked on. My Uncle Conrad taught at Southern Methodist University in Dallas, a member of the Southwest Conference (which is no longer in existence), and he got me a meeting with head coach Hayden Fry. But by the time I'd spent a year at McLennan

Community College and was ready for a four-year school, Fry had been replaced by Dave Smith. I met with Smith, who watched me lift. Good enough for a walk-on, he said, but not good enough for a scholarship. At least not at first.

SMU was not known for "cheapness." My dad informed me there was no way he could afford the tuition, even for an initial semester while I tried for a scholarship. I don't think he felt that I was a good investment. I would have to set my sights elsewhere. Elsewhere turned out to be Kingsville in South Texas, where the Texas A&I University Javelinas were about to make football history. And I was going to be a part of it.

CHAPTER TWELVE
A Walk-On Javelina

"A school without football is in danger of deteriorating into a medieval study hall."

Vince Lombardi

Few colleges or universities would ever be able to match the football excellence of the Gil Steinke–coached Javelinas of Texas A&I University in the 1970s. Now part of the Texas A&M system, and called Texas A&M University-Kingsville, A&I got its start when it was chartered in 1917 in the south Texas town of Kingsville as South Texas Normal College. Kingsville was named for Richard King, founder of the King Ranch, which served as the model for the Reata Ranch in Edna Ferber's novel *Giant*. The town initially grew up to serve as headquarters for the St. Louis, Brownsville and Mexico Railway as well as to provide infrastructure for the ranch—at 825,000 acres, the largest in the United States and, at one time, the world. Anna Creek Station in South Australia now holds the title at 5.85 million acres, with the King Ranch weighing in at number 5 on the "world's largest ranches" list.[1]

After the turn of the twentieth century, the King Ranch owners built a system of schools for its workers' families, including the Santa Gertrudis School, established in 1917, the same year that South Texas Normal College was chartered. A normal college is designed to train teachers and, ostensibly, South Texas Normal would train educators for the King Ranch schools as well as nearby Kingsville and other south Texas towns. Unfortunately, American involvement in World War I intervened, and the college was not opened until 1925, under the new name South Texas State Teacher's College. The name was changed four years later to Texas College of Arts and Industries, shortened to Texas A&I. While it was originally identified by its proximity to the King Ranch, by the '60s and particularly the '70s, it would be primarily known, at least in American popular culture, for football.

In the history of college football, only two NCAA teams have won forty or more consecutive games. Between 1908 and 1914, the University of Washington won forty straight games under the tutelage of head coach Robert Gilmour Dobie, whose record from 1908 to 1916 was 58-0-3, with one of those ties breaking the win streak. The record is forty-seven consecutive games, from 1953 to 1957, by the Bud Wilkinson–coached Oklahoma Sooners. Remarkably, just three years prior, OU ended a thirty-one-game winning streak.[2]

But that's NCAA, or the National Collegiate Athletic Association. There was also the NAIA, or the National Association of Intercollegiate Athletics, for "smaller" colleges and universities. According to Victory Sports Network, Texas A&I is the greatest NAIA football program of all time.[3] The network's rankings are based on factors that include total number of NAIA championships, total number of postseason appearances, ranking on the "All-Time Winningest" list, and how dominant the program was while in the NAIA. A&I cemented its position at the top of the list with its performance in the 1970s, when it won national championships in 1970, 1974, 1975, 1976, and 1979. During the stretch of three consecutive championships from 1974 to 1976, the Javelinas won forty-two consecutive games between November 17, 1973, and October 1, 1977, ranking second only to OU's forty-seven. That doesn't include a five-game winning streak on an exhibition tour of Europe that would bring the winning streak up to snuff with OU's. Throw in a few ties, and the consecutive unbeaten streak stretches to fifty-one.

Head coach Gil Steinke's tenure started in 1954 and ended following the third consecutive national championship in 1976. Although he retired after the '76 season, missing out on the last two games in the winning streak, which occurred in 1977, and was not coach for the '79 championship, he lays claim to additional national championships in 1959 and 1969 and won ten Lone Star Conference championships; his overall record at A&I was 182-61-4.

His attempt at coaching in the professional ranks didn't pan out so well, however, with a 9-15 record between 1984 and 1985 with the United States Football League's San Antonio Gunslingers before the USFL pulled the plug on the team. The Gunslingers had started in 1977 as the San Antonio Charros (Mexican horsemen or cowboys) in the American Football Association and were added to the USFL in 1984, with Steinke as head coach, when that competitor league to the NFL expanded to eighteen teams. But the Gunslingers had a rough time. There were reports that Steinke suffered from signs of mental decline, sometimes forgetting plays during games.[4]

But the real problems were financial. It seemed that Clinton Manges, the oilman owner who had acquired the team when it was still the Charros, dealt with declining fortunes in the oilfields by refusing to pay the team's expenses and payroll. USFL commissioner Harry Usher revoked the franchise after the 1985 season, and Manges filed bankruptcy in 1987 when Gunslingers players sued for back pay. He lost his 100,000-acre ranch in Duval County in south Texas and, in 1995, at the age of 72, was convicted in federal court on bribery and mail fraud charges. He was sentenced to two years and three months in prison,[5] but served his time in a federal prison medical facility in Fort Worth. He died in a nursing home in 2010.

★ ★ ★ ★ ★

I had known Bill Bronstad since we were little kids, though he moved to Corpus Christi before high school graduation. He didn't play football, but he knew that I did, so he suggested that I give it a shot at A&I, where he was enrolled. On the surface, it had some practical appeal. I would most likely have to walk on to earn a scholarship, which meant I had to pay my own way at the start. Tuition at a state school was a drop in the bucket compared to a private school like SMU. I also figured I would have an easier time making the team, and earning a scholarship, at a small, no-name college in a small town. Boy, oh boy, was I wrong about that. It was no-name only to me, but not to the rest of Texas, nor, for that matter, to the rest of the United States, as I would soon find out. And I had no idea how good the Lone Star Conference was, with schools like Angelo State, East Texas State, Abilene Christian, and West Texas State, all of which, like A&I, regularly turned out NFL players. Earning a scholarship would not be a gimme.

Kingsville was a small town, even compared to Waco, and it seemed like it was in the middle of nowhere. On the map, the nearest city of any size was Corpus Christi, with roughly one hundred thousand residents, more than forty miles away. Beyond that, there was the "big city" of San Antonio, but it was 160 miles away. So, for all practical purposes, Kingsville offered a bit of isolation. Given my track record in high school of . . . shall we just say "mischief" . . . I figured that I couldn't get into any mischief there.

I took Bill's advice and drove to Kingsville in the spring of 1974 to visit the campus, where Bill had arranged a meeting for me with Gene Walkoviak, one of the assistant coaches. Coach Walkoviak had played quarterback at A&I from 1966 to 1969, a stretch during which the Javelinas won three straight Lone Star Conference titles and a national championship in 1969, so he had good credentials. I did an impromptu workout for him that included running pass routes and performing drills as well as showing him how much I could bench press.

In high school, I had primarily played nose tackle/defensive tackle on defense and guard on offense. I was a smidge over six feet tall and weighed about 215 pounds. Decent size for a high school lineman at the time—certainly not like the behemoths that play in Texas high schools these days—but small for a college lineman. Even though I had worked myself into peak physical condition with Allen Stanford, and I carried the weight well on my frame, I still looked like someone who belonged in the backfield. Coach Walkoviak suggested that I move from defensive tackle to fullback, something my size was better suited for, and I agreed. Just like that, I had an invitation to walk on at Texas A&I.

Excited, I went home to Waco and started planning my future as a college football player. I also started studying the offense that Texas A&I ran so I would be prepared once two-a-day workouts started in the fall. In high school, we ran a fairly traditional offense. Some kind of I formation, if my memory serves me correctly. That type of offense was popular in the 1960s and '70s, with the fullback lined up in a three- or four-point stance directly behind the quarterback and the tailback in an upright position behind the fullback. In that formation, the fullback was primarily a blocking back, with the exception of an occasional dive play into the line, while the glory of carrying the football belonged to the tailback. John McKay popularized the I formation at USC in the '60s, with the likes of O. J. Simpson. Tony Dorsett of the Cowboys and Walter Payton of the Chicago Bears were examples of prominent tailbacks in the NFL.

Things would be a little different at A&I, which ran the Houston Veer offense. I had not played in the backfield in high school, but I had played defense against the I formation, so I sorta understood that offense. It was a different story with the veer, an offense that had been developed in the mid-1960s by University of Houston head coach Bill Yeoman around the same time that another Texas school, the Longhorns at UT, were running the wishbone. Both offenses featured the triple option.

The wishbone, which had been developed by Emory Bellard while an assistant coach at the University of Texas, used a three-man backfield, with the fullback in the center, often in a four-point stance, with halfbacks on either side, stationed about a yard or so behind the fullback. It was run to perfection at Texas with James Street at quarterback and Steve Worster at fullback, flanked by Chris Gilbert and Ted Koy as halfbacks. The veer, on the other hand, used two backs instead of three. Technically, one was a fullback and the other a halfback, but at A&I, speed was everything, so both backs were, in essence, halfbacks.

The triple option could be tricky. Ordinarily on a running play, the quarterback hands the ball to a back plunging into the line, or he fakes it to the back and pitches it, or hands it off, to the halfback. Technically those are two options, but they are preset. It's either a handoff to one back or a pitch or handoff to another. With the triple option, there truly are three options, and none of them are preordained. The quarterback plunges the ball into the belly of the fullback hitting the line straight ahead—but he doesn't let go of the ball. At least not yet. The first option, then, is to read the defense to see how it reacts to what appears to be a straight ahead handoff. If the defense lays back or appears to regard the move as a fake, the quarterback may release the ball to the fullback. But if the defense crashes down to "stuff" the hole, the quarterback can pull the ball back. To make it work, though, the quarterback must "ride" with the fullback for a second or two in order to read the defense before deciding to either release the ball or pull it back.

In the same instant, the trailing back, the halfback, pivots and runs parallel to the line of scrimmage. If the quarterback pulls the ball back from the fullback, he then also runs parallel while waiting to "read" the defense at the end of the line of scrimmage and to choose his second and third options. If the defensive end sets his sights on the halfback, the quarterback keeps the ball and cuts upfield inside. That's option number two. If the end crashes down on the quarterback, the quarterback pitches the ball, ideally at the last possible moment, to the halfback for an end sweep. Option number three. It all takes split-second timing and split-second decision-making. Nothing is predetermined other than the existence of the three options; which option is chosen depends upon what the defense does on any given play.

The problem for a rookie fullback in the triple option is being unsure exactly what to do. The fullback must "read" the defense just as the quarterback does, but if the fullback misreads it, the quarterback's read controls. That means the fullback must sense the quarterback's decision. When the ball is plunged into his gut, the fullback has to keep his arms around it loosely at first, in case the quarterback decides to pull it back. He must simultaneously be prepared to clamp it tightly as soon as the quarterback decides to let it go. There is really nothing natural about it. Maybe the quarterback gives it to you, maybe he doesn't. And you have to figure it all out in an instant. If the fullback thinks the quarterback is pulling it back and lets go, but the quarterback is actually giving it to the fullback, the typical result is a fumble. If the fullback thinks the quarterback is handing the ball to him and clamps down on it, but the quarterback intends to pull it back, the typical result is a fumble or at least a tangled-up mess between the two backs on the line of scrimmage.

Being in the backfield was a foreign experience for me, except to the extent I had occasionally crashed into the backfield from the defensive line to sack a quarterback or tackle a running back for a loss. I didn't know how to receive the ball from the quarterback, how to read the defense in synch with the quarterback, or how to let the ball go in the option. Fortunately, one of the veterans took pity on me. Our starting fullback, a big guy named Don Hardeman, mentored me on the finer points of playing fullback in the veer offense.

Don, who stood about six-foot-two and weighed about 235 pounds, was from Temple, Texas. He was one of A&I's stars and would later be a first-round draft choice of the NFL's Houston Oilers. His nickname was "Jaws" because he talked all the time. He showed me some of the techniques for a fullback in the veer.

Things like which leg to push off from, how to get your elbow high enough for the quarterback to get the ball in yet still be able to pull it back if he saw the hole stuffed. It was invaluable to me, not only to hear it but also to be able to watch him do the things he talked about. I will forever be in his debt for the kindness he showed me.

I was learning all kinds of stuff I never knew in my lifetime as a lineman. It was fun to find out there was actually life in the backfield. Then tragedy struck. Or at least it seemed like a tragedy to me. In fact, I experienced a whole sequence of tragedies over my two seasons at A&I, all involving knees. I have learned, since then, that what might have seemed like a tragedy at the time was merely a setback. In hindsight, my later-in-life tragedies made knee injuries pale by comparison. Those tragedies included drug addiction, a broken back, and a neurological disorder. I also learned that I had a half-brother who was killed during the Vietnam War. Those kinds of things shed a new light, and new perspective, on knee injuries that simply kept me off a football field. Those injuries involved a torn bursa sac, torn anterior collateral ligament, and a torn medial collateral ligament.

But first, a layman's simplistic perspective on the anatomy of the knee. A bursa is a small sac typically found around joints in the body. It is filled with fluid and acts as a cushion between ligaments, bones, and muscles. There are several bursa sacs in the knee joint, which prevent friction when the parts in and around the knee move. One of the most common afflictions associated with knees is bursitis, which is inflammation of one or more of the bursae. It can be the result of repetitive impact or repetitive friction, or even a direct blow to the knee. When it tears or ruptures, fluid leaks into the joint and surrounding tissues. It can cause increased joint pain, swelling, loss of function, and an increased risk of infection.

Ligaments are tissues in the body that connect bones to other bones. There are two cruciate ligaments in the knee, which stabilize the knee in motion, whether running, jumping, or, as in my case, pivoting: the anterior, which connects the femur to the tibia at the front of the knee (or, as the old song goes, connects the thighbone to the shinbone, or vice versa); and the posterior, which connects the same two bones at the back of the knee. Another ligament is the medial collateral ligament, which is on the inside of the knee and which also helps connect the thigh bone to the shin bone.

My first knee injury was prior to the 1974 season. I was running routes with Larry Urban, a quarterback from Kingsville High School, throwing to me. One afternoon, I was doing what we called "ten and outs," a pattern of running full bore downfield for ten yards and then cutting out to the sidelines, either left or right depending upon which side of the field you were on. It was a fairly basic pass pattern, but details mattered. Precision can be key to getting open or not. I sprinted downfield for ten, ready to cut to the right sideline. But I made one false move and ruptured a bursa sac. Fluid seeped in and my knee swelled up dramatically. The team doctor arrived and performed what could almost be termed the knee version of a tracheostomy. In a tracheostomy, a hole is made in the windpipe to insert an air tube to facilitate breathing when there is blockage. With the bursa, the doctor slit open the front of my knee, not to facilitate breathing, but to allow the bursa fluid to escape rather than, in effect, poison the joint. I was told that, if not done promptly, a possible result, though extreme, could have been gangrene.

One of the worst things about an injury (besides pain) is feeling like you are letting your teammates down. Even though I was still part of the team, technically, and was dutifully rehabbing my knee every day, I was not on the field with them. I guess they didn't really need my help, though, because they did just fine without me. The Javelinas ran the table in 1974, going 13-0, winning the Lone Star Conference and beating Henderson State of Arkansas 34-23 in the NAIA national championship game, the first of three in a row.

Texas A&I Javelina Hall of Fame trophy for Paul Heckmann. *Photo courtesy of Paul Heckmann.*

That season paid off for a lot of my teammates in other ways. As I mentioned earlier, Don Hardeman, who was a senior that year, went into the NFL Draft in 1975 and was a Number One pick. He was the latest in a line of A&I graduates who were, or had been, number one picks. Others were:

Quarterback Randy Johnson, from San Antonio, was selected first by the Atlanta Falcons in 1966. Johnson also played for the New York Giants, Washington Redskins, and Green Bay Packers of the NFL and spent one season (1974) with the Honolulu Hawaiians in the World Football League before returning to the NFL. Randy was the first Texas A&I player to be selected in the first round of the NFL draft.

Offensive guard Gene Upshaw from Robstown, Texas, was selected first by the Oakland Raiders in the 1967 AFL draft. He spent his entire career with the Raiders until he retired at the end of the 1981 season. Upshaw was a multi-time All-Pro and All-AFL

TEXAS A&M UNIVERSITY KINGSVILLE

Office of the Vice President for Intercollegiate Athletics & Campus Recreation

Texas A & M University-Kingsville
700 University Blvd.
Kingsville, TX 78363
Phone (361) 593-2800

E-mail scott.gines@tamuk.edu

July 23, 2015

Paul Heckmann
2705 E. Trinity Mills, #315
Carrollton, TX 75006

Dear Paul,

It is my great pleasure to congratulate you on your selection to the **Javelina Athletic Hall of Fame** as a member of the 1975 Texas A&I University football team. This honor preserves your team's special *mark* on Javelina Athletics for all time. The Greek definition for the word "mark" refers to character, and the character of college sport is reflected from the front porch of university campuses - it's about excelling, persisting, leading and succeeding – and your team's mark is one we are honored to lift up for perpetuity.

On **Friday, September 11, 2015** we will induct the 1974/1975 Texas A&I University football team into the Hall. You will receive two complimentary tickets to the 2015 Javelina Hall of Fame Induction Ceremony & 2015 Hall of Fame Football Game and Javelina Volleyball Tournament. Additional tickets can be purchased ($ 30.00 each banquet only) online at www.javelinatickets.com or by contacting Rosie Moreno (rosalinda.moreno@tamuk.edu; 361-593-4030). Tickets can be purchased until Thursday, September 3, 2015. Walk-up ticket sales are *not* available and tickets are required for entry. The induction social (5:30 p.m.), dinner (6:30 p.m.), and ceremony will take place in the Memorial Student Union Ballroom.

For your convenience, a limited supply of rooms is currently blocked at the Best Western Kingsville Inn (361-595-5656), the Comfort Inn (361-516-1120) and the Hampton Inn (361-592-9800). When reserving rooms, use the reservation code "Javelina Hall of Fame". Rooms are first come, first serve with a cut-off date of Friday, August 28, 2015.

Again, and on behalf of all Javelinas - past, present and future - please accept my sincere and resounding congratulations!!

Best Regards,

D. Scott Gines
Vice President for Intercollegiate Athletics & Campus Recreation

Letter to Paul Heckmann notifying him of his selection to the Javelina Hall of Fame. *Photo courtesy of Paul Heckmann.*

player, and he was inducted into the Pro Football Hall of Fame in 1987. He was active in the National Football League Players' Association and served as executive director of the union.

Cornerback Jim Hill from San Antonio was drafted first by the San Diego Chargers in 1968. He also played for the Green Bay Packers and Cleveland Browns. After retiring, he resumed a broadcasting career he had begun while a student at A&I as a disc jockey for Kingsville radio station KINE. His sportscasting career included stints in Los Angeles, on CBS and ABC, as well as being one of the hosts for Showtime's pay-per-view boxing.

Cornerback Eldridge Small from Houston was drafted first by the New York Giants in 1972, but his NFL career lasted only three seasons. In 1975, the Giants traded him to the Cleveland Browns, and the Browns released him before the start of the '75 season.

A&I has produced two other NFL Hall of Famers besides Upshaw. One is cornerback Darrel Green, a first-round pick of the Washington Redskins in 1983. A multi-time All-Pro and a Super Bowl champion, he was one of the fastest players in the NFL and was inducted into the NFL Hall of Fame in 2008. The other was defensive tackle John Randle from Hearne, Texas, who was undrafted following his senior season at A&I in 1989. He tried out for the Tampa Bay Buccaneers but didn't make the team. The Minnesota Vikings picked him up after the Bucs cut him, and he went on to become a multi-time All-Pro. He played primarily for the Vikings but spent his last three seasons with the Seattle Seahawks. He ended his career with 137.5 sacks to his credit. He was inducted into the NFL Hall of Fame in 2010.[6]

But enough about Hall-of-Famers and first-round draft picks who weren't named Paul Heckmann. By the spring of 1975, I was ready to get back on the field again during spring practice. Coach

Steinke had been watching me closely while I was rehabbing my knee. He also knew that I had been diligent in continuing my weightlifting. I saw him one day while I was at the school fitness center that had been named for him. We had weight machines there, rather than free weights, and he watched as I loaded the bench press machine as high as it would go, which, if memory serves, was 220 pounds. I benched it. Then, with Coach Steinke still watching, I had a teammate named Robert Dawson sit on the stack to increase the weight. Dawson was another medical casualty, an offensive lineman who weighed in the upper 200s, maybe 260 or so. I benched it. It sounds like a lot, and it was, but it wasn't quite like benching free weights. This was the typical Universal Gym of the 1970s, so there were angles on the arms and handle of the press that actually did some of the work for you. Still, it was a lot of weight.

Coach Steinke offered me a scholarship right then and there—and I hadn't been back on the gridiron since the injury. I say "scholarship," but that's not really what it was. I was living off campus and already buying my own groceries, so I didn't need housing or meals, which is what typically came with a scholarship. The offer was more like a grant, a stipend—I don't remember the exact amount—that should have lasted all school year. Should have, but it didn't. The first thing I did was buy a couple of Earthquake speakers for my stereo system. I don't recall how much they cost, but I do remember that they were awesome. And I just *had* to have them. A financial wizard, I was not.

In retrospect, I guess I was a little like the grasshopper in Aesop's fable of *The Ant and the Grasshopper*, frolicking while the ant stored food and prepared for the future. When the future came, I was woefully unprepared. Looking back over my life, it's apparent that I was like that grasshopper through a lot of seasons—and I'm not talking just about football seasons. And I'm not talking just about stereo speakers.

When spring practice rolled around, my knee was strong, but it was still a little tender. Rehab had gone well and I had regained a lot of strength and mobility. However, "better" is not the same as fully recovered. I should have sat out spring practice, but I felt like time was passing me by. If I was going to make it as a football player, I needed to grab my shot at the earliest. I had already lost one full season in high school to stupidity, and now I had lost one due to injury. I didn't want to lose another. Missing spring practice would likely have lowered me on the depth chart, and I could foresee myself serving as cannon fodder for the first team when fall practice rolled around. So I suited up in full pads and joined the rest of the team on the field.

On one play, I planted my foot in the ground and pushed off on my good leg but failed to pivot properly. My cleats dug in, my right knee joint swiveled as I alternated legs, but the lower leg couldn't follow. The result was the quintessential football knee injury, so common it was almost a cliché. When I pivoted, the anterior cruciate ligament in my right knee ripped in two. By many accounts, an ACL tear is the most common football injury. The result was knee surgery. My first. But not my last.

Summer came and I moved back to Waco to work on rehabbing my knee. Again. I also needed to earn a little money to tide me over when I went back to school. I got a job at a bar called The Shadows, where I worked as a barback, which is essentially a bartender's assistant. I thought I might segue into being a bartender. Unfortunately, my memory issues short-circuited that dream. You can't be a bartender if you can't remember orders or how to mix drinks. But at least I made a little money.

Then it was back to A&I for the fall season in 1975, with new grant money. I had redoubled my rehab efforts and felt that my right knee was as strong as it had ever been. Too bad I couldn't say the same about my left knee. I had worked so hard on my right that I had all but ignored my left. Something was bound to give. And it did. There was that history rhyming thing. Ligament again, this time the MCL—the medial collateral ligament. More surgery and the prospect of arthritis and maybe even canes and wheelchairs in my future. That was it as far as my football dreams were concerned. I was too young to have to think about never walking normally again. Sadly, I missed out on a second consecutive national championship and a continuation of the winning streak. The team went 12-0 in '75, winning the Lone Star Conference and beating the previously undefeated Salem University Tigers from West Virginia in the national championship game 37-0.

That summer I had an apartment on the Baylor campus in Waco while taking a few classes there. I hadn't done very well academically at A&I. My GPA typically ranged from 2.4 to 2.5, with scholastic probation after one particularly bad semester. The only course I remember taking at Baylor was Geology 101. Not a particularly helpful class for a business major, or for what my future turned out to be, but I liked it. I can't remember the professor's name, but he made the class interesting. I got a C but always felt like it should have been a B.

One afternoon, I heard an unexpected knock on my apartment door. I opened it to greet a six-foot-six-inch mop of hair named Larry Seidel. Larry was my best friend on the A&I squad and was funny as hell. He was from San Antonio, where he attended Dillard McCollum High School and started at defensive tackle. He stayed with me for a few days, and I think we played foosball every night at one of the local clubs. I was hungry for news, and he kept me in the loop on what was going on with the team. Once you quit, it's not like you're excommunicated, but it is like you've been separated from a family you once had. They're going through things and sharing experiences that you once went through and once shared, but you no longer have that common bond. It was a difficult time for me, and Larry's visit filled a gap.

I learned that one of the things I missed out on was a tour of Europe by the team. Texas A&I had been selected, along with Henderson State in Arkansas, to play games in Germany, Austria, and France. A&I and Henderson, the team we had beaten in 1974 for the National Championship, had been ranked first and second in the final 1975 poll. The series was designed as a goodwill tour to introduce American football to European fans, and there were some interesting requirements. According to Coach Steinke, "They want us to pass at least 50 percent of the time and they prefer that we throw from a drop-back pattern. They've asked that we run basic defensive patterns." Not the way A&I usually played but, Coach Steinke said, "The objective of the games is to excite the fans. To the seasoned football fan, tough defense, good faking and a veer offense are exciting. But the fan who is just learning the game wants to see the football being thrown." According to the Javelina Athletics website, A&I won all five of the exhibition games: 17-8 in Berlin, 21-7 in Vienna, 20-6 in Mannheim, 17-15 in Nuremberg, and 21-13 in Paris.[7]

★ ★ ★ ★ ★

My college days at Texas A&I weren't all about football. I realize I have pretty much skipped over my education in the narrative, but that's probably because I pretty much skipped over it while I was enrolled. Because I had taken enough freshman-level classes at McLennan Community College, I entered A&I as a sophomore. My classes, even at the sophomore level, were much harder than I was expecting. Or, perhaps better said, much harder than I was prepared to work for. My memory issues reared their ugly head once again. Tests were exceedingly difficult for me. I could study all night if I wanted to, yet I still ended up with a blank slate when taking exams. Besides, I was a football player. Nobody expected football players to be rocket scientists, and I obliged that stereotype.

Being a football player had other perks, too. Like popularity. Javelina football players, particularly in the midst of an unprecedented winning streak, were treated like gods on campus and in town. I joined Bill Bronstad's fraternity, Lambda Chi Alpha, and was elected vice-president for two years while Bill served as president. If you've seen the movie *Animal House*, you get an idea of what it was like—at least a tiny bit. Unlike Delta House in the movie, we kept a clean front yard at our house, which was just off campus, as were all the other frat houses. I was elected Party Chair my first year before "ascending" to the vice-presidency. That meant I planned all the parties—at least the ones that required preplanning instead of simply spontaneous get-togethers and beer blasts. I remember one in particular at the King Ranch Museum. We brought in a band, along with kegs of beer and Purple Passion for the ladies. The latter was a makeshift drink concocted from whatever booze we had in the house closet, combined with beer and Welch's Grape Juice, all mixed together in a trash can. It was a great time for me, socially. But it also helped fuel some of my bad habits. Beer and pot, primarily.

And even the occasional trip into the desert in search of peyote, a small spineless cactus that grew wild around a lot of the fences in the cattle ranches nearby. Native Americans had long used peyote, ingesting it for medicinal and also spiritual and ceremonial purposes. It acts as a hallucinogenic and can give a sense of well-being and heightened perception, particularly with sounds and colors. A little reminiscent of LSD. I used it only a few times, but I was open to experimentation. My serious drug use was still ahead of me.

★ ★ ★ ★ ★

The fall of 1976 was my last semester at Texas A&I. The football team had come off of its third consecutive national championship, going 13-0, winning the Lone Star Conference again, and beating Central Arkansas in the championship game, 26-0. What a great time to be a Javelina! Although I had been a part of the first two of those three consecutive championships—and in 2015 was named to the Javelina Hall of Fame for that—I was no longer one. And I had made up my mind that it was time to move to the bright lights of the big city.

Dallas.

CHAPTER THIRTEEN

Anything, Anytime, Anywhere[1]

"I did Air America for two reasons: to be in a movie with Mel Gibson and to make a bunch of money. And then underneath there was the hope that in doing this formulaic thing I would be launched into a whole new realm of opportunity to do A-list movies. By the time we were done, the only positive thing was meeting Mel Gibson."

Robert Downey, Jr.

Popular culture refers to the influence on society of cultural products that are consumed by a majority of that society's population, including music, art, literature, television, film, radio, and mass media. In other words, it is how society is led to perceive some particular subject or aspect of that society. Too often, it provides a skewed frame of reference for history. Take, for example, the Vietnam War.

There are numerous films about Vietnam and the veterans who served in the war. Mary Hamilton wrote in her master's thesis about the popular culture image of Vietnam veterans as depicted in nine of the earliest movies to address the war. Titled *And the Enemy Was in Us: Vietnam War Films and Complicating Visions of American Masculinity, 1976–1989*, Hamilton's work tackled these smash films: *Taxi Driver*, *Apocalypse Now*, *Platoon*, *The Deer Hunter*, *Born on the Fourth of July*, *Coming Home*, *Full Metal Jacket*, *First Blood*, and *Rambo: First Blood Part II*.[2] Of the nine, only *The Deer Hunter*, *Taxi Driver*, and *Coming Home* garnered less than $100,000,000 domestically, but they were still considered commercial successes based on the box office return when measured against production costs.[3] *The Deer Hunter* won an Academy Award for Best Picture while the other two were nominated in that category.

However, there are few films about the "secret war" in Laos. Fortunate, perhaps, because the lack of films limits the distortion pop culture might impose on certain little-known, and even lesser understood, aspects of that particular episode in American history. One of those little-known or understood aspects is the role of Air America.

It's a good bet that, to the extent the general American public knows anything about Air America, its perception may have been shaped by the 1990 film *Air America*, an action comedy directed by Roger Spottiswoode, starring Mel Gibson and Robert Downey Jr. as Air America pilots. The movie was adapted from the nonfiction book of the same name by British journalist Christopher Robbins.[4] Not particularly successful at the box office, it garnered $31,053,601 domestically and a little over $3 million worldwide. The combined total barely exceeded its production budget.[5]

Upon release, the film became mired in controversy. Caryn James of *The New York Times* called it a "muddled film" and wrote that it "fails on every possible level."[6] Film historian Alun Evans called it a "tawdry, unfunny war comedy"[7]—the latter adjective, "unfunny," being perhaps the most devastating description of a comedy. The author of the book from which it was adapted didn't even have nice things to say about it, claiming it didn't accurately portray the true story.[8] Historian William M. Leary wrote, "The exploits of CAT[9]/Air America form a unique chapter in the history of air transport, one that deserves better than a misleading, mediocre movie." Elaborating, Leary said:

> Air America's public image has fared poorly. The 1990 movie *Air America* is largely responsible for this. It featured a cynical CIA officer who arranged for the airline to fly opium to the administrative capital of Vientiane for a corrupt Asian general—loosely modeled on Vang Pao, a military leader of the mountain-region-based Hmong ethnic group. The film depicts the CIA man as having the opium processed into heroin in a factory just down the street from the favorite bar of Air America's pilots. The Asian general, in return, supplied men to fight the war, . . . which was fought for control of the area's opium fields.
>
> Air America pilots in this film are portrayed as skilled at landing damaged airplanes, but basically as a wildly unprofessional menagerie of party animals, including a few borderline psychotics. These ill-disciplined airmen are not the villains of the story; they are merely pawns in a drug game that they either disdain or oppose outright.[10]

The movie did, at least, boast a great soundtrack, featuring music from Aerosmith, B.B. King, Bonnie Raitt, Steely Dan, Edgar Winter, The Temptations, The Mamas & the Papas, and even the Four Tops. But that is poor recompense for distorting Air America's track record.

So what, really, was Air America, and what was its role in the secret war in Laos?

★ ★ ★ ★ ★

In simplest terms, Air America was a charter airline the CIA operated as a front for its covert paramilitary activities in Indochina during the Vietnam War, particularly in Laos. Its history traces back to a nationalist Chinese airline, Civil Air Transport (CAT), created in 1946 by Claire Chennault and Whiting Willauer. Chennault was an aviator who commanded the First American Volunteer Group in World War II, nicknamed "Flying Tigers," which operated primarily in the China-Burma-India theater during the war. Willauer was executive secretary of China Defense Supplies, Inc., during the war and, immediately after, served as director of the Far East and Special Territories branch of the Foreign Economic Administration until teaming up with Chennault to found CAT.

CAT was originally created for primarily benevolent purposes, such as delivering food and medicine to war-decimated areas of China. Chennault and Willauer acquired war surplus cargo planes and hired World War II veterans, including Flying Tigers pilots as well as veterans of the US Army Air Forces, Navy, and Marine Corps. It operated by authority of the Chinese National Rehabilitation and Relief Association, established by the government of the Republic of China, and worked in conjunction with the United Nations Relief and Rehabilitation Administration.

Air America headquarters at Udorn, Thailand. *Public domain.*

CAT's tenure included the communist takeover of

China that ultimately deprived CAT of its ability to carry out its mission. As stated on the CAT Association website,

> We provided hope to thousands of freedom-loving refugees by flying them to Taipei. We rescued the Government's Bank of China silver ingots. And we had precluded a brain drain by supporting doomed cities until the city fathers arranged orderly departures to the island of Taiwan, a 240-mile long island approximately 90 miles east of the China Mainland. But we had become an airline with no place to go.[11]

Starting in 1950, CAT occasionally contracted with the CIA, rescuing refugees and wounded soldiers during the communist takeover of China. By 1960, it had become integrated into the CIA through a series of business transactions under the name of Air America. Air America's website notes the unevenness of how CAT became part of the CIA.

> The concept of ownership in the case of Air America is far from straightforward. Documents on the CIA website state that while the Central Intelligence Agency purchased the assets of Civil Air Transport, it had to obtain permission from the Department of State. The contradictions are numerous, but it's a given, based on letters and statements in several presidential libraries, that the Department of State, Defense, USAF, and USAID used the company, and none of these agencies needed CIA permission. Through one or more of its agencies, the federal government shifted employees to other corporations classified as front organizations at the federal government's whim and caprice, defying the classic defini-

tion of ownership. The shift did not affect employees' status, despite front corporations being in different states and everyone being on one seniority list. No other legal corporation could accomplish this act except the federal government, which didn't make it legal but rendered it complicated and almost impossible to determine.[12]

In the meantime, the CIA was looking to reorganize some of its activities. In 1957, it created the Delaware-based Pacific Corporation as a holding company, which took over the assets of American Airdale Corporation. It then bought out CAT and formed Air America in 1959, ostensibly as a private charter firm, with the slogan "Anything, Anytime, Anywhere, Professionally." In August of 1960, the CIA bought an air cargo firm called Southern Air Transport, which operated on four acres in Florida, with one C-46 that it owned and a lease on another. Air America crews and planes were transferred there to operate. At its peak, Pacific Corporation employed more than twenty thousand people. Air America employed 5,600 to 8,000 (counting support personnel) and owned or leased 167 aircraft. By 1970, it averaged thirty thousand flights a month.[13]

Air America Helio U-10D Courier aircraft on a covert mountaintop landing strip in Laos. *Public domain.*

Air America played a significant role in the "secret war" in Laos. Much of its original involvement was humanitarian, similar to that of CAT in China. That included dropping military supplies but also dropping food such as rice (weapons drops were euphemistically known as "dirty rice"), wheat, cornmeal, and salt. Air America also assisted in airlifting wounded Hmong tribesmen and even some Americans to hospitals. Air America's role escalated to surveillance operations, then delivering military aid, moving troops, and searching for downed American pilots.[14] According to former diplomat Peter Dale Scott, Air America flights out of CIA operations headquarters in Pakse, in southern Laos, were originally "to observe and harass the Ho Chi Minh trail," but by late 1969, as the war expanded, "Air America planes are reported to be flying arms, supplies and reinforcements in this larger campaign."[15]

Air America suffered casualties, just as CIA paramilitary operators and advisors did. *The Washington Post* reported on a missing CIA airliner over Laos in December of 1971. The article led, "An Air America C-123 transport plane was missing over north Laos yesterday, according to the airline's office here. Reports from Vientiane, capital of Laos, speculated that the plane had been shot down by Chinese anti-aircraft known to be deployed in parts of northern Laos."[16]

The McDermott Library at the University of Texas at Dallas has a special History of Aviation archives, with a section devoted to Air America. A memorial graces the wall, reading, "This memorial is dedicated to the air crews and ground support personnel of Civil Air Transport, Air America, Air Asia, and Southern Air Transport, who died while serving the cause of freedom in Asia from 1947 to 1975." There are 242 names on the memorial.

★ ★ ★ ★ ★

One thing the Mel Gibson movie got right—sort of—was the issue of drug smuggling, particularly heroin and opium. Although it appears to be undisputed that there was some transport of drugs on Air America aircraft, there is no real indication of knowledge or involvement by Air America personnel. Historian Leary wrote,

> My nearly two decades of research indicate that Air America was not involved in the drug trade. As Joseph Westermeyer, who spent the years 1965 to 1975 in Laos as a physician, public health worker, and researcher, wrote in *Poppies, Pipes, and People*: "American-owned airlines never knowingly transported opium in or out of Laos, nor did their American pilots ever profit from its transport. Yet every plane in Laos undoubtedly carried opium at some time, unknown to the pilot and his superiors—just as had virtually every pedicab, every Mekong River sampan, and every missionary jeep between China and the Gulf of Siam."
>
> If the CIA was not involved in the drug trade, it did know about it. As former DCI William Colby acknowledged, the Agency did little about it during the 1960s, but later took action against the traders as drugs became a problem among American troops in Vietnam. The CIA's main focus in Laos remained on fighting the war, not on policing the drug trade.[17]

CIA paramilitary operator Anthony Poshepny, AKA Tony Poe, complained of opium being carried on Air America aircraft. Richard Gough, author of *Tony Poe's CIA War*, reported that Poe was a "zealot in trying to wean the Hmong away from opium culture," and that he once threatened to throw a Lao soldier from a plane when he discovered the soldier was carrying opium.[18]

Memorial for Air America personnel at McDermott Library. *Courtesy of Mike Farris.*

Historian Alfred W. McCoy argued that the CIA was an accomplice in the drug traffic, turning a blind eye to smuggling. "In most cases, the CIA's role involved various forms of complicity, tolerance or studied ignorance about the trade . . . The CIA did not handle heroin, but it did provide its drug lord allies transport, arms, and political protection."[19]

The issue of drug smuggling was widely known in the United States, particularly after publication of McCoy's book while he was still a graduate student at Yale. *The Miami Herald*, in reviewing the book on January 16, 1973, raised the question, in a headline, whether US involvement in Southeast Asia was "A War to Help Sell Heroin?"[20] Headlines in other newspapers included "Airline accused of shipping opium," "Politics and History of Heroin," "Heroin Road In SE Asia," "U.S. Is Backbone of Laos Drug Trade," "Our Allies, Opium, and the CIA: When the Embarrassed Chuckling Stopped," "Smuggling? Yes; collusion: No," "CIA Dope Tie in Charged," and "Uncle Sam—drug pusher."[21]

The issue raised such a ruckus that President Nixon threatened to cut off economic aid to governments participating in, or protecting, drug trafficking. He also praised the Central Intelligence Agency for its role in fighting the international drug traffic and said the agency has been "much maligned."[22] In December of 1972, a staff survey team of the House of Representatives Committee on Foreign Affairs released a report entitled *The U.S. Heroin Problem and Southeast Asia.* The report concluded that there was no evidence linking General Vang Pao to narcotics trafficking, although drugs "have been and probably still are being smuggled out of Laos on Royal Laos Air Force aircraft, on Lao and other commercial aircraft, by trucks, automobiles, and by foot and caravan." However, the report did not lay blame at the feet of the CIA.[23]

★ ★ ★ ★ ★

There is an interesting footnote that relates to General Chennault, the father of CAT. During the countdown to the 1968 presidential election, the Johnson administration announced a cessation of bombing in North Vietnam in order to allow for serious peace negotiations. Democrat Hubert Humphrey and Republican Richard Nixon were racing neck-and-neck in the polls, and an agreement for peace might well have ensured a Humphrey victory. South Vietnamese president Nguyen Van Thieu put the kibosh on any peace talks, turning the election in Nixon's favor.

Subsequent events revealed that Thieu had been encouraged to stand firm through the intercession and surreptitious encouragement of Nixon loyalists, including the chairwoman of the Republican Women for Nixon Committee, Anna Chennault, widow of Claire Chennault. According to journalist Seymour Hersh, Chennault acted as a go-between on behalf of Nixon.[24] FBI wiretaps revealed that she contacted Ambassador Bui Diem and transmitted a message from "her boss," who is not identified but clearly a reference to Nixon, to "hold on, we are gonna win."[25]

CHAPTER FOURTEEN

Big D-Little-A-Double L-A-S[1]

"Whether your destination is heaven or hell, you always have to change planes in Dallas."

Kinky Friedman

I arrived in Dallas in late December of 1975, unaware that I had lost a brother three years earlier. A brother that I didn't even know I had. The new year of 1977 would open doors for me, and it would also present challenges. Although the expression "sex, drugs, and rock and roll" wasn't popularized until the 1977 song by Ian Drury, it might easily have been the motto for the 1960s. Now that era was giving way to the '70s and a mantra of sex, drugs, and disco, and I found myself slap-dab in the middle of it. I was a small-town boy from Woodway by way of a small college town. Kingsville had a population, according to the 1970 census, of 28,995, which would explode (tongue in cheek, of course) by 1980 to 28,808. Dallas, on the other hand, boasted a population in 1970 of 844,401, growing to 904,078 over the decade. The Dallas-Fort Worth metropolitan area claimed more than 2.3 million residents in 1977.[2] I was in the big city now, and it, like me, was transforming.

Dallas was finally shaking its reputation as a safe haven for far right "nuts" and as the town that killed JFK, with the dubious nickname "The City of Hate." On the fiftieth anniversary of the JFK assassination, journalist Mark Byrnes wrote that, following the assassination, "Dallasites faced years of trouble while traveling around the country. They were sometimes even denied service because of their hometown."[3] Danny Gallagher, writing for the *Dallas Observer*, said, "The city of Dallas took the full brunt of the country's wrath even though one man who wasn't even from Dallas pulled the trigger."[4]

But it wasn't all bad. Darwin Payne, historian and expert on all things Dallas, wrote that, while the "city could not easily accept the world-wide opprobrium that came" from the assassination, the impact on the city was, to a degree, positive. "The new mood which was to dominate the city for the coming years was one of moderation, rejection of extremism, and encouragement of introspection." Gloom and doom about the tragedy's adverse economic impact remained unfulfilled. Rather than a slide into stagnation, Dallas registered greater business growth in the following years than its fiercest Texas economic competitors, Houston and San Antonio. The city also experienced actual growth, moving up from the fourteenth largest city in the nation to the eighth.[5]

By 1970, *Look* magazine named Dallas an "All-America City." Tom Peeler, writing in *D Magazine*, described the designation as a "coveted honor at the time."[6] According to Darwin Payne, in 1974 *Newsweek* had labeled Dallas "the city that works" and, in 1981, *Time* magazine declared that it "still works."[7] Dallas seemed to be running on all cylinders; not just business but also sports and entertainment. But while the road ahead may have looked smooth, it still had some bumps.

Sports

Dallas was a football city. The Dallas Chaparrals basketball team started in the late 1960s as a charter member of the American Basketball Association but moved to San Antonio prior to the 1973 season. They were renamed the San Antonio Spurs and joined the National Basketball Association for the 1976–77 season as part of the merger between the NBA and the ABA. The Dallas Mavericks didn't debut until 1980, and the newly transplanted baseball team from Washington D.C., the Texas Rangers, hadn't quite found their footing by the end of 1976. The Dallas Cowboys owned the city. In fact, the Cowboys owned north Texas.

When Texas Stadium opened in the fall of 1971, with its hole in the roof so God could watch his favorite team play (an observation generally credited to linebacker D. D. Lewis), the Cowboys moved from the Cotton Bowl in Dallas to the suburb of Irving. Team president Tex Schramm changed the character for the team's cheerleaders from traditional high school–type cheerleaders to glamorous showgirls who performed dance-style cheer routines, traveled the globe on goodwill tours, inspired movies, and courted litigation.

Following the prior year's devastating 16-13 loss in Super Bowl V to the Baltimore Colts, the '71 Cowboys won the National Football Conference (NFC) East, beat the Minnesota Vikings 20-12 in the Divisional Playoffs and the San Francisco 49ers 14-3 in the NFC Championship. Then, on January 16, 1972, in Super Bowl VI, they beat the Miami Dolphins at New Orleans's Tulane Stadium, 24-3, to claim their first ever NFL championship. The victory threw off their tag as "next year's champion," also the title of sportswriter Steve Perkins's book published in 1969, which detailed the annual heartbreaking playoff losses that led to the tag being applied—the notion that, with each disappointing playoff defeat, the team proclaimed, "we'll be champions next year."[8]

They would win another Super Bowl in 1977, 27-10 over the Denver Broncos in Super Bowl XII, sandwiched between losses to the Pittsburgh Steelers in Super Bowl X (21-17) and Super Bowl XIII (35-31). A drought followed until Super Bowl XVII against the Buffalo Bills (52-17) in 1993. That sixteen-year futility now seems like a pittance compared to the team's current three decades and counting absence from the so-called "ultimate game." Then again, who can forget Cowboys running back Duane Thomas's question following the 24-3 win over the Dolphins in Super Bowl VI: "If it's the ultimate game, how come they're playing it again next year?"

There was also, as noted, baseball. In 1972, Major League Baseball made its debut in Dallas—well, technically Arlington, in the mid-cities between Dallas and Fort Worth, but no need to quibble over a few miles. After all, following a stint in Texas Stadium in Irving, the Dallas Cowboys of today play in Arlington, right next door to the Rangers. Thanks to an offer from Arlington mayor Tom Vandergriff, Bob Short moved his MLB team from Washington D.C., where it had played under the name of the Washington Senators. The newly-arrived Rangers struggled mightily in the 1970s and 1980s, finally making the playoffs for the first time in 1996 and winning their first, and only, World Series championship in 2023.

The early '70s were, at best, ignominious for the Rangers and baseball fans in the area, with just a few bright spots. Turnpike Stadium (because it was located on the Dallas-Fort Worth Turnpike; clever, really), a former minor league stadium for the

Dallas-Fort Worth Spurs, served as their home. They were managed by Hall of Famer Ted Williams, who proved he knew more about hitting, with his career .344 lifetime batting average, than he did about managing. In 1972, their first year in Arlington, the Rangers ended the season with a record of fifty-four wins and one hundred losses, finishing sixth in the American League West—dead last. They also finished last in the major leagues in batting with a .217 team batting average. Williams retired after the season.

Williams's replacement was Whitey Herzog, but he was ousted and replaced before the end of the second season by former New York Yankees second baseman Billy Martin. In 1974, the Rangers finished second in their division, with an 84-76 record. Martin was named Manager of the Year, first baseman Mike Hargrove was A.L. Rookie of the Year, Jeff Burroughs won the A.L. Most Valuable Player, and twenty-five-game-winning pitcher Ferguson Jenkins was named Comeback Player of the Year. Overall, though, the middle '70s were not the heyday of the Texas Rangers. *Fort Worth Star-Telegram* sports reporter Mike Shropshire was explicit about the problems in his book *Seasons in Hell: With Billy Martin, Whitey Herzog, and the Worst Baseball Team in History: The 1973–1975 Texas Rangers.*[9]

But the 1970s-era Rangers were colorful, to say the least. When the Rangers acquired shortstop Bump Wills, son of Hall of Famer and Dodger great Maury Wills, prior to the 1977 season, manager Frank Lucchesi (who had replaced Billy Martin after Martin was fired ninety-five games into the 1975 season) telegraphed his intention to start Wills at second base in front of the previous year's starter, Lenny Randle. Sportswriter Randy Galloway quoted Randle as saying, "Too bad I'm not Jackie Robinson's nephew, maybe I'd get more respect around here."[10] According to news reports, Randle packed his bags and arrived at the ballpark on March 24, ready to confront Lucchesi and leave training camp, but sportswriters clued in Lucchesi on Randle's plans. Lucchesi reportedly said, "There's no way Frank Lucchesi is going to kiss anybody's ass or ask them to stay in camp." Apparently the trigger for what happened next was Lucchesi's postscript: "I'm sick and tired of some punks making $80,000 a year moaning and groaning about their situation."[11]

It all came to a head in Orlando on March 28, prior to an exhibition game against the Minnesota Twins. Randle approached Lucchesi on the field. They spoke heatedly and then Randle delivered a series of punches. One fractured Lucchesi's right cheekbone; another knocked him to the ground on his hip. Randle continued swinging until he was restrained by shortstop Bert Campaneris. Lucchesi was diagnosed with, in addition to the fractured cheekbone, a cerebral concussion and a lacerated lip, plus significant back pain. Renowned *Dallas Times Herald* (and, later, *Dallas Morning News*) sportswriter Blackie Sherrod wrote that he had seen "the hand speed of Sugar Ray Robinson and the cobra strikes of Muhammad Ali, but the flurry of Randle's punches, all landing on the manager's face, must have broken all speed records."[12]

Fran Lucchesi, Frank's daughter, was a student at the University of Texas at Arlington at the time. She recalls she was in class when a friend, who had heard about the incident on the radio, summoned her. She said that, in later years, when people found out that Lucchesi was her dad, they treated it as nothing more than a fight between a player and the manager. But that wasn't the case. "He was attacked," she told me. "A lot of people didn't realize it; they just thought it was a brawl. Dad really suffered so many years with that, jaw pain and teeth issues and trauma to the head."

Randle was suspended, fined, and later traded to the New York

Mets. He was also charged with aggravated assault in Florida. He pled no contest to a misdemeanor battery charge and was fined. Lucchesi, upset that Major League Baseball didn't impose any fine or suspension, sued Randle for $200,000, but the two settled out of court for $20,000. T. R. Sullivan, beat writer for *Rangers Today*, viewed the event with understated irony. Eyebrows were raised when the Mets traded for Randle, but Donald Grant, the Mets owner, said his team believed Randle deserved a second chance. "He lost his head once, and I don't think it will ever happen again." Sullivan noted, "Grant was right. Randle never beat the shit out of another manager again."[13]

For the Rangers, 1977 was a notable year in another respect as well. It was the famous season of four managers. Lucchesi started the year and was fired on June 21 with a 31-31 record. Former MLB player Eddie Stankey was introduced as the new manager on June 22, but he lasted only one game (that might be some kind of record) before quitting and returning home to Alabama. Next up was Connie Ryan, the Rangers bench coach, named interim manager for six days, then Billy Hunter was hired as the permanent manager.

No question about it, Dallas was a football city in the mid-to-late 1970s, and the Cowboys owned the town. This was the height of the Tom Landry era, with twenty consecutive winning seasons that spanned from 1966 to 1985, and playoff appearances in eighteen of those years. That twenty consecutive winning seasons still stands as the NFL record, recently challenged by the New England Patriots, but they fell one short, with nineteen consecutive winning seasons between 2001 and 2019. In 1978, John Facenda narrated the team's highlight film with the opening, "They appear on television so often that their faces are as familiar to the public as presidents and movie stars. They are the Dallas Cowboys, 'America's Team.'"[14] The '70s featured players such as Roger Staubach, Bob Lilly, Calvin Hill, Lee Roy Jordan, Mel Renfro, Cornell Green, Tony Dorsett, Drew Pearson, Randy White, Harvey Martin, Ed "Too Tall" Jones, Charlie Waters, Cliff Harris, and Thomas "Hollywood" Henderson." Remember that last name.

It was a golden time to be a Cowboys fan.

Music

In 1974, on its fiftieth anniversary, MGM Studios released a film called *That's Entertainment*, which was a compilation of musical performances from the studio's fifty years of films. Archival footage included such stars as Judy Garland, Nelson Eddy, Jeanette MacDonald, Gene Kelly, and Frank Sinatra. Dallas could have put together its own compilation and wouldn't have had to go back nearly as far as MGM did.

Dallas has always been a good music town, stretching back for decades, but the 1960s and 1970s were prime examples. Two weeks after Woodstock, on the weekend of August 30 to September 1, 1969, Angus Wynne III put together the Texas International Pop Festival, which was held in Lewisville, about 25 miles northwest of Dallas. Acts included Texas's own Janis Joplin (from Port Arthur), Santana, Grand Funk Railroad, Delaney and Bonnie and Friends, B. B. King, and Led Zeppelin. Though it might not have had the cachet (or notoriety; pick your poison) of Woodstock, the three-day event drew an estimated one hundred twenty thousand attendees.[15]

Texxas Jam was the nickname for the Texxas World Music Festival, the first of which was held in Dallas at the Cotton Bowl in 1978. Performers included Van Halen, Eddie Money, Ted Nugent,

Aerosmith, Journey, and Atlanta Rhythm Section. A reported one hundred thousand people attended that first year on a hot summer Fourth of July weekend—100-plus degrees with temperatures around 120 degrees on the field (it's always hot in Dallas in July).

Yes, Dallas was a bit of a Mecca for music in the '70s. But Dallas—and, in particular, Dallas high schools—also originated more than its fair share of musical talent, including a number of recording artists who were at their zenith in the '70s. Although the Steve Miller Band may have started in San Francisco, and although Miller may have been born in Wisconsin, he was raised in Dallas, where he attended St. Mark's School, at least for a while. His parents were both musicians (of sorts), his mother Bertha a jazz singer and his father, although a physician by profession, a jazz buff and amateur recording engineer.

In Dallas, Miller formed his own band, The Marksmen, and taught guitar chords to St. Mark's classmate Boz Scaggs. When he was kicked out of St. Mark's, he transferred to Woodrow Wilson High School in East Dallas. He graduated from Woodrow (as its alumni call it) in 1961 and attended the University of Wisconsin-Madison, where he continued his music career, forming a band called The Ardells. His old St. Mark's classmate, Boz Scaggs, played with The Ardells and Steve Miller Band for a while in the 1960s. Classic '70s hits for Miller included "The Joker" in 1973, "Take the Money and Run" and "Fly Like an Eagle" in 1976, and "Jet Airliner" in 1977.

Boz Scaggs started his solo career in 1969. The '70s saw "Lowdown" and "It's Over" in 1976 and "Lido Shuffle" in 1977. One of his biggest hits would come in 1980 with "Look What You've Done for Me" to the motion picture *Urban Cowboy*.

Another Woodrow product was Dusty Hill, who played the

cello (of all things) while at Woodrow, but he also played blues music with his older brother Rocky. When they formed their own band, Hill learned to play the bass. The two Hill brothers and a drummer named Frank Beard, who graduated from Irving High School (the suburb that was the site of Texas Stadium), played in several local bands in Dallas, the last being American Blues. In 1968, Rocky left the band, and Frank and Dusty moved to Houston, where they combined with Houston native Billy Gibbons to form ZZ Top. Seventies hits for ZZ Top included 1973's "La Grange," 1975's "Tush," and 1977's "Arrested for Driving Blind."

While Dallas's Woodrow produced Miller and Hill, another Dallas high school, Thomas Jefferson, turned out a duo of artists who were prominent in the 1970s. Marvin Lee Aday graduated from TJ in 1965. According to Aday, his father convinced hospital nurses to place the name "Meat" on his crib because "he looked like nine pounds of ground chuck." In junior high, he sometimes went by his initials M. L., but classmates, following the lead of his football coach, dubbed him Meat Loaf.[16] And it stuck. His 1978 discography included "Two Out of Three Ain't Bad," "Bat Out of Hell," and "Paradise by the Dashboard Light." He also had some acting credits in the '70s, perhaps best known for playing the role of Eddie in *The Rocky Horror Picture Show* in 1975.

The other TJ alum was Robert Michael Nesmith, who preceded Meat Loaf by a few years. He first rose to fame as a member of The Monkees, a group created for television. He left the Monkees in 1970 and scored his first top-forty hit as a solo artist with "Joanne" that same year. His ninth album, *From a Radio Engine to the Photon Wing*, was released in 1977. One single from the album, called "Rio," was released worldwide.[17]

One of the more interesting bits of trivia about Nesmith

is that his mother Bette, a high-school-dropout-turned-secretary-who-made-frequent-typographical-errors at Texas Bank and Trust in Dallas, invented the first correction fluid in her kitchen in 1956, when Nesmith was thirteen years old. According to the United States Patent and Trademark Office, she was unable to afford the $400 necessary to pay a patent application fee. She earned only $300 a month and, having been divorced a decade prior, her salary and whatever she could make selling the fluid were her sole sources of income to support herself and her son. She marketed the fluid under the brand name "Mistake Out." She opened her own home business, the Mistake Out Company, producing bottles of correction fluid in her kitchen and then, as the business grew larger, upgraded to her garage. She renamed the product Liquid Paper and, in 1980, sold it to the Gillette Corporation for $47.5 million—nearly two hundred million in 2026 dollars—plus a share of future royalties.[18]

Another Dallas high school, W.W. Samuell in southeast Dallas, produced a trio of talent. Its products include Dan Seals and John Ford Coley, classmates who reached fame as England Dan & John Ford Coley. Their '70s hits included "I'd Really Love to See You Tonight" and "Nights Are Forever Without You" in 1976, "It's Sad to Belong" and "Gone Too Far" in 1977, and "Love Is the Answer" in 1979. And to keep the talent in the family, a third Samuell alumnus to make it big in the music business was Jim Seals, older brother of Dan Seals, who teamed with Dash Crofts of Cisco, Texas, to form Seals and Crofts. Their '70s hits included "Summer Breeze" in 1972, "Hummingbird" and "We May Never Pass This Way Again" in 1973, "I'll Play for You" in 1975, "Get Closer" in 1976, and "My Fair Share" from the 1977 movie soundtrack for *One on One*, starring Robbie Benson.

Dallas's W.H. Adamson High School also produced a trio of

music stars who made it big in the '70s. One of them was singer-songwriter and leader in the so-called progressive or "outlaw" country movement Michael Martin Murphey. After graduating from Adamson, he attended John Kearns's alma mater, North Texas State University in Denton, where he studied Greek before transferring to UCLA to study poetry, creative writing, and medieval history. His personal website touts original songs he wrote that were performed by such notables as The Monkees ("What Am I Doing Hangin' 'Round?"), Kenny Rogers (an entire album of Murphey songs called *The Ballad of Calico*, performed by Kenny Rogers and The First Edition), The Nitty Gritty Dirt Band ("Lost River"), Johnny Cash (who performed "Tennessee Stud" as a duet with Murphey), and Jerry Jeff Walker (who performed "Little Bird" with Murphey).[19] His hits as an artist included "Wildfire" and "Carolina in the Pines" in 1975, "Cherokee Fiddle" in 1977, and "Backslider's Wine" in 1979, which was also performed by Jerry Jeff Walker.

Speaking of Jerry Jeff Walker, one of Murphey's high school classmates at Adamson, as well as in college at North Texas State, was Ray Wylie Hubbard, who first achieved prominence as a songwriter when Walker recorded his "Up Against the Wall, Redneck Mother" in 1973. Hubbard toured and recorded with The Lost Gonzo Band and, in 1976, he released an album called *Ray Wylie Hubbard and the Cowboy Twinkies.*

Another Adamson alum is on at least one "one hit wonders" list with a song from the '70s: B. W. Stevenson. Born Louis Charles Stevenson, also sometimes known as Buckwheat Stevenson, he released his biggest hit in 1973, "My Maria," which he cowrote with Daniel Moore. "My Maria" was a Top 10 hit on the pop chart in the United States and reached No. 1 on the US Adult

Contemporary chart. That same year, Stevenson also released "Shambala," cowritten with Moore. "Shambala" reached as high as sixty-six on the Billboard Hot 100. In 1973, Three Dog Night released a version of "Shambala," which made it to No. 3. Stevenson died prematurely in 1988 at age thirty-eight after developing a staph infection during heart valve surgery. His primary legacy is as a songwriter. In 1989, Poor David's Pub in Dallas created The Annual B.W. Stevenson Memorial Singer-Songwriter Competition.

Another Dallas musician and product of a Dallas high school worthy of discussion is Trini Lopez. Lopez's long career spanned both the '60s and the '70s, and on into the twentieth century. Born to Mexican parents who moved to Dallas shortly after their marriage in Guanajuato, Lopez grew up in what was known as the "Little Mexico" area of Dallas. He attended the now-defunct N.R. Crozier Tech High School, which was also the alma mater of former Supreme Court justice Tom Clark and Domingo Samudio, better known as rock and roll singer Sam the Sham. Sam the Sham and the Pharoahs' "Wooly Bully" was a *Billboard* magazine number one hit in 1965, and Samudio performed with Lopez while in school.

Lopez dropped out of Crozier Tech short of graduation to help support his family financially. One of his earlier gigs with the first band he formed was at The Vegas Club in the mid-1950s, owned by Jack Ruby. Lopez was known for, among other hits, "Lemon Tree" and a cover of Pete Seeger's "If I Had a Hammer," which sold over one million copies after its release in 1963. "Lemon Tree" got a humorous mention in 1991 on a *Seinfeld* episode titled "The Phone Message." Looking for a code for George Costanza to alert Jerry Seinfeld that someone was coming, the two decide that George should sing "Lemon Tree." Although perhaps not as well-known in the 1970s, Trini and his brother Jesse occasionally performed at the Playboy Club in Dallas.

One more Dallas high school product worthy of note is Stephen Ray Vaughan from Justin F. Kimball High School. Better known as Stevie Ray Vaughan, he made his first studio recording in 1970 on an album called "A New Hi," which was a compilation of songs from Dallas teenagers. One of Vaughan's band members on the album, listed as performing vocals, guitar, and piano, was Kimball classmate Steve Tobolowsky, later more commonly as Stephen Tobolowsky, an actor who appeared in such movies as *Groundhog Day* and *Memento* and television shows *Deadwood* and *Californication*.

Dallas produced its share of harder rockers, as well. Stephen Stills was raised in a military family and moved around quite a bit, but Dallas can claim him as a native son by birth. Best known for his time in Buffalo Springfield, Crosby, Stills and Nash, and Crosby, Stills, Nash and Young in the '60s, his '70s hits primarily reflect his years as a solo act. They include "Love the One You're With" in 1970, "Change Partners" in 1971, and "Long May You Run" in 1976.

Saxophonist Bill Tillman, originally from Houston, moved to Dallas in the late '70s after spending a portion of his career with Blood, Sweat and Tears. In Dallas, he appeared as a featured soloist for the Dallas Symphony & Jazz Orchestra, in addition to playing in clubs with his Bill Tillman Band. Noting that prior stint with BS&T, Tim Schuller wrote in *D Magazine* in 1978 that "his current jazz efforts better display his musical versatility. One of the city's best jazz improvisors, he can intensify a solo to a degree well beyond the reach of many better-known players."[20]

Movies and Television

Perhaps not as well known, or popular, as the musicians it produced were a few movies and television shows shot in and around Dallas in the 1970s. Most of them were B movies, although a few were studio projects. The '60s saw films like Twentieth Century Fox's *State Fair* in 1962, a production musical scored by Rogers and Hammerstein starring Pat Boone, Bobby Darin, and Ann-Margret. In 1967, there was Arthur Penn's *Bonnie and Clyde*, starring Warren Beatty and Faye Dunaway, released by Warner Brothers. *Executive Action* in 1973 created a fictional account of the JFK assassination starring Burt Lancaster and Robert Ryan. It was written by Dalton Trumbo, who had been blacklisted during the Red Scare of the late '40s and '50s. In 1974, a small dog captured America's hearts in *Benji* and, in 1976, the war of the ages was fueled by MGM's *Logan's Run*, starring Michael York. In 1978, Ron Howard, probably better known at the time as Opie Taylor from *The Andy Griffith Show* or Richie Cunningham from *Happy Days*, wrote and directed *Cotton Candy*. The movie starred his *American Graffiti* costar Charles Martin Smith, who played Terry "The Toad" Fields in *Graffiti*, and Howard's brother Clint, who cowrote the *Cotton Candy* script with Ron.

As time ran out on the '70s, one low-budget effort married the city's love affair with the Dallas Cowboys to film. *Squezze Play*, from 1979, starred Cowboys tight end Jay Saldi, wide receiver Drew Pearson, linebacker Thomas "Hollywood" Henderson, and defensive end Ed "Too Tall" Jones as Vietnam War buddies who returned home from the war and were having trouble adjusting to life. It sounds like a bad imitation of the prior year's *The Deer Hunter*, only the returning vets in that film were played by real actors: Robert DeNiro, John Savage, and Christopher Walken, and the movie won five Oscars—Best Supporting Actor for Christopher Walken, Best Director for Michael Cimino, Best Editing, Best Sound, and Best Picture.

Not so *Squezze Play*. The director of the film, Anthony Lanza, was quoted as saying,

> It was a bad movie, just a bad movie. It had four Dallas Cowboys in it. At the time, they were very popular. It had two or three people that were starlets that were just starting out, didn't really have any background, didn't want to be told what to do or how should I direct them and the action. It was just very unprofessional, and I didn't enjoy putting that together at all.[21]

That's a lot like a parent telling the world their own kid is ugly. It appears that the director, who passed away in 2010, had other ugly kids as well, both preceding *Squezze Play*. At least the earlier films had actors instead of athletes in their casts. For example, 1967's *The Glory Stompers* starred Dennis Hopper and Jody McCrea (son of Western star Joel McCrea and actress Frances Dee), while *The Incredible 2-Headed Transplant* in 1971 starred Bruce Dern and Pat Priest (better known for her role as Marilyn in *The Munsters* television show).

A new pop culture phenomenon was about to explode onto the scene. It would sweep the country and lock in how the world viewed Dallas and Dallasites. It also raised the imponderable question that plagued television viewers for one entire off-season: Who shot J. R.?

The nighttime soap *Dallas* premiered on April 2, 1978, ran

until May 3, 1991, and starred Larry Hagman, who was born in Fort Worth to Broadway actress Mary Martin. Previously best known as Barbara Eden's long suffering "master," Major Anthony Nelson, in *I Dream of Jeannie*, Hagman portrayed oil tycoon J. R. Ewing for all 357 episodes of the original Dallas series. The last episode of the 1980 season ended in a cliffhanger with J. R. shot by an unknown assailant. The identity of the shooter and J. R.'s life-or-death fate remained unknown until the beginning of the next season. At the time, the cliffhanger was the most-watched episode in television history, surpassing the series ender of *The Fugitive*, starring David Janssen. It was bested a few years later, in 1983, by the finale of *M*A*S*H*, and it still ranks second to *M*A*S*H* but just ahead of the final episode of *Roots*.

Paul Heckmann would get a chance to be involved with the production of *Dallas*.

CHAPTER FIFTEEN
Small Town Boy in the Big City

"If you've ever driven across Texas, you know how different one area of the state can be from another. Take El Paso. It looks as much like Dallas as I look like Jack Nicklaus."

Lee Trevino

Being a member of a national championship football team was great. Being a member of a history-setting football team, winning two consecutive national championships, took "great" to another level. But being injured all the time—not so great. Because of my injuries, I didn't play on the '76 team, which again won the national championship. I was never much of a student, though in my defense I had some issues that not everyone had to deal with. By December of 1976, just after the Javelinas capped off that third straight championship, I decided I'd had enough of school.

My old college roommate, Bill Bronstad, had a three-bedroom apartment in a Dallas complex called Land's End, located on Skillman Street, just north of Northwest Highway at what is now called Retail Road. He offered me a place to stay if I wanted to try life in the big city. There was nothing left for me in Kingsville, so I accepted his offer. Getting there posed a bit of a problem. My 1972 Chevy Vega had suffered a catastrophic death at a four-way stop sign in Kingsville. I had run out of gas and was pushing the car through the intersection when it got whacked by the very traffic I was trying to avoid. Fortunately I still had my Kawasaki 750 motorcycle. Dad drove down from Waco and we loaded the same trailer I had pulled behind my Vega when I first went to Kingsville. We ran the motorcycle up a ramp into the trailer, along with the rest of my meager belongings. Then we headed from Kingsville to Dallas, a journey of more than four hundred miles.

Survival instincts kicked in almost immediately when I got there. Dallas drivers were not kind to motorcycles, and the apartment was in the area of some of the busiest roads in East Dallas—Central Expressway, Northwest Highway, Abrams Road, Skillman Street, just to name a few. I needed a car. On a prior trip to Dallas, I had interviewed for a sales position at Kenray Ford in north Dallas at the corner of Forest Lane and Marsh Lane. Not only were they hiring car salesmen but they would also let salesmen drive demo models. A match made in heaven. I got a job and a car. A nasty-looking brown Granada, but at least it was a car!

The dealership paid salesmen a commission of forty percent on the net, one of the best, if not the best, rates in town. We worked on an "up" system, which essentially meant you were in a rotation. When the next customer walked in, whoever was "up" in the rotation got them. Of course, this led to prank calls from coworkers, but not really so funny. For example, when I was "up," I might get a summons on the intercom that told me I had a customer on the used car lot, or that I had a call waiting on line two, when I really didn't. In my absence as I searched for the nonexistent used car customer or went to take the phone call, another salesman would snatch the next new car customer away from me. It could be a little cutthroat.

I didn't like selling cars, but I was decent at it. I set the company record in 1977 for the biggest gross profit on a transaction when I took a Porsche Targa with nine hundred miles on it as a trade-in for the "new" version of the downsized Thunderbird, loaded to the max. Still, there was *waaaay* too much down time for me between customers. I was bored. So, I left after a year. That meant farewell to the Granada, but I was able to trade in my motorcycle for a car, an older Chevy Caprice, a '66 or '67 model, green four-door with a darker green vinyl top. It didn't look like much but it had good air conditioning (a necessity in north Texas) and electric windows. I was in the lap of luxury. And so, even though the match made in (not quite) heaven turned out to be short-term, at least it got me settled in Dallas.

During that time selling cars, I met Gene Cook, who almost instantly became my best friend. We often covered for each other on the sales floor, which helped cut down on losing customers to pranks. Gene was one of the most loquacious people you will ever meet, but that was a fit for my personality. He was smooth with the ladies, something I had not yet mastered—still too shy—but he opened doors for me. He introduced me to Debbie Kepley, a Dallas Cowboys cheerleader he had been dating. Cute, funny, energetic, Debbie fit the cheerleader mold perfectly. She had an amazing smile that, despite every other great physical attribute, was the first thing you noticed. Her great sense of humor made me feel energized just being around her. When I got into modeling a little later, she went out of her way to help me. Same for acting. I'm not sure I ever would have tried either of those without her encouragement and help.

When Gene and Debbie stopped dating, she called to ask me out. Even though she and Gene were no longer dating, it seemed like a betrayal to accept. I decided to handle it by saying yes and

Paul Heckmann and Debbie Kepley. *Photo courtesy of Paul Heckmann.*

simply not telling him. No need for that kind of drama. At least not yet. I did tell him later—much later. By then he and Debbie were ancient history, and he turned out to be cool with it.

After Debbie left the Cowboys Cheerleaders, she was part of a group of former Cheerleaders who posed for *Playboy* magazine for the December 1978 issue, calling themselves Texas Cowgirls, Inc. Their attempt to capitalize on their past as Dallas Cowboys Cheerleaders, including wearing white hotpants, carrying pom-poms, and posing in a parody—and highly revealing—version of a popular Dallas Cowboys Cheerleaders poster led to unsuccessful litigation by the Cowboys for, among other things, copyright infringement, service mark infringement, and unfair competition.

The Cowboys were more successful in 1979 suing the producers and distributors of the X-rated *Debbie Does Dallas* movie. A federal district court granted an injunction against showing the movie, noting that it "has no other purpose than to display sex acts in minute detail."[1] The United States District Court for the Second Circuit Court of Appeals affirmed the ruling, and the movie was pulled from theaters. In its opinion, the appellate court described the movie as a "gross and revolting sex film whose plot, to the extent that there is one" involved a cheerleader at a fictional high school who becomes a "Texas Cowgirl" and performs sexual services as fundraising for a trip to Dallas.[2]

I didn't know much about the Playboy lawsuit at the time, but it didn't change my opinion about Debbie, who I ended up dating for only a brief time. Debbie was a model for the Sarah Norton Agency in Dallas, which specialized in providing models for print and television ads. Nowadays, Sarah is still in business but mostly works in promotions, not as a talent agent. Debbie wanted me to meet her, to have her size me up as a model. I had never considered modeling. In fact, I didn't really know what all it entailed. But I figured it couldn't hurt.

I met Sarah at her office in the old European Crossroads complex on West Northwest Highway, which was also home to one of Dallas's hottest disco clubs at the time, The #3 Lift. Sarah's office was in the interior on the second floor. It wasn't exactly a Lana Turner at Schwab's Pharmacy moment, but she signed me on the spot. And there I was, a small town boy from Woodway, Texas, now a big-time model in Dallas. Who would ever have believed it?

Sarah sent me on several small gigs at first, but I needed to build a portfolio if I wanted to get into the big-time. I didn't yet have a resume that could show anything other than "car salesman." I tried to create a portfolio with some photos taken by friends, but it was pretty bad. Amateurish. That was the bad news. The good news was that for each of the gigs I worked, I got a professional photo. Accumulating them was taking too long, so I hired a professional photographer named Jihad Nijar to take some headshots. Those came out pretty good, so I redid my resume and portfolio and made modeling my primary occupation.

Paul Heckmann modelling headshot. *Photo courtesy of Paul Heckmann.*

Sarah sent me to do a television commercial for a jeans company called Pants West. I still have the pay slip from them: $190. Not bad for a day's work in 1977. In 2026 money, that would be about $1030. Not bad for a day's work today, either. I weighed about 195 pounds at the time and Sarah wanted me to lose some weight. Debbie took me to her weight control doctor. I'm not sure what his specialty was, but he was well known in some circles for helping with weight loss. He didn't actually prescribe anything. Rather, when you departed his office, you left carrying a bag of pills. In street parlance, they were known as "Black Mollys," and sometimes "Black Beauties." To me they were just "diet pills." I now know a bit more about them. They were a combination of amphetamine and biphetamine, commonly used in the '60s and '70s as diet pills. They were also given to soldiers in the Vietnam War to decrease fatigue and to help them stay awake. I have even heard them described as a cheap alternative to cocaine. But I didn't know any of that at the time.

I ended up losing about twenty pounds, and Sarah got me more work. But I started having issues with the pills' side effects, which included constipation, inflamed hemorrhoids, lack of appetite, and grinding my teeth. I had to get other pills to counteract the effects of the first pills, creating a vicious cycle. I never thought about addiction then, but this might have been a harbinger of things to come.

While I was with the Norton Agency, Jerry Ford came to Dallas to scope out the Texas talent. Jerry was the husband of

Eileen Ford and co-owner with her of Ford Models in New York City, one of the most successful agencies in the country. *Vanity Fair* described the agency as "synonymous with the freshest most iconic faces in the business." Candice Bergen modeled for the agency in the '60s, Lauren Hutton in the '70s, and the '80s would see Brooke Shields and Ali MacGraw on the runway. The following decade produced the likes of Naomi Campbell and Christy Turlington, who—although they didn't invent the term—popularized the concept of "supermodel."

My specialty was suits and tuxes. Notwithstanding my background as an athlete and my training regimen, I didn't really have the swimsuit body, so that was never on my agenda. Jerry Ford thought I was at least worth a look in The Big Apple, so the agency paid for my trip and accommodations for a brief—very brief!—stint in New York. I was there for only a week or two and did some runway work, but that was it. I didn't have the "sleek" form they wanted, so we weren't a fit.

Besides, New York City wasn't for me. Too big and, in the '70s, too dirty and crime-infested, with one of the highest crime rates—and murder rates—in the nation. So, this small-town boy returned to Dallas, where I continued building my portfolio and resume. I did gigs for newspaper and print ads, including *The Dallas Morning News* and *The Houston Post*, and various trade magazines. I even had an ad in *Gentleman's Quarterly*. That made me a bit of a celebrity back home. Or at least a mini-celebrity. Or maybe more of an oddity. Most of the folks I knew in Woodway were

Paul Heckmann modelling shot. *Photo courtesy of Paul Heckmann.*

blue-collar workers and white-collar commuters to Waco. They didn't really pay attention to things like modeling, or if they did, it was with raised eyebrows.

I got a regular gig with Southland Corporation. It was a good gig. Not great pay, but okay. It was regular work and always seemed to go smoothly. Until it didn't. Most Texans recognize Southland as the owner of 7-Eleven convenience stores. It was founded in Dallas in 1927 as the Southland Ice Company, operating a storefront icehouse that also sold milk, eggs, and bread, before proliferating into convenience stores everywhere. And I mean everywhere. Its website boasts that it operates more than 85,000 stores in nineteen countries.[3]

A training film cast me as the "klutz manager" who kept knocking over stuff in the store. One of the camera crew lay down on a pad (like the kind to pad furniture when moving it) so as to film me while shooting upward. The way the script had it, I was supposed to knock over an oxygen-type tank for the Icee machine. The frozen slush is actually called a "Slurpee," which was the brand sold by 7-Eleven when it entered into a licensing agreement with The Icee Company in 1966. Part of the deal with The Icee Company was that 7-Eleven was only allowed to sell the drink in the United States and had to use a different name. There was also a noncompete clause in the agreement that prohibited 7-Eleven from going head-to-head with Icee. Bob Stanford, a 7-Eleven advertising executive, coined the term "slurpee" as a play on the sound made when "slurping" the slush drink through a straw.[4]

By the way, the Slurpee or Icee was the inspiration for Woodrow Wilson High School graduate Mariano Martinez's frozen margarita machine, which he invented in 1971 for his restaurant in East Dallas. The original machine can be seen today at the

Smithsonian National Museum of American History.

But back to the training film. The reason I, as the "klutz manager," was able to knock over the tank was because I, the "klutz manager," had failed to put a safety chain around it. The camera guy was supposed to move out of the way at the last minute when the tank fell but for some reason he failed to do so. The heavy tank hit the front of the camera and shattered its very expensive lenses. I had played the scene the way I was supposed to. In fact, wasn't this exactly the kind of accident the safety chain was supposed to prevent? Seemed like a perfectly good example. But the camera crew talked as if the accident was my fault. And that was the last time I worked for Southland.

The television show *Dallas* was filming in the area, on its way to enormous worldwide reception. I managed to get a short gig on the show. Not in front of the camera, other than a few scenes as "background" (or an "extra" in layman's parlance), but as a stand-in for both Patrick Duffy and Larry Hagman. A "stand-in" was called "second team." Before shooting a scene, the real actors, the "first team," will take their positions and maybe read through their lines while crew members mark the spots with different color tape. Then, after the first team goes back to their trailers, or wherever, the second team comes in and takes position on the colored marks, depending upon whom we are standing in for. Stand-ins are typically the same height and weight as the actors so as to allow cameras and lighting to be properly set up before shooting the scene. I had risers to put in my shoes, so I could stand in, without the risers, for Larry Hagman, at six feet, or, with the risers, for Patrick Duffy, at six feet two inches. It wasn't glamorous work, but it was necessary. And it was a thrill just to be on the set of a big-time television production.

I read for several speaking lines on the show, but my poor short-term memory, which had plagued me my whole life, betrayed me. Reading the lines was one thing, but as soon as the cameras rolled, I couldn't remember a thing. One time, while preparing to film a buffet scene in which I was "background," someone grabbed me from behind in a bear hug. It was Larry Hagman. The cast had decided it would be fun to play tricks on each other and Larry wanted my help. "Make Linda laugh during the shot," he said. Linda was Linda Gray, who played Sue Ellen Ewing, onscreen wife to Larry's J. R. Ewing.

How could I turn that down? "Just don't get me fired," I said.

Larry said, "Don't worry, you'll be fine."

Linda Gray publicity shot inscribed to Paul: "Keep your fingers out of deviled eggs." *Public domain, photo courtesy of Paul Heckmann.*

As the scene was being shot, I stood directly across the buffet table from Linda. As she began to deliver her lines, I grabbed a handful of deviled eggs from a platter and squeezed them. Squished deviled eggs shot out from between all my fingers. Linda simply started laughing and couldn't get her lines out. The entire cast broke up. Director Larry Katzman had been in on the set-up, but he wasn't sure what I had planned. I saw him rolling on the floor, laughing. Later, Linda sent me an autographed photo with the inscription, "Keep your fingers out of deviled eggs! Love Linda Gray."

As an aside, if you've ever seen the movie poster for *The Graduate* from 1967, with a shapely female leg across the frame as the owner of the leg pulls on a stocking in front of Dustin Hoffman as Ben Braddock, don't automatically assume the leg belongs to the on-screen Mrs. Robinson, Anne Bancroft. Bancroft was not on set that day, so the leg belongs to Linda Gray, an aspiring model and actress at the time. She later said she got $25 for the gig.

Unfortunately, even with modeling and the occasional commercial, film, or tv gig, I was having trouble paying my bills. I didn't want to go back to selling cars, but I needed a regular job. Or at least some regular income. It was time to check out the club scene.

CHAPTER SIXTEEN

Oh, It Was a Scene, Man![1]

"The night club had a curious and diverse appeal. To some it was a sex-exciter. To others, frequenting a night club and throwing away money was a form of exhibitionism."

Stanley Walker

What Dallas may really have been known for in the 1970s was its nightclubs. Disco clubs, to be specific. Of course, Dallas had long had a reputation for its "club scene." Or maybe "club scene" isn't exactly the right word, but vice in Dallas had a long history, and clubs were where much of Dallas's vice played out. Gambling and prostitution, jazz and booze, red light districts and shootouts, with names like Boggy Bayou and Hell's Half Acre. John Henry "Doc" Holliday even plied his trade for a short while in Dallas as a dentist, gambler, and gunfighter—well, at least one gunfight, in which apparently neither participant was either killed or arrested.

Honolulu had its Hotel Street while Dallas had Frogtown,[2] so-called "red light districts" where prostitutes were permitted to shop their anatomical wares without interference from law enforcement. Frogtown, or "the reservation," near the southwest-ern edge of downtown, was a sort of haven for "fallen women" and the "social evil" (euphemisms for prostitution) in early twentieth-century Dallas. A crackdown on prostitution spearheaded by First Baptist Church's Rev. George W. Truett broke up the "reservation" but simply succeeded in dispersing the trade from a centralized location into other venues, including clubs and saloons. According to the *Dallas Dispatch*, "immorality now existed in almost every neighborhood of the city rather than safely within the confines of the reservation."[3]

In the first half of the twentieth century, the mid-cities between Dallas and Fort Worth offered two of the best-known clubs: the Baghdad Supper Club, east of Grand Prairie, and Top O' Hill Terrace in Arlington. The Baghdad Club, perhaps the more "legitimate" of the two, operated as a theater and entertainment venue, with dining and dancing, along with live music, from the late 1920s until it was destroyed by fire in 1953.

Top O' Hill Terrace started as a tearoom in the early 1920s but evolved into a casino during Prohibition, with gambling and prostitution. Fred and Mary Browning bought the club in 1930 and, at one point, partnered with Benny Binion, with his cohort Bennie Bickers, to run the casino. It was known as the finest in the Southwest and "one of the most elegant in the country."[4] Journalist Rena Pederson called it "a hush-hush hideaway for millionaires and mobsters" and "an underground Casino Royale."[5] The club had racehorse stables on the grounds, a swimming pool, and a boxing ring where fighters from heavyweight champion Max Baer to lightweight champion Lew Jenkins, the "Sweetwater Swatter" from Sweetwater, Texas, sparred. Entertainment included the likes of Tommy Dorsey and Benny Goodman; customers included John Wayne, Ginger Rogers, Howard Hughes, H. L. Hunt, Gloria

Swanson, Clint Murchison, Don Amache, and Bob Hope. Even crooks and mobsters like Bonnie Parker and Clyde Barrow paid an occasional visit, as did Bugsy Siegel.[6]

Just as Frogtown fell victim to a crusading Baptist preacher, Top O' Hill's demise began with a shut-down campaign by J. Frank Norris, pastor of First Baptist Church of Fort Worth, who vowed to someday own the place. In 1956, The Bible Baptist Seminary, part of First Baptist of Fort Worth, bought the property. Norris had died earlier in 1956 and didn't get to see his promise fulfilled, at least in spirit. Today, the former casino is part of the grounds of Arlington Baptist University.

But while Baghdad and Top O' Hill were not in Dallas proper, two later, and perhaps more notorious, clubs were. The first was the Carousel Club, owned by Lee Harvey Oswald assassin Jack Ruby. The second was the Colony Club, owned by Abe Weinstein, which featured a burlesque dancer named Candy Barr, née Juanita Dale Slusher. Although she was born in Edna, Texas, on the Texas Gulf Coast, she ran away from home at the age of thirteen and ended up in Dallas, where she gained fame.

But the heyday of the club scene in Dallas came in the late 1970s and on into the 1980s when disco exploded. Although disco actually got its start in the '60s among people of color and the gay community, it reached its zenith in the mid-1970s, thanks in large part to the John Travolta film *Saturday Night Fever* in 1977 and the frenetic disco beat of the Bee Gees soundtrack that accompanied it. Not everyone appreciated disco, though, as evidenced by Memphis, Tennessee, disc jockey Rick Dees' satirical "Disco Duck." Some credit Colleen Hoover's 2014 novel *Maybe Someday* as the origin of a quote about preferring to eat barbed wire to listening to disco, but a popular T-shirt in the late '70s pictured

Looney Tunes cartoon character Yosemite Sam (or perhaps a rip-off of the character) saying, "I'd rather chew barbed wire than listen to disco."

D Magazine provided an entertaining list of club mishaps in the '70s and '80s in an article entitled "Low Moments in Dallas Bar History." They included a dance contest at élan in 1977 in which the sponsor, a "snappily attired man with an exotic Middle Eastern accent," doled out more than a million dollars in worthless checks for winners and runners-up.[7] It's not clear if this is accurate. While *D Magazine* lists it as occurring in 1977, it seems to reflect a 1978 event reported in *The Dallas Morning News*. That story told of a wealthy Pakistani named F. Masood Khan, nicknamed the "Pakistani cowboy," who spent an expensive few days, and millions of dollars, in Dallas, including at élan but also at NorthPark Center and Neiman Marcus. According to the *News*, Khan "streaked through Dallas . . . in a star-studded limousine blazing a trail lined with jewels, furs and $1 million tips." The *News* story reported on a dance contest, with $500,000 checks being given to each of the dancers, and "conflicting statements" as to whether the checks were good. élan's manager reported that, when he ran a check on the checks, he was told, "The money is there."[8]

In 1979, Gene Street closed his bar J. Alfred's when a "hulking biker" hit him with a beer mug. He replaced it with Dallas's initial fern bar, The Wine Press. Punishment enough. A 1983 performance by Joe "King" Carrasco at Tango on Lower Greenville was broken up by a tear gas grenade, and a cat burglar crashed through the ceiling of Dick's Last Resort at its grand opening in 1985.[9]

One of the more famous (or perhaps "infamous" is a better word) mishaps in a Dallas club occurred in 1984. Dallas Cowboys offensive tackle Jim Cooper, while eating dinner and watching Monday Night Football on a wall-mounted television, slipped on a slick floor at a club called Confetti. *The New York Times* reported, "Jim Cooper, a mainstay at offensive tackle for the Dallas Cowboys, suffered a broken leg during the Monday night game and was lost for the season. That was surprising, since the Cowboys weren't playing."[10]

Among the more popular clubs of the '70s were Bowley and Wilson's Up Your Alley (or simply the "Alley"), Old Plantation, Lizard Lounge, The Village Station, the Beggar, The Joint, Louann's (an institution in Dallas for over thirty years), and #3 Lift in European Crossroads. Journalist Hillary Juster wrote,

> The disco era really glittered in Dallas. As you might imagine, hippies weren't all that welcome here, and women's lib never seemed to take off either. Disco and drugs, flash and cash, those got Dallas buzzing in the late '70s and the early '80s. If your parents lived here as young professionals, chances are they were caught up in some aspect of the outrageous party scene. Do they deny it? Maybe they just . . . can't remember.[11]

Kirby Warnock, writing in *Buddy Magazine* (named as a tribute to Lubbock's Buddy Holly), said this about the Dallas club and music scene in the '70s:

> This was in the era of vinyl and dozens of record stores such as Sound Warehouse, Hastings, and Peaches, as well as FM radio powerhouses KZEW (aka The Zoo) and Q102. It was also a time when Dallas was shaking off its deeply conservative trappings and starting to walk on the wild

side. Cocaine had burst onto the scene, finding its way into just about every niche of Big D society, from Highland Park to Industrial Boulevard. But it was also the age of a huge live music scene in Dallas that only the aging baby boomers can now recall. There were so many clubs offering live music nightly that *Buddy* ran pages and pages of their schedules, as well as photos of the local bands that played there. Not only that, but every national rock and country act had to play Dallas-Fort Worth because their record companies demanded it. Back then, artists went on tour to sell records, and their concerts were available for just $5 a seat. (Now they give away their music on the internet and charge $100 for a concert ticket.)

It was the decade before MADD and heavy penalties for DWI. From 1973 to 1981, the drinking age in Texas was 18, and you could carry an open container in your car as long as you weren't drunk. Bars regularly had two-for-one happy hours or ladies' nights when the women drank for free. Dallas also had a huge pool of 18- to 24-year-olds who moved here after graduating from college or high school and were able to find jobs and cheap rent.[12]

But the club scene of the '70s brought problems of its own (besides disco music itself, of course). Number one on the list might well have been the newfound popularity of a drug that was more than a century old: cocaine.

CHAPTER SEVENTEEN
Bombs Away

"Laos . . . Once a storybook kingdom of misty mountains and opium. At one time a protectorate of France. A mysterious land-locked nation bordered by China, Thailand, Cambodia, and, as fate would have it, Vietnam."

Anthony Bourdain

Laos is routinely referred to as "the most bombed country" in the world. More bombs were dropped on Laos during the so-called "secret war"—more than 2.1 million tons between 1964 and 1973—than the total dropped on all countries during World War II.[1] "In 1969 alone, according to several accounts, the United States dropped more bombs on Laos than it did on Japan during all of World War II. By 1973, when the bombing campaign ended, America had launched over 580,000 bombing runs in Laos."[2]

The Laotian Times, in a 2016 article, said the tonnage represented a planeload of bombs every eight minutes, twenty-four hours a day, for nine years. In total, 270 million cluster bombs were dropped on Laos, which included 80 million that failed to explode, resulting in more than twenty thousand people later killed or injured by delayed explosions of that ordnance.[3] *The Laotian Times* derived its information from ABC News, which reported that President Obama pledged $90 million over the course of three years to help remove undetonated bombs in Laos, calling it a "moral obligation to help Laos heal."[4]

Much of the bombing was strategic, largely a direct US military operation, such as along the Ho Chi Minh Trail. It was nevertheless part of the overall covert strategy in Laos. While the United States was making plans to launch a campaign of sustained bombing in North Vietnam in March of 1965, called Operation Rolling Thunder, US ambassador to Laos William Sullivan masterminded his own bombing campaign for neighboring Laos. Called Operation Barrel Roll in the northern part of the country and Steel Tiger in the south, both would involve American bombers, notwithstanding the Geneva Accords of 1962. "It was dirty, bare-knuckle warfare, but [Sullivan] had no regrets. The North Vietnamese were playing dirty, too."[5]

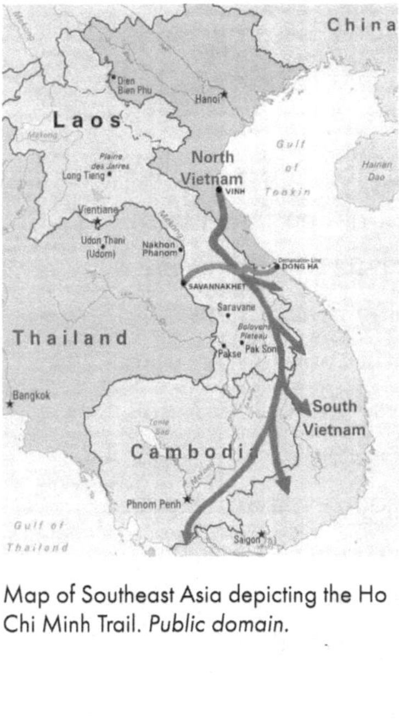

Map of Southeast Asia depicting the Ho Chi Minh Trail. *Public domain.*

The primary goal was to stop delivery of equipment and supplies along the Ho Chi Minh Trail to the communist guerillas in South Vietnam. Originally called the Annamite Range Trail (or, in Vietnamese, Duong Truong Son) because of the mountain region it passed through, the Ho Chi Minh Trail was actually a network of trails, footpaths, tracks, and roads. It stretched over nine hundred miles from Hanoi in North Vietnam to the Mekong Delta in South Vietnam, running along the border between those two countries and Laos, but was predominately inside Laos. On the Trail, the communists trekked weapons, supplies, and men from the North to aid the communists in the South.

The Geneva Accords of 1962 had several provisions that, arguably, outlawed this use of the Trail, but there were certainly loopholes or ambiguities in language. For instance, it was the Royal Government of Laos that resolved not to enter into any military alliance that was inconsistent with Laos neutrality and not to allow any foreign "troops or military personnel" into Laos. Laos then "appeals" to the other signatories not to introduce any foreign troops or military personnel into Laos, nor to connive at the introduction of such troops or military personnel. Article 1 of the attached Protocol defined "foreign military personnel" quite broadly and included "foreign citizens connected with the supply, maintenance, storing or utilization of war materials."[6] That language would seem to have resolved any ambiguities that would allow a benign interpretation of North Vietnam's activities on the Trail.

But there were more clarifications. Article 5 of the Protocol prohibited the "introduction into Laos of armaments, munitions and war material generally."[7] A good lawyer might make the argument that the communists were not introducing those things *into* Laos but were merely using Laos as a conduit for introduction of them into South Vietnam. But more likely, the North Vietnamese knew it was violating the Accords. British journalist Christopher Robbins wrote,

> It became clear that the United States had underestimated the enormous ambitions of the Lao Dong, the North Vietnamese Communist Party, which saw the Geneva Accords as nothing more than a tactical ploy. A measure of the agreement's failure can be taken by the enthusiasm

Transporting material on the Ho Chi Minh Trail. *Public domain.*

with which it was received by the North Vietnamese, who hailed the Accords as a "success and a victory." Far from reducing the number of troops in Laos, the North Vietnamese continued to build up and strengthen their forces while enlarging the Ho Chi Minh Trail—activities they pursued in secret.[8]

The United States treated activity on the Trail as violations of the Accords, thereby justifying its own violations. By the summer of 1963, Operation Hardnose had begun, which was primarily a CIA-led and -run espionage and surveillance operation on the Trail. President Kennedy authorized Hardnose, which was commanded by General William Westmoreland, Secretary of Defense Robert McNamara, and CIA case agent Mike Deuel. In a December 21 memorandum, McNamara advised the new president, Lyndon Johnson, who had been in office for scarcely a month following Kennedy's assassination, of the extent of activity along the Trail. He told the president that plans had already been drawn for interdicting the flow and awaited the president's go-ahead. These plans included "cross-border operations into Laos," and, he conceded, "would not be politically acceptable or even militarily effective."[9] This memorandum would be exposed to the public seven-and-a-half years later as part of the Pentagon Papers.

In January of 1964, Chairman of the Joint Chiefs Maxwell Taylor advised that the United States "must be prepared to put aside many of the self-imposed restrictions which now limit our efforts, and to undertake bolder actions which may embody greater risks."[10] Some of those "bolder actions" were already in motion, in the form of the Butterfly program. This was part of a covert air initiative in 1963 by the US Air Force and the CIA, under the supervision of William Sullivan, ambassador to Laos, and his successor, G. McMurtrie Godley. The Butterflies, American noncommissioned officer pilots who were "sheep-dipped"—stripped of any military identity and assigned civilian covers—helped direct targeting for Thai and Laotian pilots under Project Water Pump.[11]

In the spring of 1967, when Lieutenant General William W. "Spike" Momyer, commander of the Seventh Air Force, first learned the Butterfly pilots were noncommissioned officers and, for the most part, not even pilot-rated, he put the kibosh on the program. According to one account, Momyer "hit the roof" and said, "That will cease. I'll take care of that."[12] Thus endeth the Butterflies. Enter the Ravens.

Prior to 1964 and the commencement of Operation Barrel Roll, the CIA, rather than the US military, had controlled pretty much all of the airstrikes in Laos, maintaining the pretext of compliance with the 1962 Accords. Soon enough, the United States began taking direct military action in Laos, albeit still in secrecy. Airstrikes began under Barrel Roll in December of 1964, primarily

Butterfly forward air controllers with a Pilatus PC-6 Porter in Laos, 1966. *Public domain.*

along the Laos/Vietnam border, while Steel Tiger commenced in April of 1965. The United States acted under the authorization of Laos's prime minister, Souvanna Phouma, with the proviso that the operations would be covert.[13] This was in keeping with Secretary McNamara's insistence that "more ambitious operations" should require Laotian approval.

Unfortunately, there were not enough American air controllers available with sufficient knowledge of conditions in Laos. As a result, "[c]ollateral damage incidents began to mount."[14] One of those, known as the "Sam Neua Incident," occurred when US Air Force pilots mistakenly bombed a town while searching for North Vietnamese 105-millimeter gun positions. Coincidentally, an air force photo-reconnaissance plane piloted by Captain Charles E. Shelton was shot down in the area on April 29, 1965. He evaded capture for three days before falling into the hands of the Pathet Lao. He was first imprisoned in the Sam Neua city jail, escaped twice, but was recaptured both times. He was ultimately held, along with other American captives, in caves near Sam Neua, from which he also attempted to escape. The Pathet Lao later claimed Shelton died in captivity, but unconfirmed reports suggested he was still alive as late as 1987. He has never been accounted for.[15]

By January of 1968, bombing runs into Laos had expanded beyond simple interdiction along the Ho Chi Minh Trail. Planes were flying fifteen to twenty sorties per day, which might peak to forty or fifty if a battle was ongoing. By the end of 1969, that number had increased to three hundred sorties per day. Much of these were still directed at the Ho Chi Minh Trail, and much of them repetitious since the North Vietnamese emerged from cover almost every night to repair damage from the prior day's bombing attacks. According to Captain Jerry Brown, who was the US Air Force targeting official for the bombing of Laos, the North Vietnamese could build a mile a day of road under bombing.

> So where you had one road in 1964, now you had four . . . with four, five, six bypasses going in different directions. To stop a bypass, let's say we put 25 or 50 aircraft in on one day. They made an awful lot of holes in the road. They would then use one of the alternate bypasses to go around the holes until they filled them up. Or it would be the next day and you'd go in and put a lot of holes in the other bypass, but that also didn't make any difference because they'd have fixed the other one up.[16]

Brown, who said he knew the Ho Chi Minh Trail better than anybody else, agreed with the typical American assertion that the North Vietnamese violated the 1962 Accords first. Sometimes there might be as many as two hundred trucks coming into Laos at night, he said. Nevertheless, despite an abundance of targets, bombing was hit and miss. "Guys coming in at 15,000 feet would drop at 12,000; consequently, you had bombs dropping all over the countryside, had bombs going anywhere from one-fourth of a mile to five miles off target. And five miles off target could conceivably be a village."[17] The results were devastating to the landscape, leaving massive craters and defoliating jungles, and destroying human life.

Bomb craters along the Ho Chi Minh Trail. *Public domain.*

Despite the merciless bombing, the airstrikes still weren't having their desired effect. Equipment, weapons, supplies—there seemed to be no end to the flow southward. Brown said,

> Bombing wasn't necessarily working militarily in Laos or North Vietnam then [late 1968], and—according to recently published United States intelligence estimates—it still has failed to slow down the Pathet Lao and North Vietnamese operations, despite causing widespread damage and deaths in both North Vietnam and Laos.[18]

There are civilian casualties in every war, but the incessant and overwhelming bombardment, much of it off the mark, created particular horrors in Laos, such as those at the Plaine des Jarres—the Plain of Jars— an archaeological landscape of stone "jars" that was strategically located in the central part of northern Laos. It was primarily inhabited by a Hmong peasant population of about two hundred thousand, but it was also coveted territory by the Pathet Lao, who occupied the plain in May of 1964. Part of the United States' bombing plan was to force the communists off the plain and to retake it, only to have the Pathet Lao return later and the cycle start all over. That meant increased frequency of sorties and dropping of bombs. And the bombs, of course, did not distinguish between friend or foe, combatant or civilian. People living on the plain were forced to move out of their homes and into trenches, holes, or caves to avoid the attacks. They farmed only at night when they felt safe—or at least safer—from overhead danger.

Fred Branfman, an educational advisor in Laos, asked the inhabitants of the area to write first-hand accounts of bombing raids. He included a compilation of their stories in his book *Voices from the Plain of Jars*, first published in 1972. Although the curtain of secrecy of the war in Laos had already, to some extent, been pulled back, the stories of terror not only further exposed the United States' covert activities but also the brutality of its impact on the innocent. In introducing the stories, Branfman wrote,

> The major goal of its [the United States'] air warfare was simply, in the words of a September 1970 Senate Subcommittee on Refugees staff report, to "destroy the social and economic infrastructure of Pathet Lao held areas." This time war did not mean an attempt to supplant the Pathet Lao. Rather it was meant to hurt them by depriving them of local food supplies, disrupting transport and communications, killing off potential recruits and rice porters, demoralizing the civilian population, and eventually causing a refugee flow away from the Plain.[19]

While that was the official goal, the reality was that "villages were struck frequently . . . and virtually everything was destroyed." Branfman explained,

> The bombing was characterized above all by the heavy toll it took on the civilian population. In our interviews with more than one thousand Plain of Jars refugees, we recorded on film and tape dozens and dozens of case histories of villagers killed or wounded by the bombing. Refugees explained that much of this was because the children lacked discipline and the older people were often too infirm to reach a safe place fast enough. Relatively few soldiers were reported to have been struck by the bombs. Refugees explained that the

The Plain of Jars. Photo by Ernest Kuhn, courtesy of Ernest and Phaythoune Kuhn Image Collection, Southeast Asian Images & Texts Project, University of Wisconsin Digital Collections.

> troops hid deep in the forest and kept on the move constantly in small groups at night. They said that it was mostly civilians who were struck because families could not survive on the run and had to remain near the villages—which were the targets most often hit.[20]

Historian Alfred McCoy,[21] writing the foreword to the second edition of *Voices*, said that more than 321,000 tons of bombs were dropped on the plain. The United States Information Service did an official survey of refugees from ninety-six villages, the results of which Senator Edward Kennedy cited at a Senate subcommittee hearing. He noted that, out of a population of nearly three million in Laos, there were approximately seven hundred thousand refugees. According to the results of the survey, 97 percent of those surveyed said they had seen a bombing attack, 61 percent had seen a person killed, 75 percent said their own homes had been damaged, and 2 percent said they thought the bombing intentionally targeted civilians.[22]

The stories Branfman collected are particularly heart-wrenching. Here are some excerpts.

> There was one man who ran for the holes when he heard the sound of a plane but before he reached the hole he was shot by the plane and died outside the hole. His wife ran up but his heart had already given out and he had died.[23]
>
> **—a forty-nine-year-old farmer**

> Ours was the first village in the canton. Four planes of the jet type dropped their bombs together to destroy my village and returned to shoot twice in the same day. They dropped eight napalm bombs, the fire from which burned all my things, sixteen buildings along with all our possessions inside, as well as maiming our animals. Some people who didn't reach the jungle in time were struck and fell, dying most pitifully. By the time the fire died down, it was dark. Everyone came out of hiding to look at the ashes of the houses. Even the rice was all burnt. Everyone cried at once—loudly and agitatedly. Some families had been wounded. We were all heavy-hearted and mournful almost to the point of losing our minds. The other villagers and I got together to consider this thing. We hadn't done anything, nor harmed anyone. We had raised our crops, celebrated the festivals, and maintained our homes for many years. Why did the planes drop bombs on us, impoverishing us this way?[24]
>
> **—a thirty-nine-year-old farmer**

In my village there was a young man who went to graze his buffalo in the forest. The airplanes dropped bombs and killed the buffalo. The young man ran away from that place, but not in time. He was hit in the waist—cut right in half. For two days you could see him like that.[25]

—a twenty-two-year-old-man

There was an old woman who went to the village to get rice for her children and family to eat in their holes. But that day the planes bombed and she died apart from her family.[26]

—Unknown

This village woman was a person of good character. She spoke softly and sweetly and never gave sorrow to any person for any reason. Why did she have to die so pitifully? She died in the middle of the forest beside the cow she tended. She died in misfortune with unsurpassed sadness. The outlaws in the airplanes did this, bringing fear to our country such as we had never before seen.[27]

–Unknown

One friend of mine went to the village to get rice for his mother and father to eat. He crossed the field to the hill and the airplanes saw him and shot and killed him so that you couldn't even see his body. It was scattered all over the field.[28]

—a twelve-year-old boy

One time in the year of 1967, my old aunt carried things to sell in the market as was her old custom in the countryside. That day she arose at six in the morning, put fruit into her basket and then walked out of the village on her way. Just as she arrived at a place where there was a small stream, she stopped to rest. An airplane saw her and shot a smoke bomb at her. She was afraid and then as she sat there her body was hit. Blood came out everywhere. She decided to run and just as she arrived at the house she died, before she could say any last words. Her children and her husband were most angry that they had lost her so. Everyone was disconsolate. After that day no one ever went to the market anymore.[29]

—**Unknown**

CHAPTER EIGHTEEN
Opening a Dark Door

"The notion that Playboy turns women into sex objects is ridiculous. Women are sex objects."

Hugh Hefner

Lenny Licht made a bet and the payoff was a Playboy Club in Dallas.

He and a group of friends used to occasionally meet at the 2001 Club atop Bryan Tower, at 2001 Bryan Street in downtown Dallas. On one occasion, one of the group, as spokesman for the others, bet Lenny $5,000 that he couldn't bring Playboy to Dallas. The year was probably 1975 or 1976, so the current value of that $5,000 is about $24,000. If the bet was serious, it was not a trivial thing.

Lenny had "no experience in the restaurant business. Just a dream."[1] And, apparently, an extra $5,000 he was willing to gamble. As it turned out, what he lacked in experience he made up for in luck. He had been accepted to Harvard Law School but had to complete some undergraduate courses at Harvard first. While working on those classes, he happened to meet Christie Hefner, daughter of Playboy founder Hugh Hefner, at a bar in Boston, where she worked for the *Boston Phoenix*, writing movie reviews. He told her about the bet, and one thing led to another, including a trip to Chicago to meet Hefner, then back to Boston to find a manager. Joe Cimino, who had been recommended by Playboy, owned clubs and restaurants in Boston, and he could fill Lenny's lack-of-experience gap. The next thing you knew, Lenny was opening a Playboy Club in Dallas, the first to be franchised outside the Playboy empire.[2]

The original plan was to buy an old building on Commerce Street on the southwest edge of downtown Dallas and turn it into the club. Lenny said:

> It's kind of a funny deal. Do you know where the downtown McDonald's is on Commerce Street? That was where the Playboy club was supposed to be. It used to be the Aaron Brothers Fur and the Dorsey Building. It was a 6 story building that everyone tried to buy but nobody could get the deal done. I was friendly with the people that owned it though. The reason I wanted to buy it, is it is an entire city block. You could make an entire circle around the location which was highly unusual in downtown Dallas. So anyway, I knew the guys that owned it and went ahead and bought it with the idea we were going to put the Playboy Club there.[3]

What is that old saw about mice and men and their plans going astray? Well, sometimes that is for the better. A space opened up in the Expressway Towers on Central Expressway at the intersection of Yale Boulevard (now SMU Boulevard), near the SMU campus. Expressway Towers, owned by the Murchison family, was the same building that held the offices of the Dallas Cowboys, owned by Clint Murchison. The vacant space had previously housed a restaurant called Chateau Madrid, but it had gone out of business. So Lenny cut a good deal on the Expressway Towers space, sold the building downtown for a hefty profit, and Dallas's Playboy Club was born, opening in August of 1977.[4]

Keyholders in the Playboy Club included many Cowboys players and local celebrities, and its shows were second to none. Lenny said that, during his ownership, which lasted about a year before he sold his interest, he had a half-million-dollar entertainment budget. The club competed for the same acts as other prominent entertainment venues in Dallas, such as the internationally acclaimed Venetian Room in the Fairmont Hotel. But despite initial interest, and anywhere between thirty-five and fifty thousand keyholders (depending upon which source you rely), the club had a short life in Dallas. After going through three owners in five years, it was shut down by bankruptcy.

Opinions abound as to the reason for the club's ultimate failure. Playboy bunny Mary Ann Russell said that the club's demise was because of "the strip clubs that opened around that time. Guys thought, 'Why should I see a woman in a bunny suit when I can see a practically naked woman?'"[5] It may also simply have been inexperience or mismanagement on the part of the succession of owners. *The Dallas Morning News* said, "The Dallas Club has had a troubled history. The second franchise holder, Pete Couvall, fought a well-publicized battle to retain ownership of the club after Playboy International contended that he had not operated the club according to standards."[6]

Lenny reminisced on his good luck, at least at the inception.

> In retrospect, the crazy thing is, if my . . . dad hadn't been a lawyer, my brother-in-law hadn't been Dean at the University of Dallas and wrote me the letter of recommendation for Harvard, if I hadn't met Christie Hefner there in Boston doing

some undergrad work, hadn't gone to the Playboy Club, if Mike McCullough hadn't bet me $5,000 I couldn't get the Playboy to Dallas—any one of these dominoes would have stopped Playboy from ever coming to Texas.[7]

★ ★ ★ ★ ★

Having already quit the car business, and unable to fully support myself with modeling and acting, I got word out that I was looking for regular work—regular as in steady income and steady hours. A friend named Pat Applewhite told me she wanted to introduce me to a friend of hers who worked at the newly opened Playboy Club in Dallas. I figured they might be hiring so I agreed. I also knew it was too pricey to be a member and, if I didn't get hired, this might be my only chance to see it. What red-blooded American male wouldn't want to at least see the Playboy Club?

Pat introduced me to manager Joe Cimino, who hired me on the spot, even though I didn't have any nightclub experience other than as a bouncer. A bouncer's job was pretty simple: if somebody started something, you finished it and "bounced" the troublemaker out. 'Nuff said. Since I had at least some prior experience as a bouncer, I thought Cimino was hiring me for that job. Or maybe as a floorman, which was essentially the same as a bouncer. As I would learn, Playboy handled its rowdiness problems, which were rare, with a little more finesse and discretion than most clubs. Sometimes you had to strongarm a "bad guy" outside, but dialogue was the preferred option. There were other times when, as a last resort, you had no choice but to call the police. When I later worked at Papagayo, their policy was to *never* call the police unless a gun or other deadly weapon was involved.

It turned out that Cimino needed an assistant maître d'. "Can you find a tuxedo and work tonight?" he asked. I could and I did. I flew out of the club to find a cheap tux to rent and just barely made it back in time for my first Playboy shift to start.

The bunnies worked four areas of the club—the front door/gift shop, the disco/buffet, the front room, and the showroom. In those days, the minimum age for serving alcohol was twenty-one, so bunnies who were younger than that typically worked in the gift shop, which sold everything from coffee mugs to shoes and T-shirts. Occasionally a bunny got reassigned to the gift shop if she was recovering from a medical issue—like falling off high heels and suffering an ankle injury. Yes, that was a real risk!

Most of the action took place in the front room, so that's where I was stationed. I was also assigned to back up the bunnies at the front door/gift shop. I felt as if life was coming together for me. Since I had moved to Dallas, I had dated a Dallas Cowboys cheerleader, modeled menswear, walked a runway in New York City, been on one of the hottest shows on television, and now I was working at the Playboy Club. If only the kids back home could see me now.

Working at the Playboy Club was everything I imagined it to be. Beautiful women in their bunny costumes and the beautiful people of Dallas, including celebrities all across the spectrum of entertainment. The only problem at the start was . . . well, I didn't know what I was doing. Little things evaded me, like opening champagne bottles without shooting someone across the room with a cork. Or pouring wine. I learned it wasn't like filling a glass with Dr Pepper or opening a tap at the bar. You started by popping the cork using a corkscrew. Then you folded a napkin over your arm and moved around to the right (as opposed to the left, not right as opposed to wrong; although I suppose left would be wrong) side. You always had to ask the "one in charge" if he or she wanted to first taste the wine. Sometimes it was hard to figure out who was in charge, but alphas usually had a way of letting everyone know. Then, of course, there was always someone who wanted to sniff the cork. You never poured until you got the okay.

I didn't even know how to take tips for seating. Once I realized that was a good way to supplement my income, I mastered it pretty quickly. Some customers liked to be near the action—the part of the club that always seemed to be moving, with folks coming in and out (so you could see who was there), disco dancing, and just general activity. Perfect for people-watching. The better the table you led a customer to, the better the tip. Usually. After a while, you learned to spot the big spenders and, of course, there were repeat customers. You learned which were the good tippers and which weren't. We didn't make a huge salary at the club, so tips for seating were the primary source of income.

When the maître d' left the club a few weeks later, I moved up to the top spot. Sounds good, doesn't it? Except now it meant doing everything by myself that had once been split between two people, including those things I was still learning. The room was big enough that it required two people to work it right. I needed help. I had been bugging management to hire my buddy Gene Cook. That meant I also had to sell Gene on the idea. He was a busy guy, but I knew he and I were pretty much always on the same wavelength. I figured we could tag-team the room like a shortstop and second baseman turning a double play. They hired him and suddenly things fell into place. I had the help I needed, I had a friend to work with, and we both made money.

Gene said,

> You kept bugging me to come to work with you, so I finally relented. Wow. We probably made $100 each the first night, pretty good money for 1978 [close to $500 in 2026 money]. I guess you and I worked together for about a year running the front room at Playboy. We really learned how to work it because we communicated so well. Who would have thought there was an art to seating people? There were folks you wanted close to the action that helped that action, other folks that preferred to be in the back, you learned pretty quickly to read people. And because we learned how to do that, the tips were pretty generous. We were really making great money.[8]

Boogie Machine: Rick Marshall, Fran Lucchesi, and Gene Cook. *Photo courtesy of Rick Marshall, Fran Lucchesi, and Gene Cook.*

Gene also performed in a dance group called Boogie Machine, along with Cathy Lucchesi, who also goes by her first name Fran, and Rick Marshall, a guy with the quickest feet I ever saw. Boogie Machine performed regularly at the Playboy Club, sometimes on the same nights that Gene worked the front room. That didn't cause any hiccups—I just had to cover for him while he was performing. And he had a chance to make a little more money. "[M]y dance group came on board and I was double dipping," Gene said. "I would be in my tux working the front room, run to the dressing room and change for our dance gigs, do them—then run back and change into my tux, sweat dripping from every pore. Whewwww! And then we started doing two shows a night. That was absolutely crazy!"[9]

Things were good for me at the Playboy Club. I was loving my life. But then it took a turn. In hindsight, I can see the red flags I missed. Working in the Dallas club scene in the 1970s, I guess it was inevitable. It would change my life—and not for the better. I was still drinking a lot. Mostly clear liquor, vodka, and gin. In fact, I drank so many screwdrivers that the citric acid from the orange juice created sores in my mouth. But one day I walked into the restroom and saw one of the managers doing a drug he was about to introduce me to.

CHAPTER NINETEEN
Blow

"There is no happy ending to cocaine. You either die, you go to jail, or else you run out."

Sam Kinison

In 1977, Eric Clapton released a single called "Cocaine." Written by J. J. Cole, it was the B-side to "Lay Down, Sally." Although the song might appear to be a tribute to the drug, Clapton claimed it was just the opposite, and that its intent was to warn against the drug's addictiveness. He said, "If you study it or look at it with a little bit of thought . . . from a distance . . . or as it goes by . . . it just sounds like a song about cocaine. But actually, it is quite cleverly anti-cocaine."[1]

Viewed objectively, though, the lyrics are, at best, ambiguous, which is why Clapton, a recovering addict, stopped performing the song for a time. "I thought that it might be giving the wrong message to people who were in the same boat as me." But he later added it back to his playlist, determined to perform it as "a reality check about what it does."[2] Regardless of the lens through which one interprets the lyrics, the song can be seen as an anthem for Dallas in the late 1970s.

Cocaine—also known as blow, coke, or snow—is a stimulant made from the leaves of the coca plant. South American indigenous peoples chewed the leaves to get a high-energy high, which allowed them to be more productive. Cocaine was first isolated from coca leaves by European scientists in the 1850s. The result was lauded as a medical breakthrough. Researchers attributed its effectiveness as a stimulant to its capacity to increase the amount of dopamine in "parts of the brain that control reward or motivation."[3] Users typically described a feeling of euphoria, which *Merriam-Webster* defines as "a feeling of well-being or elation."[4] Users also experienced increased energy and hyperactivity, and sometimes feelings of paranoia.

Sigmund Freud wrote a paper in 1884 called *Uber Coca*, in which he analyzed the drug "cocaine hydrochloride," the powder form of cocaine commonly thought of today. This stuff and its impact is real, he said. "[O]ne must reject the view sometimes expressed, that the effect of coca is an imaginary one and that through force of circumstance and with practice the natives would be able to perform the feats attributed to them even without the aid of coca." He noted that "Indians under the influence of coca can withstand exceptional hardships and perform heavy labor, without requiring proper nourishment during that time."

He described the effects of cocaine this way:

> . . . one experiences a sudden exhilaration and feeling of lightness. One feels a certain furriness on the lips and palate, followed by a feeling of warmth in the same areas; if one now drinks cold water, it feels warm on the lips and cold in the throat. On other occasions the predominant feeling is a rather pleasant coolness in the mouth and throat.

He described the "psychic effect" this way:

> . . . exhilaration and lasting euphoria, which does not differ in any way from the normal euphoria of a healthy person. The feeling of excitement which accompanies stimulus by alcohol is completely lacking; the characteristic urge for immediate activity which alcohol produces is also absent. One senses an increase of self-control and feels more vigorous and more capable of work; on the other hand, if one works, one misses that heightening of the mental powers which alcohol, tea, or coffee induce. One is simply normal, and soon finds it difficult to believe that one is under the influence of any drug at all.

He advocated that cocaine, which he called a "magical substance" in a letter to his fiancée Martha Bernays, could be used as a stimulant. "Protracted use," he said, might lead to lasting improvements in "human mental powers," and "there is no danger to the body as is the case with the chronic use of morphine." He also said that "coca, if used protractedly but in moderation, is not detrimental to the body."

Perhaps more telling, particularly as relates to the "free love" movement that "hippies" espoused during the '60s and '70s, Freud wrote that South American natives "did not doubt the stimulative effect of coca on the genitals," and that some of the persons to whom he had given the drug "reported violent sexual excitement which they unhesitatingly attributed to the coca."

Freud concluded that cocaine did not have any addictive qualities:

> It seems to me noteworthy—and I discovered this in myself and in other observers who were capable of judging such

things—that a first dose or even repeated doses of coca produce no compulsive desire to use the stimulant further; on the contrary, one feels a certain unmotivated aversion to the substance.[5]

Freud ended up addicted to cocaine for more than a decade.

★ ★ ★ ★ ★

The 1980s were a time of transition in Dallas, at least on the drug scene. The Starck Club, designed by French architect and designer Philippe Starck, opened in 1984 under Woodall Rodgers Freeway on the northwestern fringe of downtown. Tom Foster wrote, "If 1980s Dallas was the ultimate ego city, awash in new money and glitz, the Starck Club was its unchecked id—the pleasure center pulsing beneath its conservative costume."[6] The Club had another basis for its reputation, a drug that swept across the Dallas-Fort Worth metroplex in that decade. "Perhaps the Starck Club is best known as the place where a new drug called MDMA proliferated and took hold, eventually (under the name ecstasy) becoming synonymous with raver culture."[7]

Other drugs gained prominence in Dallas in the '80s, as well. A Frontline documentary on PBS in 1988, called *The Dallas Drug War*, depicted Dallas as "a major drug trafficking center." According to the report, more than ten thousand drug arrests were made in the city the prior year, including marijuana and LSD arrests. In addition to the "traditional" drugs, an uptick in robberies on the club scene was the result of a spree Dallas police labeled the "Mickey Finn club," based on a knockout drug slipped into a person's drink to render them unconscious. "Slipping a mickey" gained some notoriety in the Dallas club circuit in the mid-1980s.[8]

But when it came to the 1970s, cocaine was king.

Michael Cain, producer of a documentary on Dallas's Starck Club, said, "You had sexual freedom, which had come of the '70s, and the drug culture was still going on. At that point you could have a party in Highland Park and someone might have cocaine on a tray and no one would think a thing of it."[9] Emily Freeman of *D Magazine* wrote, "Stick heroin in your veins or speed in your mouth and people call you a junkie. But put cocaine up your nose, and you've got status."[10]

Cocaine claimed more than its share of victims in Dallas, and its victims cut across socioeconomic lines, right up into the Dallas world of celebrity. Steve Gerkin, a car dealer involved in a multimillion dollar a year cocaine ring, was sentenced to forty-eight years in federal prison for killing a rival drug dealer with a bomb.

Bob Hayes was once billed as the world's fastest human after winning two gold medals in the 1964 Olympics in Tokyo, in the hundred-meter dash and as the anchor for the four-by-one hundred meter relay team, where he sprinted from fifth place to first place. Drafted out of Florida A&M as a wide receiver by the Dallas Cowboys, his speed changed the complexion of defense in the NFL. He was part of that first Super Bowl winning team in 1972 and retired from football following the 1975 season.

In 1978, Hayes was arrested for selling cocaine. He claimed to simply be a middleman in the transaction, introducing the seller to a buyer named Danny Kelly, who turned out to be an undercover cop for the City of Addison. But, he said, there were no drugs involved at the meeting. "Alfred [the purported seller] didn't have any cocaine, and we all left after I told them that I didn't want anything to do with their business." When he was arrested and charged, "There seemed little question that Kelly had entrapped me. The cocaine Kelly bought wasn't mine, and I didn't get any money for it."[11]

Still, concerned that the charges brought a possible life sentence, he pled guilty in 1979 to two charges of delivery of cocaine and one of delivery of methaqualone. He was sentenced to two five-year-terms in prison, to run consecutively. Texas Governor Bill Clements described Hayes as a "deserving, model prisoner" and paroled him after ten months. Hayes wrote in his memoir, "I pleaded guilty to a crime I don't honestly believe I committed, lost ten months out of my life while I was in prison, and had my reputation and finances ruined—all without cause." In short, "[g]oing to prison destroyed my life."[12] Among other things, it kept him out of the NFL Hall of Fame until 2009. Unfortunately, he had passed away in September of 2002 at the age of fifty-nine.

Hayes said that his real problem was alcohol but acknowledged that, after his release from prison, he occasionally turned to cocaine. "I don't think I used cocaine more than twenty-five times in my life, but when I did, it increased my reflexes and stimulated me. It gave me an incredible high, just like liquor, but cocaine works faster than alcohol and gives you a better high." He also recognized the role of a friend in coming to grips with his addiction. "You don't tell yourself you're crazy; someone else has to tell you that. People don't just walk into a rehabilitation center and say, 'I'm a drug addict.' Someone else has to recognize your problem and take you or make you go for help. For me, that person was Roger Staubach." In fact, when Hayes relapsed, Staubach recommended a rehab facility and personally paid the $25,000 fee for him. Staubach, Hayes said, "was determined to get me straight, and he saved my life."[13]

In 1983, the names of four Cowboys players were mentioned as part of a federal drug investigation as cocaine users: Harvey Martin, Tony Dorsett, Ron Springs, and Larry Bethea. According to *The New York Times*, the four were implicated on wiretaps as "users of small quantities of cocaine." The same article noted that another Dallas Cowboy, wide receiver Tony Hill, had been subpoenaed, along with Harvey Martin, to testify in the cocaine smuggling trial of a Dallas man.[14]

A prominent Dallas Cowboy felled by cocaine was linebacker Thomas "Hollywood" Henderson, who became addicted in the 1970s. In his memoir, he tells of his introduction to the drug in 1976, just prior to Super Bowl X against the Pittsburgh Steelers. "I whooped it up one nostril. Didn't feel anything at first. The cocaine was so clean that it wasn't until a minute later that I got that drain, that anesthetizing feeling down my throat. Then I got the smell of the coke. I don't know what it was washed with but it smelled pure, it smelled good." No real rush from that first dose, he said. But a feeling of well-being.[15]

It wasn't long before he was hooked. Following the team's dismantling of the Denver Broncos in Super Bowl XII, he developed his own off-season routine: "By that time I had a ritual. Every morning I would smoke a joint, then do some heavy lines of cocaine, then blow my nose raw, then do some more lines of coke, then go out into the day and start to get loaded."[16] After a long slide into addiction, Hollywood found himself in prison, sentenced to four years and eight months as part of a plea bargain that included pleading no contest to sexual battery and bribery.

Sometimes you have to hit rock bottom before you can start to ascend again. And so, upon his release from prison in October of

1986, and sober, Henderson began a new career of helping others who were addicted.

> Confronting someone can be a tough and tricky proposition. But to me, if you think he's in trouble and you don't say anything, you're obviously not much of a friend at all. To be quiet is to be an enabler in the sense that you're doing nothing but enabling him to continue heading down the same path of running, denying, and abusing. It's a path that only leads to awful places, places I've been.[17]

Hollywood's path would cross with that of Paul Heckmann.

CHAPTER TWENTY

Lima Site 118A

"What do you call it when the assassins accuse the assassin? They lie. They lie, and we have to be merciful for those who lie. Those nabobs. I hate them. I do hate them."

Colonel Walter E. Kurtz in *Apocalypse Now*

In 1971, Douglas Bonner III, then on the cusp of his teen years but currently a D.C. attorney, had the rare opportunity to see something very few, if any, outsiders had ever seen, or would ever see. His grandfather, Douglas Bonner Sr., served as station chief in Accra, Ghana, during World War II for the Office of Strategic Services (OSS), predecessor to the CIA.[1] In 1971, his father, Douglas Bonner Jr., served as a CIA case officer in Vientiane, Laos, operating undercover as part of the CIA's paramilitary operations in the "secret war." Although Bonner III didn't follow the two preceding generations of Douglases into the CIA, it's not exactly accurate to call him an outsider, at least not when he lived, and attended the American School, in Vientiane. CIA blood runs in his veins. So when his dad invited him along on a "business trip" up near the Chinese border with Laos, he jumped at the chance.

Transported by an Air America PC-6 Pilatus Porter turboprop, designed by Pilatus Aircraft of Switzerland as a "short take-off and landing" aircraft, he and his father landed on a dirt airstrip surrounded by mountains. It was like no other airport he had ever seen. There was no hangar, no terminal, no parked aircraft. Down below he saw a primitive village that they reached on foot, crossing a wooden bridge over what may, or may not, have been a tributary of the Mekong River. The village was nothing more than a series of wooden huts on stilts, populated by traditional Yao tribeswomen, but Bonner was struck by an absence of men. The only thing that distinguished the village was a concrete building that resembled a warehouse and, farther down the road, their destination: a multistory wooden building and another concrete building. In an excellent essay about the trip, Bonner III writes, "I suddenly felt like I was in the remotest corner of the world."[2]

Welcome to Nam Yu. Or, in CIA parlance, Lima Site 118A.

Lao General Vang Pao and CIA's Douglas Bonner, Jr. *Photo courtesy of Douglas Bonner III.*

The CIA, sometimes derisively called Christians in Action[3] or Catholics in Action, due to the number of Catholics who have served as director,[4] had ratcheted up its activities in Laos by the late 1960s. A top secret memorandum (which has since been declassified) from Secretary of Defense Melvin Laird to President Nixon, dated October 6, 1969, reported, "Based on recent combat activity on the ground and in the air over Laos, the war in Laos has been intensifying." That same memorandum also warned that "provision of additional US arms, equipment, and advisory personnel in Laos undoubtedly will increase the intensity of the military conflict," and expressed concern that the United Stated had not "fully explored the risks associated with providing additional US personnel in Laos to operate (or train Laotian forces to operate) the sophisticated new equipment." On a political note, Laird warned that "[r]ecent Congressional and public discontent with our current level of involvement in Laos would probably increase significantly with any commitment of additional arms and military personnel."[5]

Many of the CIA's activities in Laos, like its operations out of Lima Site 118A—and, in fact, that site's very existence—were still relatively secret. But when you follow the money, it is inevitable that secrets come out.

> In 1970, the Department of Defense began to spend funds directly in support of CIA operations in Laos. John Eisenhower, who worked in the policy office of the Secretary of Defense from 1969 to 1971, recalls that money began being transferred overtly and directly from the DOD budget to support the use of Thai irregulars in Laos.[6]

And, in late September of 1970, a journalist named Michael Morrow would blow the lid off Lima Site 118A.

★ ★ ★ ★ ★

When John Kearns graduated from North Texas State University in 1968 with a degree in Far East Studies, the CIA came a'knocking. After signing with the CIA as a contractor, John had to undergo a rigorous training regimen to prepare for his duties in Laos. First stop, Fort Benning, Georgia (now Fort Moore), for the US Army

Ranger Course, generally accepted as the most stringent the army had to offer.[7] Just as working with the Army Security Agency foreshadowed his duties with the CIA, so, too, did Ranger training.

The army first instigated Ranger Training in 1950 and, by all accounts, it has changed very little. Fort Moore provides this "Student Information" about the course on its website:

> Ranger Course is the Army's toughest course and the premier small unit tactics and leadership course. The Ranger Course is a mentally and physically challenging [sic] that develops functional skills directly related to units whose mission is to engage the enemy in close combat and direct fire battle. For 62 days, Ranger students train to exhaustion, pushing the limits of their minds and bodies. The course incorporates three phases (Darby, Mountain, and Swamp) which follow the crawl, walk, run training methodology. In Darby phase, the students become trained on squad operations and focus on ambush and recon missions, patrol base operations, and planning before moving on to platoon operations. In Mountain phase, students develop their skills at the platoon level in order to refine and complete their training in Swamp phase. After these three phases, Ranger Students are proficient in leading squad and platoon dismounted operations around the clock in all climates and terrain. Rangers are better trained, more capable, more resilient, and better prepared to serve and lead Soldiers in their next duty position.[8]

After successfully completing the Ranger Course, where he earned his Ranger tab—a badge that traces its roots back to Darby's Rangers, under Major William O. Darby, in World War

II—John's next stop was Fort Gulick in Panama for the Jungle Warfare course.[9] The Jungle Operations Training Center, an area along the Panama Canal, had been established near the end of the Korean War but ramped up operations during the 1960s with the Vietnam War and the need for special training for jungle warfare, sometimes referred to as "Green Hell." Again, a foreshadowing of John's CIA service in Laos.

At Fort Gulick, John earned his Jungle Warfare badge. Then it was off to Fort Bragg, North Carolina, for the HALO course and Special Forces Training Course. HALO training involved instruction in high-altitude low-opening (as opposed to HAHO—high-altitude high-opening) parachuting, which is exactly what it sounds like: jumpers depart the aircraft at high altitudes, sometimes as high as thirty thousand feet or more, then free fall to an altitude as low as three thousand feet before opening the parachute. This allows for covert insertions of manpower. High altitude minimizes radar detection of the airplanes while low opening minimizes visual detection of the jumpers by ground personnel.

The HALO technique, at least as a concept, dates back to the Korean War but was not used in combat until the Vietnam War. The Military Assistance Command, Vietnam-Studies and Observation Group (MACV-SOG), which was established in 1964 to perform highly classified, secret, unconventional warfare operations during the Vietnam War, used the HALO tactic as part of its covert operations.[10] On November 28, 1970, a MACV-SOG team led by Staff Sergeant Cliff Newman jumped into Laos from a C-130 at eighteen thousand feet. The team spent five days behind enemy lines conducting reconnaissance before being exfiltrated successfully. "This was the first known HALO combat jump in history."[11]

On June 22, 1971, another team jumped in combat, this time

in South Vietnam. One of the team, Madison Strohlein, was injured in the jump and radioed for emergency medical evacuation. A rescue team later found his weapon but did not find Strohlein. He was listed as missing in action, but "it can be safely assumed that Sgt. Strohlein was captured or killed by the enemy in the area he was last seen."[12]

Today, Special Forces training is conducted at the US Army John F. Kennedy Special Warfare Center and School at Fort Bragg, North Carolina. It traces its history back to Fort Riley, Kansas, in 1950 under the auspices of the US Army's Psychological Warfare Division of the Army General School. With a name change to Special Warfare School in 1956, it expanded its responsibilities to counterinsurgency operations in 1960 and, in 1962, "established a Special Forces Training Group to train enlisted volunteers for operational assignments within the SF groups. The Advanced Training Committee was formed to explore and develop sophisticated methods of infiltration and exfiltration."[13] The vertical wind tunnel at the John F. Kennedy Special Warfare Center and School in Fort Bragg is named in honor of Sergeant Madison Strohlein.[14] John Kearns received his Special Forces Qualified and Combat patches from the school before taking his first assignment with the CIA as a paramilitary contractor in Vientiane, Laos. From there, he was assigned as a paramilitary officer to Nam Yu, in northwest Laos close to the Mekong River.

John Kearns on Mekong River in 1969.
Photo courtesy of Malone family.

Lima Site 118A.

★ ★ ★ ★ ★

Nam Yu was one of four substations in Laos operated during the "secret war" under the direction of the CIA base at Udorn, Thailand. The others were:

> Long Tieng, sometimes spelled Long Cheng, south of the Plain of Jars. This substation, where John would later serve twice, was originally set up in 1962 as a headquarters for Vang Pao, the Laotian general in command of an army of Hmong people. Sometimes called the "Secret Army," Pao's army was trained and supported by the CIA. By the time a 4,100-plus foot runway was built there in 1964, Long Tieng had become one of the United States' largest foreign installations.
>
> Savannakhet, a city located on the western border of southern Laos with Thailand, on the Mekong River. In 1968, CIA operations in Savannakhet created a specialized force of irregular Laotians initially intended to operate as guerrillas along the Ho Chi Minh Trail. Known as the Commando Raiders, they did so quite successfully.
>
>> Such triumphs on the Trail, explained one CIA advisor at Savannakhet, were due to the unique understanding the guerrillas had of the local terrain and population. "They were just some good old boys working within earshot of their hometown." Indeed, time and again it was local guerrillas on the simplest of operations that surprised their case officers with bursts of excellence.[15]
>
> John Kearns would serve as CIA Commando/Raider officer

during his first tenure at Long Tieng.

Pakse, about forty miles east of Paksong, in the southern Laos panhandle. John was assigned to Pakse in the late summer of 1972. It would be his last duty station.

★ ★ ★ ★ ★

To say that Nam Yu, or Nam Thieu, was primitive might be an understatement. "Unlike nearly every other CIA station in Asia—even ones in relatively remote places—Nam Yu had virtually nothing of the modern world, not even hot showers."[16] One writer called it a "remote military backwater."[17] Air America pilot Terry Burke described it as "a hell hole."[18] Another noted that, surrounded by mountains, it was "difficult as hell to get into."[19] Wild animals, such as tigers and various types of leopard, prowled the jungles in the area. Even during the dry season, roads were barely passable.

Nam Yu landing strip in northwest Laos (Lima Site 118A). Photo by Ernest Kuhn, *courtesy of Ernest and Phaythoune Kuhn Image Collection, Southeast Asian Images & Texts Project, University of Wisconsin Digital Collections.*

And just try and find it on a map! An Internet scribe, self-dubbed "The Wanderling," proclaims that Nam Yu was only one of several "secret" places during the secret war but that, while much has leaked out about most of the others, "such is not the case with Nam Yu, otherwise known as Lima Site 118 A." Here is how he describes its location:

> There are a couple of major geographical features that [. . .] once located on a Google map will help pinpoint where LS 118A is in Laos and how it fits into the world. The most prominent feature [. . . .] is the Mekong River and how it makes a sharp right turn toward the east before swinging back in a hairpin U-turn toward the west. At the top of the hairpin just as the river turns south for a short distance is a city named Ban Xieng Kok. Go straight down the map and a short distance to the west, on your right of LS 118A, is a community named Ban Ta Hou. If you put "Xieng Kok, Laos" into Google search a map comes up that is both clickable and expandable. Using the measurement function go about 23 miles south from Xieng Kok and by enlarging the map you should be able to find Ban Ta Hou . . . which doesn't show up until you really enlarge the map. If you go to the west, your left, a little ways you will be able to [. . .] locate fairly close where LS 118A was located. It is, however, NOT designated on the Google map.[20]

Located in the so-called opium-rich "golden triangle," where Laos, Burma (now known as Myanmar), and Thailand converge, Nam Yu was established by the CIA's Bill Young to serve as his paramilitary base in the area, moving from Long Tieng. Young was the grandson of a Baptist missionary to Burma. Young's father, Harold, later took over the grandfather's mission, but he also became a source of intelligence on activities in the region for the CIA. Bill Young grew up in Burma, a background that made him "the only American capable of operating in the boondocks of Laos by himself without Paru to help him."[21] The Police Aerial Reinforcement Unit, or PARU, was a Thai paramilitary unit made up of members of the Royal Thai Police and trained by the CIA. Alfred McCoy described Young as "one of the CIA's most effective agents," whom the CIA regarded, because of his fluency in five of the local languages, as its "tribal expert."[22]

Bill Young took his own life in 2011 at the age of 76. He was reportedly found clutching a gun in one hand and a crucifix in the other. Young's obituary in *The New York Times* noted that some "used to jokingly call him the American warlord."[23] British journalist Edward Loxton reported that Young was an "American missionary's son who became a top CIA Vietnam War–era hit-man in the jungles of Burma, Laos and Thailand." He quoted Young as saying, "Killing was part of the job."[24]

Nam Yu is where John Kearns was first dispatched to ply his skills for the CIA in signals intelligence and as a paramilitary operator. We don't have an exact record of John's activities at Nam Yu, but we know how that substation operated, which gives a good sense of John's service during his time there. In addition to training "tribal mercenaries,"[25] and as befit John's training and skillset, Nam Yu was a center for intelligence gathering:

> Using four-pound radios with a broadcast radius of four hundred miles, the teams transmitted their top-priority data directly to a powerful receiver at Nam Yu or to specially equipped Air America planes that flew back and forth along the Laos-China border. After these messages were translated at Nam Yu, they were forwarded to Vientiane for analysis

> and possible transmission to CIA headquarters in Langley, Virginia. The radio messages also served to pinpoint every team's position, all carefully recorded on a huge relief map of Yunnan Province mounted in a restricted operations room at Nam Yu.[26]

The intelligence gathering was not limited to North Vietnamese communications. In September 1970, journalist Michael Morrow, writing for the *Dispatch News Service* (which won a Pulitzer Prize for picking up Seymour Hersh's reporting of the My Lai massacre), blew the lid off Nam Yu and sparked a little heartburn within the Nixon administration. Morrow reported that US eavesdropping activities actually crossed the border into China. He quoted "highly reliable sources" as saying that "there is always a team in China," and he described the CIA-directed activities this way: "The teams are equipped with American small arms, a special three-pound radio with a range of 400 miles, and other special gear. Their missions are to tap Chinese telegraph lines, watch roads, and do other types of intelligence gathering. Teams have gone as far as 200 miles into China." Morrow wrote that the teams, typically consisting of about fifteen Yao tribesmen, were flown to a small sod airstrip about twenty kilometers north of Nam Yu, called "Site 93," then would cross the Mekong River into Burma in inflatable rafts. From there, they would head northwest and enter China about fifty kilometers from Site 93. They were typically gone for three to four months, all the while maintaining radio contact with Nam Yu.[27]

"Several of the teams inserted into China have been captured, and some have switched allegiances, returning to Nam Lieu [Nam Yu] as counter-spies," Morrow wrote. On one occasion, he reported, an Air America Porter aircraft lost parts of both wings to antiaircraft fire near the border of Burma, Laos, and China but managed to return to base.[28] Hugh Tovar, who was CIA station chief in Laos from 1970 to 1973, confirmed the report in a 2007 interview. Tovar said the Chinese "had a huge investment in anti-aircraft defenses up there" and that "an Air American [sic] plane got blasted up there and almost went down."[29]

Morrow reported that these activities were directed from CIA headquarters in Udorn, Thailand, and that there were several Americans, both CIA and military, at Nam Yu. In September he said there were four, but by the following January of 1971, he reported that the number had increased to more than ten. Americans at Nam Yu "help to direct a joint operation of SGU (special guerrilla units) and the Thai army," and "[t]hey run intelligence-gathering missions on a road being built by the Chinese government (under an agreement with the now defunct coalition government of Laos) in the same vicinity."[30]

Tovar confirmed Chinese involvement, which explained why incursions were made into that country.

> I think the Chinese had a very complex sort of approach to this war, as you well know. They backed up the North Vietnamese in their effort over there, did a lot to contribute there to it, and I think they visualized and wanted to see the North Vietnamese victory. But when it came to Laos, which was kind of in-between territory, I think the Chinese figured they had a hand in this. They were not going to let the North Vietnamese or any Vietnamese have a hand up there, and they swung around the back there and moved down form [sic] Chinese territory all the way down to—almost to Thai

> territory, at the very minimum to say, "Hey, look, we're here. Don't forget, you can't count us out, we're part of this equation."[31]

Jerome A. Cohen, a law professor at Harvard University Law School and an expert on Chinese law who had studied China under a grant from the Rockefeller Foundation, was alarmed by Morrow's reporting. After meeting with Henry Kissinger in December of 1970, he wrote to Kissinger on January 6, 1971. He enclosed a photocopy of a September 3, 1970, article in *The Boston Globe* under Michael Morrow's byline, which bore the headline "CIA Sending Laos Tribesmen into China on Spy Patrols." Referring to testimony before Congress by Ambassador to the Republic of China Walter P. McConaughy, Cohen raised the inquiry:

> You have access to the substantial deleted portions [of McConaughy's testimony], but even what remains indicates that the U.S. itself is at least engaging in unmanned reconnaissance flights over China and that we are helping the GRC [Greater China Region] with maritime raids and other forms of hostile penetration. China, of course, has listed hundreds of American aerial and naval intrusions, many since January 1969. Are all of these fictitious? Past Chinese claims have often been verified by capture of pilots or wreckage of our planes. . . . I wonder what "the Agency" and the Pentagon will report on these activities.[32]

Kissinger solicited input from the CIA on how to respond to Cohen, and Frank M. Chapin provided him with two options, both nonresponsive. One was to consider Cohen's letter as having been "overtaken by events and therefore requiring no reply at this time," while the other option was to acknowledge the letter but to "not respond specifically to each of the points he raises." Chapin's letter to Kissinger provided a box beside each option for him to check to either "approve," "disapprove," or "other." If Kissinger chose the second option, he was advised to "sign the letter at Tab A," which he did. That letter said, in its entirety:

> Dear Jerry:
>
> It was good to see you on the 19th. I enjoyed the session immensely.
>
> I have done some checking into the matters you raised in your letter of January 6th and can assure you that your concerns appear to be based on exaggerated reports.
>
> Perhaps we will have an opportunity to chat about this on a future occasion.
>
> Warm regards,
>
> Henry A. Kissinger[33]

Chapin also told Kissinger that Morrow, a conscientious objector to the Vietnam War who had refused to report for induction, was "one of three newsmen captured by the Viet Cong in Cambodia. Upon his release he wrote a series of uncritical articles which were good propaganda for the Viet Cong."[34] Morrow, along with Richard Dudman of the *St. Louis Post-Dispatch* and Elizabeth Pond of *The Christian Science Monitor*, were first reported missing in Cambodia in early May of 1970. It was later determined that they had been captured by the Viet Cong. They were held for forty days before being released.[35]

Chapin seemed to imply to Kissinger that Morrow's character was suspect and, thus, his reporting was not credible—although Chapin did not dispute any of the factual statements in Morrow's articles. The question arises as to how credible, in fact, were his stories? Morrow is still alive as of this writing, living in Mongolia. In an email exchange, he sourced his story for the first time—the "highly reliable sources"—although without providing any names. On September 18, 2025, he wrote that "the articles were based on information given to me totally off the record in a small, otherwise empty Vientiane bar opposite the Hotel Constellation by an intelligence officer in the Vientiane embassy attached to Ambassador [to Laos George McMurtrie] Godley."[36]

This was the world into which John Kearns arrived when he first set foot at Nam Yu. His posting most likely resulted in his crossing paths with one of the Vietnam War's most infamous characters: Tony Poe.

Former marine and active CIA operator Tony Poe, real name Anthony Poshepny, had been sent to Nam Yu from Long Tieng in 1969. At Long Tieng, he had clashed with Laotian general Vang Pao on a number of matters, including use of Air America aircraft to transport opium. Poe had a visceral disdain for drug trafficking, but Vang Pao viewed the opium trade as the means to finance the war. To Poe, "selling and moving opium was, from the start of the war, central to Vang Pao's life—that he was in business as much as in war."[37]

Additionally, Poe disliked Vang Pao's "political style."

> It bothered Poe that Vang Pao skimmed soldiers' pay and gave Hmongs from the more powerful clans the best jobs. Poe thought Vang Pao should stick to soldiering and stay out of politics. It did not occur to him that without all the graft and patronage, Hmong support for the war would evaporate overnight.[38]

Despite his clashes with Pao and notwithstanding his slide into depression and, perhaps, insanity, Poe's superiors still viewed him as having significant value in the war in Laos. Hence, the move to Nam Yu. By the time John Kearns arrived there, Poe was already "infamous" for his alcohol consumption. There were reports that he required foreigners who stayed overnight in Nam Yu to join him in getting drunk. Then there was the crazy stuff.

> Poe also admitted cheerfully to his bosses that he had been carrying out extreme measures to scare veteran North Vietnamese troops. The CIA operative had started sticking heads of dead communist fighters on spikes and leaving them out by the roadside like a Southeast Asian Vlad the Impaler. One time, he convinced an American pilot to fly over communist-controlled territory in Laos. As the pilot zoomed low, Poe tossed the severed heads of dead North Vietnamese soldiers down onto enemy forces.[39]

And that possible slide into insanity?

> Poe had never been known for his stability, but with the war

> not going the way he wanted, he began losing his mind completely. Though Poe had wanted to live rough up at Nam Yu, he had become so isolated in the northwest—no television, nothing much to do, few foreign visitors—that he had started having conversations with himself as if he were on a desert island.[40]

He screamed at pilots and relentlessly criticized Vang Pao. Finally, Poe made so many enemies that the CIA had no choice but to remove him from Laos altogether. He was transferred to a training camp in Thailand and retired in the mid-1970s.

Ostensibly, Morrow's September 1970 article that first opened up Nam Yu to scrutiny ultimately led to the transfer because it had blown Poe's cover. Morrow referred to Poe by his conflated name—Anthony Poe—and called him a "rough-and-tumble veteran clandestine guerrilla organizer." He said Poe was "known best for his dislike of journalists, disregard for orders and radio codes, capacity for Lao whiskey and expertise at clandestine guerrilla operations." Poe would not allow his picture to be taken, was infected with a "brusque and stubborn manner," and "preferred working with Laotian hill tribes over Americans."[41]

CIA case officer Tony Poe celebrating Lao New Year with Colonel Khamphay Sayasith and his wife, 1970. Photo by Ernest Kuhn, *courtesy of Ernest and Phaythoune Kuhn Image Collection, Southeast Asian Images & Texts Project, University of Wisconsin Digital Collections.*

But blowing Poe's cover may have been just an excuse for the CIA to do what it already wanted to do, which was "to get rid of Poe, whose mountainman [sic] style had been a source of long-term friction with members of the American mission in Laos, including Ambassador Godley."[42] That latter observation is interesting, particularly in light of Morrow's assertion that his articles were based on information given to him by someone attached to Godley. In his emails, Morrow wrote, "In hindsight, and with no proof, I suspect I was used by the ambassador in a feud with Poe, or perhaps in a feud at a higher level between Kissinger and [CIA Director Richard] Helms (whom I was later told quietly visited Laos in the wake of my story) over emerging US China policy, or perhaps by the CIA itself to corral a rogue Poe."[43] In other words, the ambassador wanted Morrow to blow Poe's cover to provide the excuse needed to remove him.

Morrow also speculated that a "corollary intent, of course, might have been to put an end to my run in Laos. If any of that is true, it was clever and at least somewhat successful."[44] Whichever motivation might have been true, both ends were achieved. Poe was removed from Nam Yu. And as for "putting an end to Morrow's run in Laos"? Morrow had written that the Pathet Lao put a price on Poe's head, and Poe must have felt that some sort of retribution was required for that. Morrow said that he was told by the proprietor of the Constellation Hotel, where he stayed in Laos, that Poe had put a $10,000 bounty on his head. "I took the threat seriously. I immediately left Laos and didn't return until after the war was over."

John Kearns would have reported to Poe when he arrived at Nam Yu. Although the authors were unable to find specific documentation of any encounters between the two men, it is virtually impossible that their paths would not have crossed. According to Morrow's first article in September 1970, there were only four Americans in Nam Yu at that time. We can only imagine how the highly disciplined Kearns responded to Poe.

To a great degree, Tony Poe presented himself as a sort of real-life Colonel Walter E. Kurtz, the character played by Marlon Brando in Francis Ford Coppola's *Apocalypse Now*. Essentially an adaptation of Joseph Conrad's 1899 novella *Heart of Darkness*, a critique of European colonialism in Africa, Coppola reset the story in the Vietnam War. Based loosely on Conrad's character of an ivory trader in the Congo named Kurtz, Brando's character was on the brink of—if not full-fledged into—insanity. Based on conduct, a good argument can be made that Poe represented the real-life version of Brando's Kurtz.

In *Apocalypse Now*, the old adage "just because you're paranoid doesn't mean they're not out to get you" rang true. Martin Sheen's Captain Willard, a member of MACV-SOG, was sent to "terminate Kurtz's command . . . with extreme prejudice." Much as Brando's Kurtz isolated himself in the jungles of eastern Cambodia, Tony Poe did so in northwestern Laos. His brutality, "which had always been a part of his character and his operation, became much more extreme."[45]

In addition to sticking the severed heads of enemy combatants on spikes along the roadside, Poe issued bounties for communists' ears, amassed dead bodies, and stuck captured North Vietnamese doctors in holes dug in the ground. When the doctors complained, he shot them. Poe also developed a deep paranoia while at Nam Yu: "the isolated Poe started to see enemies all around him, though in his mind, the enemies were all within the group of Americans in Laos and Washington who were running the war. . . . he believed everyone connected to the US government was out to get him."[46]

British journalist Adrian Levy, who coauthored, along with Cathy Scott-Clark, a profile and interview with Poe for the *London Sunday Times Magazine* in 1998, concluded Poe was Kurtz. In 1999, a documentary was produced for The History Channel's *History Undercover* program, also cowritten by Levy and Scott-Clark, about Levy's search for the man behind Kurtz. The documentary's synopsis says, "Levy discovers the real Colonel Kurtz is a former American Marine and CIA operative in charge of 'Operation Momentum,' the CIA's secret war in Laos. His name is Anthony Poshepny, aka Tony Poe."[47]

Writer and filmmaker Ashish Arora suggests that Kurtz was a composite character based on Poe and another Special Forces officer in Vietnam, Colonel Robert Rheault. Many agree, though, that Poe was one of the inspirations for Col. Kurtz.[48] Writer Blake Stilwell, on the other hand, gives the nod wholly to Colonel Rheault:

> The Army's Special Forces command came down to one man during the Vietnam War. His job performance earned him the nod from screenwriter John Milius, who turned retired Army Colonel Robert Rheault's legacy into something more enduring than he ever imagined. He was immortalized forever by actor Marlon Brando in *Apocalypse Now*.[49]

Rheault doesn't really fit the bill. Stilwell even admits, "Unlike Col. Kurtz, there was nothing insane or dark about Col. Rheault."[50] He was a key figure in what was known as Project GAMMA, an operation of covert intelligence-gathering by a Special Forces group in Cambodia, and the killing of a double agent working for the Viet Cong that came to be known as the Green Beret Affair. But other than the rogue killing, Rheault falls lightyears short of Kurtz, or Poe, in his conduct.

Both Coppola and Poe deny that Poe was the inspiration. Coppola, like Stilwell, gives the nod to Rheault.[51] Pop culture has speculated about other inspirations as well. One writer credits an Australian Army officer named Arthur Barry Peterson who was sent to Vietnam by the Australian Secret Intelligence Service but who was commanded by the CIA.

> The character of Colonel Kurtz, played by Marlon Brando, has become legendary in cinema history. But what if I told you that this seemingly fictional character was inspired by a real person? Buckle up, because we're about to dive into the extraordinary true story of Captain Barry Peterson, the Australian Army officer who became known as the "Tiger Man of Vietnam."[52]

Writer Genevieve Carlton says that Kurtz was based on David Hackworth, who became the youngest colonel in Vietnam.[53]

Regardless of the merits of any other claims, it's hard to study Poe's descent into insanity in the isolation of the jungles of Laos and discount the possibility, if not probability, that he was the real-life embodiment of Brando's fictional character, who descended into insanity in the jungles of Cambodia. Ultimately, it was Poe's bizarre behavior and, perhaps to some extent his notoriety, that led to his removal from Laos altogether. He had simply made too many enemies there.[54]

It's worth noting that Poe was twice awarded the CIA

Intelligence Star. The first was for his work in a Bangkok-based CIA front company where he trained Tibetan and Chinese Muslims in 1959. In 1975, the CIA awarded him a second Intelligence Star, this one for his heroism in Laos. Poe died in 2003 from diabetes complications that had resulted in his left foot being amputated. He outlived John Kearns by nearly thirty-one years.

CHAPTER TWENTY-ONE

Oh, It Was a Scene, Man—Part Deux

"Night life is when everybody says what the hell and you do not remember who paid the bill."

Ernest Hemingway

Wow!

That was my first reaction to cocaine, when the Playboy manager pulled out a plastic bag full and suggested that I "give it a shot." I had been smoking pot since high school, but that was nothing like cocaine. In some ways, cocaine was like taking a trip on acid, which I had tried, but without all the psychedelics. The rush hit me much faster than I expected. It was as if, for the first time in my life, my eyes had been opened—metaphorically, of course. Opened to new ideas and new concepts and new ways of thinking and perceiving things. A wave of energy coursed through my body. Everything felt sharper, brighter, and more alive. I was hyperaware of my surroundings and felt an increased sensitivity to my senses. On high alert. My vision was clearer, my hearing more sharply attuned. I could feel my heart racing, could hear the muted *thump thump thump* of its beat. Then I felt this overwhelming sense of euphoria and well-being. My body was energized, like I could run a marathon and not breathe hard at the end. My confidence soared. I felt unstoppable. Unconquerable. Invincible.

The feeling from that first hit faded quickly, and it would never feel that good again. I thought maybe the trick was to do more and to do it more often. But even if I followed up the first hit with a second, and a third, the high would never again be as high, the euphoria never again as euphoric, my senses never again as sensitized. My eyes never again as open.

Life is an exacting teacher and its lessons are hard earned. Sometimes they come at a cost. Using cocaine was one of those. Because your body builds a tolerance to cocaine, you need more volume, and more frequent hits, just to achieve a lesser high. That means more money. But unless your blood runs blue, or you have a boundless trust fund, money is finite. Especially for a small-town boy trying to make his way in the big city. By the time I figured out that I would never repeat the first experience, it was too late: I was hooked. And broke. I made good money working at Playboy, but I spent lavish amounts on my newfound friend, cocaine.

After about a year at Playboy, Lenny Licht decided to sell his interest in the club. With a new owner came a new management team. I never clicked with them. I didn't want to stick around but I didn't have another job lined up—and I needed the money to support my new habit. So I stayed. For a while. I guess my attitude showed because, when they started downsizing and laying off staff, I saw the handwriting on the wall. Better to leave voluntarily than to get fired.

Fortunately, I had been talking to a friend named Rod Keishnick about a new club that had just opened called Papagayo. It was located across Central Expressway from NorthPark Center, an enclosed shopping mall in north Dallas that was first opened in 1965. It was at the time, and still is, one of the most prestigious shopping malls in the country, where Dallas's elite shopped. A guy named Duane Thompson, who was the former co-owner of Red Dog Saloon near European Crossroads on Northwest Highway, and #3 Lift in European Crossroads, owned Papagayo, but it was Rod, who was either the assistant manager or door manager, who actually hired me. Our friendship would quickly extend beyond the club. We worked out together at Doug's Gym in downtown Dallas—had to keep my football player/model physique in tune—and, unfortunately, shared a passion for marijuana and cocaine.

Papagayo was a huge club. My recollection is that the Dallas Fire Department set something in the upper eight hundreds as the building's capacity, but we had well over a thousand when the Chippendale Dancers appeared. In 1982, *D Magazine* described Pagagayo like this:

> Pagagayo . . . is home to the serious disco regulars and is one of the grandest disco caverns in the city. If you tire of dancing on the very large, incredibly lit, multilevel floor, retire to one of the several bars that encircle Papagayo and make a few friends. Or a few hundred friends. The clientele—let's call them a crowd—is highly mixed, with a large percentage of youths and no small number of bizarrely attired attention-seekers. And since some of us are just getting warmed up by 2 a.m., Papagayo stays open until 4 on Fridays and Saturdays.[1]

People "dressed to the nines" when they came to the club. I may be showing my age with this expression, but in common parlance, it means dressed elegantly or stylishly. They would practice for hours just so they could show off on the dance floor. I think Duane, the owner, saw Papagayo becoming a Texas version of New York's Studio 54. He hired a hot DJ from the Bronx named Julio Morales who received new releases directly from New York, so the music was always cutting edge. I worked the door, and I felt like a kid in a candy store. The most beautiful women in Dallas frequented the club, and they paid a little extra attention to the door guys. The energy was always high. Cocaine might have had something to do with that feeling, at least for me.

One year the club threw a massive Valentine's Day party and Duane had us wearing tuxedoes. I still had mine from Playboy, so I was set. There were eight hundred or more customers inside when Rod summoned me to deal with a problem. One of the waitresses was "having issues" with a customer. That phrase covered a wide range of possible malefactions, up to and including a customer inappropriately laying hands on a waitress. I approached the table with the "controlled anger" of a bouncer. You wanted the malefactor to see the anger, but also to see that you had it under control.

This particular customer had been loud and obnoxious, and he had grabbed several of the waitresses' rear ends. I could tell he was gearing up for a fight when he saw me coming. I politely informed him, in unmistakable terms, to knock it off or I would "help him leave," with all the force that implied. He responded by sticking a finger in my face—use your imagination as to which one. I grabbed his finger and then his arm and pulled him to his feet.

I was escorting him out in what could best be described as a headlock when he bit me. Not a nip, but a full-blown, sinking his teeth into the sleeve of my tuxedo, ripping out a chunk of cloth, and into my arm, bite. The pain was excruciating. My controlled anger switched immediately into uncontrolled anger. I managed to get him out of the club, but then a trip to the doctor ensued for a tetanus shot. Who knew where he might have been!

On another occasion, we had problems with a few guys drinking heavily and harassing one of the waitresses. I joined the bouncers in showing them to the door. Rod and I always made it a practice, when the club closed, to escort the waitresses to their cars in the parking lot. That night, it was a good thing we did, because we found these guys waiting outside, still mad at being tossed out of the club. Things quickly got pretty dicey.

The odds didn't favor us. It was just Rod and me, and the four of them. Luckily, while they might have been experts at harassing waitresses, they were inept at brawling. Rod and I managed to put three of them down pretty quickly, giving us the advantage. The fourth guy took off on foot, presumably for his car. I chased him—stupid, on my part—and quickly closed the gap. He opened his car and got in, but I was right there on the other side. I opened the passenger door to grab him . . . and found myself staring down the barrel of a handgun. Fortunately, he didn't pull the trigger or this book would have ended right there. But he did start the car, throw it into gear, and drive off, with me holding onto the door for dear life. He dragged me along the parking lot for a first down or two. Finally able to think clearly, I let go of the door and rolled across the pavement. Not too much worse for the wear. Just a few holes in my pants and some scrapes on my legs.

But no hole between my eyes.

★ ★ ★ ★ ★

My first tenure at Papagayo ended after about six months, suddenly, unexpectedly, and ignominiously. The club was managed by a couple of brothers that I thought were a little sketchy and, soon enough, I found out just how sketchy. One day I walked into the men's restroom and stumbled onto one of them in the midst of shooting up something. I might have had my problems with cocaine, but straws and needles were worlds apart. I immediately spun on my heels and walked back out. Of course, I had already seen what I had seen, and he knew it. I was fired without explanation, but I knew why.

The next day I received a call from another club, daVinci, a spectacular facility tucked into a relatively small space on Greenville Avenue near Walnut Hill. The club had been built by the Pratt Brothers (Jack, Ed, and Bill), who had built and opened Holiday Inn franchises in Texas and Mexico. I don't know how they found out I was available so soon after I was terminated at Papagayo, but I started right away as the assistant manager.

D Magazine described daVinci this way:

> The latest local contribution to discomania, daVinci does at least one important thing right—they've made their dance floor larger than a ping-pong table. The dance floor is, in fact, an impressive affair—a mirrored disco dome with a fast flashy, multicolored floor lit from beneath, flanked by a gleaming wall of electronic equipment. (The only questionable elements are the slide screens in the dome above—during the day, when the luncheon buffet occupies the dance floor; they show slides of things like garnished chicken breasts; at night they switch to ungarnished women's breasts.) But the dance floor is the focus here; daVinci's main intent is disco chic. The obvious comparison is to élan, the pleasure palace down the street. Both are exclusive (literal-

ly) in that they are membership clubs ($100 to join daVinci, $200 after May 1), they enforce dress codes, and they attract an odd amalgam of self-appointed "beautiful people" . . . . It is as an environment, though, that daVinci will likely lure some of the "in crowd" away from élan—daVinci is glossier, flashier, and classier. Slick with glass and chrome, but tasteful in its use of dark greens, tans, and browns, the place drips expense, and it's money well-spent. The trappings can get excessive, however—do they really need a hair dryer in the men's room? Nice as daVinci is (including a friendly and competent staff), the style of a place like this is dictated by its clientele. And putting a $200 price tag on a dance floor does not guarantee the customers will be an enlightened elite.[2]

At daVinci, I reported to a guy who simply went by JJ. The thing that stands out most was his irritating habit of running background checks on the staff. Ironically, nobody really knew anything about his background. I found out later that his name was not really JJ and that he was apparently on the run from the law. He knew his own background was sketchy so I guess he assumed everyone else's was as well.

After being at daVinci for a couple of months, Rod Keishnick, who had now been named manager of Papagayo, asked if I wanted to come back, this time as assistant manager. He said the brother team that previously managed the club, and who'd unceremoniously fired me, had moved on. Notwithstanding JJ, things were going well at daVinci, and I still had a bad taste in my mouth from being fired at Papagayo, so I declined the offer. In retrospect, I should have taken it. A little later, after the JJ-is-not-really-JJ kerfuffle came to light, I called Rod back and, nonchalantly, asked if the job was still open.

It wasn't.

But Rod was a good friend. He talked to owner Duane Thompson, who still had good memories of me, and Duane authorized Rod to hire me as a co-assistant manager. That second tenure was more fun than the first, but with more authority came longer hours. It was my responsibility to close out the registers, run the tabs, and count the bar drawers every night. I would occasionally see the sun coming up in the morning after having been there all night.

Sometimes I needed a little pick-me-up to get through the long hours.

★ ★ ★ ★ ★

My cocaine habit was starting to collide with yet another bad habit, threatening my financial well-being as well as my psychological well-being: gambling. I always sucked at cards, but I felt I had a bit of useful football knowledge from my days as a Javelina at Texas A&I. So I bet heavily, and almost exclusively, on football games. Unfortunately, cocaine tends to create a false sense of confidence. And then the combination of cocaine and gambling threatened my physical well-being. Maybe even my very existence.

In September of 1979, the once-defeated Cowboys headed to Cleveland Municipal Stadium to play the undefeated Browns. Because the Browns had several key players supposedly out for the game, as was reported in the press, the Cowboys were favored. Coked up and drunk, not a good combination for decision-making, I bet a bundle on the Cowboys. I don't remember exactly how much, but it was in the thousands. Turns out, all three of those supposedly "out" Browns played, and Cleveland reeled off the first twenty points in the game, a missed extra point the only reason it wasn't twenty-one. The Cowboys scored on a forty-eight-yard pass from Roger Staubach to Tony Hill before the first quarter ended, but they would get no closer. The team I had bet thousands on lost 26-7.

My bookie was a six-foot-ten-inch monster named Max. Not long after the game ended, he showed up at my apartment to collect. When I opened the door to let him in, I was totally freaked out. Scared out of my wits. We had a brief discussion about how I didn't have the money but I darn sure needed to get it. The last thing he said to me—well, it wasn't so much what he said but the show-and-tell that accompanied it. He was wearing a long, black trench coat. He opened it wide and showed me a live grenade. At least I think it was live. He said, "If you don't pay up by Wednesday, someday when you don't expect it, this is going to come flying through your window."

I called in every marker I had all over town, looking for a financial favor from anyone who could and would provide it. I called cousins and uncles, friends, former teammates and coworkers. All to no avail. Dad wasn't a lot of help, either, other than to offer some advice. "You need to move out of town," he told me, "and change your name."

Papagayo's owner, Duane Thompson, came through for me. He paid my debt to Max, in exchange for which I agreed to work for a reduced salary for a year. I will always owe Duane a debt of gratitude for that. But maybe Dad was on to something. Maybe it was time for me to get out of town.

CHAPTER TWENTY-TWO
Adrift

"To reach a port, we must set sail—Sail, not tie at anchor—Sail, not drift."

Franklin D. Roosevelt

During my second tenure at Papagayo, Gene Cook and I moved into a duplex behind Monopoly, a club at the southwest corner of Northwest Highway and Abrams Road near Medallion Center. Shortly after that, Gene and his girlfriend/dance partner Fran Lucchesi got jobs as entertainers on Carnival Cruise Lines. Carnival was founded in 1972 and, by the 1980s, was one of the most popular cruise lines. The television show *The Love Boat*, which premiered in 1977, helped springboard cruising into the public consciousness. Capitalizing on that, and with an advertising campaign featuring Kathie Lee Gifford that would air later in the mid-1980s, Carnival continued to grow throughout the decade. I was looking to make a change in vocation, as well as a change in location. I hoped to distance myself from Max the bookie, and also from the easy access to cocaine in Dallas. Cruising seemed to be the perfect solution. It might have slipped my addled mind just how easy access would be in places like Jamaica and other Caribbean drug hubs. Maybe even easier than in Dallas.

With Gene's assistance, I set up a meeting with Brendan Corrigan, Senior Vice President of Marine Operations for Carnival. He invited me to Miami, so I put some of my stuff in a rented storage unit, packed everything else, and made the 1,100 mile drive to southern Florida. The meeting with Corrigan went well. He appeared to be impressed with me (or at least I thought he was) and even commented on my "great people skills." But then he caught me off guard. "This is just an interview, at this point."

I had misunderstood. I thought I had already been hired, so I put those people skills to work. I told him I really wanted to work for Carnival, that I had all my personal belongings in my car in the parking lot, and that I was ready to board the next ship. I don't know if he simply felt sorry for me or if he appreciated my enthusiasm, but he gave me an assignment right away, aboard the *TSS Carnivale*, which sailed weekend cruises out of Miami. I may have been on board simply as an observer, but at least I was on board.

From Friday at 5 p.m. to Monday morning at 8 a.m., my task was simply to watch, listen, and learn. My berth was a passenger/crew cabin in the hallway of the lower gangway. Apparently my presence was known to only a few. Once, when I used the cabin to shower before debarking the vessel, I found the cabin doorway completely blocked with luggage when I tried to leave. The chief steward either had forgotten, or didn't know, that I was using that cabin and had stacked suitcases almost to the ceiling. With the help of a kind steward who heard me calling for help, I was able to climb my way out.

If that was a test, I apparently passed with flying colors. After I was officially hired, I joined the *TSS Mardi Gras* as a junior purser. (By the way, TSS refers to turbine steam ship, a vessel powered by steam turbines.) The purser handles administrative responsibilities on a cruise ship, and a junior purser is essentially an assistant to the purser. Responsibilities include handling financial transactions for passengers and overseeing guest services, like dealing with customs issues, implementing safety rules and regulations, and tending to documentation issues for passengers and crew. Think Gopher on *The Love Boat*, played by actor Fred Grandy. Just before embarking on that first cruise aboard the *Mardi Gras* as an actual full-time employee, someone handed me a cash tray with about $8,000 in it and put me at the purser's window. I was officially the paymaster. Boy oh boy, did I have a lot to learn! It turns out that I was an excellent paymaster. In three years, dealing with nothing but cash and hundreds of crew members, I was only off about $100.

Gene Cook and Fran Lucchesi onboard Carnival Cruise Lines *Tropicale. Photo courtesy of Gene Cook and Fran Lucchesi.*

I loved my job at Carnival. I had some great friends there already, Gene and Fran, and made others along the way. And I went to places that I probably never would have otherwise. I certainly never dreamed of visiting those destinations as a boy growing up in small-town Texas. On the *Mardi Gras*, my territory included the Caribbean and parts of the Florida side of the Gulf of Mexico. My favorite island was Cozumel, off of Mexico's Yucatán Peninsula, opposite Playa del Carmen. The chief purser on the *Mardi Gras* was a Canadian named Alain Chabot, who took me scuba diving from a little dive shop called Blue Angel. There was a worker named Mary who never took off her wet suit, or so it seemed, in the whole year and a half that I ported there. Cozumel's night life was great! I did a lot of drinking in Cozumel, where I spent my thirtieth birthday. All I really remember about that birthday is lying on the floor of a disco called Hippopotamus. My favorite beach in the Caribbean was Seven Mile Beach on Cayman. Beautiful white sand with Australian pines. It has become very commercialized now but was not so much that way in the early 1980s.

Later, I was transferred to the *MV Tropicale* (MV means "motor vessel" as distinguished from "steam turbine"), traveling up and down the western coast of Mexico. I was able to dust off and use the smattering of Spanish that I had picked up working for Dad in our rental store or Gulf Station back in Waco. I should have taken Spanish in school, but I went with Latin instead. There was nobody on the cruise route to talk to in Latin.

★ ★ ★ ★ ★

A standard risk of working on cruise ships is the possibility, if not probability, of hurricanes, particularly in the Caribbean. There are protocols in place for protecting passengers and ships, including itinerary adjustments, route changes, and port cancellations, not to mention measures taken onboard for safety. It can be as simple as securing outdoor areas and closing pools and decks. When you're in port, though, sometimes the ship has to get out of the harbor because the waves generated by hurricane winds roll in like tsunamis and can knock larger ships into smaller boats that are tied up.

In November of 1984, I was aboard the *TSS Festivale* for Carnival Cruise Lines when we were in port at Charlotte Amalie in the US Virgin Islands. Hurricane Klaus was taking aim at the Leeward Islands, the group of islands where the northeastern Caribbean joins the Atlantic Ocean, including the Virgins. The harbor master instructed our captain to get out of the harbor, which he did, pronto. Once we reached open ocean, there was no choice but to ride out the storm. Our instructions were to keep our life jackets on and be ready to abandon ship if necessary. Then we sat in the officer's lounge and waited.

With each rise and fall of the ship, our chairs rolled from side to side across the floor. That was probably the most scared I have ever been in my life. You can prepare all you want, know all the emergency procedures in the world, but in a moment like that, everything is completely out of your control. I kept waiting for that *Poseidon Adventure* moment when a mega-wave would flip us upside down. I wondered who would lead us to the bottom, now the top, of the ship for rescue. I wasn't sure I was made of Gene Hackman stuff. Or even Red Buttons stuff. I'm not exaggerating when I say we came very close to sinking. But I lived to tell about it. And probably had to change my pants.

★ ★ ★ ★ ★

I moved up the ladder as a purser on the *Tropicale*, ultimately rising as high as second purser, but I aspired to be chief purser. When Admiral Cruise Lines, which operated on both coasts of the United States, offered me a position as first purser right off the bat, I jumped at the chance. Admiral was the result of the merger of three other lines, Eastern Cruise Lines, Western Cruise Lines, and Sundance Cruise Lines. In 1988, Admiral would merge with Royal Caribbean Cruise Lines (RCCL).

Once again, I loved my job. Great folks, most of whom I am still in touch with today. I spent two years on board the *Stardancer*, porting out of San Pedro (lower area of Los Angeles). That ship would later become the *Viking Serenade* for RCCL. Not only did it hold a thousand passengers, it could also accommodate a hundred full-size RVs. When we did our summer cruises out of Vancouver, passengers would bring their RVs and we would drop off in Alaska, in either Skagway or Haines, and then pick them up weeks to months later. Once again, I got to see places that I never would have imagined visiting. I made my first chief purser job for Admiral.

Life was good.

★ ★ ★ ★ ★

On February 13, 1988, while I was first purser on the *Stardancer*, the chief purser summoned me to his cabin to talk with a passenger named Scott Roston and to take notes of the conversation. As we listened, Roston told a tragic story. He and his new bride, Karen, had taken the cruise for their honeymoon. That night, Karen had been running around the track that encircles the top of the ship when a strong gust of wind forced her over the rail and into the ocean. He had some pretty serious scratches on his face, which he said he got when he tried to grab her to keep her from going overboard and hit his face on a gangway control box. At least that was his initial story.

Later, Roston said that she had fallen overboard, not that she had been blown overboard, and that he tried to grab her—that's when he hit his face on the control box, about the only consistency in his story—and couldn't. That didn't make a lot of sense to us. The odds of her falling overboard seemed long, since she was five feet three inches tall and the railing was three feet six inches high.

That would make the railing about chest high on her. Unless a dramatic updraft of powerful wind had lifted her over the rail, it seemed impossible that she could have simply fallen over it. No such winds had been reported that night, which was probably why he changed his story. Someone checked the control box but didn't find blood or any other indication that his face had hit it.

Paul Heckmann, cruising. *Photo courtesy of Paul Heckmann.*

Our ship's doctor examined him and was also skeptical of the story. He asked the captain to put Roston in a guarded cabin, which the captain did. Roston was later arrested and charged with his bride's murder. According to an opinion written by the United States Court of Appeals for the Ninth Circuit, which affirmed his conviction for second degree murder, there was compelling evidence at trial to establish that Roston had strangled her unconscious and then thrown her overboard, that she was unconscious when she hit the water, and that she ultimately drowned. The court said,

> [Roston] cruelly killed his wife of nine days. For no reason that appears to this court, he saw fit to physically assault her, beat her, choke her into unconsciousness and throw her body into the sea over twenty miles from land in the dark of night off the coast of Mexico knowing, as he must have

known, that she was certain to perish.[1]

The chief purser and I didn't know that at the time, of course, sitting in the cabin, listening and taking notes. We thought we were listening to a tragic tale of woe—until some of the parts of the story simply didn't make sense. But it was still a tragic tale of woe.

★ ★ ★ ★ ★

While working on the *Stardancer,* I met a beautiful blonde passenger that I fell head over heels in love with, and she with me. I'd had some steady girlfriends in the past, though nothing ever advanced to a stage serious enough to contemplate marriage. But I believed that she was "the one" to take me out of bachelorhood. She was from a suburb of San Francisco and would drive down to Los Angeles when we were in drydock. We were making plans to get married, and when she became pregnant, that seemed to be a sign that the time was right. I was determined to be the best father possible. Becoming a father meant I was going to have to clean up my act, particularly relating to drugs and drinking. Additionally, although I loved my adoptive father, I had learned from him how not to be a parent. I was determined not to make the same mistakes I perceived him to have made.

It was also a second chance for me. When I was seventeen, back in Texas, I found myself an unexpected expectant father as the result of youthful indiscretion . . . or maybe call it youthful irresponsibility . . . with a girl I knew from school. It happened during that period when I had dropped out and was facing the possibility of being drafted when I turned eighteen. I was not prepared for fatherhood and so I gave up my parental rights. She, by that time, was dating someone else. They got married and he raised what turned out to be a baby boy as his own. I moved on.

Yes, I recognize the irony of having given up a child as an infant when I had been given up as an infant. And now, years later, I had a second chance at fatherhood. But we lost the baby. That was devastating for both of us. Somehow, through no fault of ours, our plans for marriage fell apart, too. I suppose, in hindsight, if the baby was all that had been holding us together, maybe we weren't ready to get married anyway. It kinda started a downward cycle for me in relationships. I also threw out all those "clean up my act" good intentions.

The company transferred me to the *Azure Seas* at some point. I really liked being on the *Stardancer* and had made a lot of friends there, but when the company said, "Jump," you said, "How high?" The move turned out to be wrong for me. Liquor flowed freely on the *Azure Seas*, and I got a little wild with drinking and drug usage. I was mourning the loss of my unborn son, as well as a relationship with the woman I had planned to marry, and I had no one to talk to about it. This was the beginning of a new job, and I was a stranger to the crew. Instead of searching for a listening ear, even if that meant getting professional help, I "self-medicated." I put that in quotation marks because what I did was in no way medicinal, just self-destructive.

A large part of my job as purser involved handling cash. I quickly found that drugs, alcohol, and the weekly intake of cash in six figures did not merge any better than cocaine and betting on the Dallas Cowboys. I made several careless errors in accounting for the cash, and that did not go unnoticed. There was one time in particular, after I had come into possession of some cocaine. I was one of those folks who, once I picked up the straw, I couldn't put it down. I screwed up the payroll royally and, when I was summoned to meet with the ship's representative, I was wired on cocaine. You can guess what happened.

I can't say I didn't expect to be fired. Sooner or later, it was bound to happen. In fact, I deserved it. Even before I was let go, I had already put out some job feelers. The Bermuda Star Lines, which was later absorbed by Commodore Cruise Lines, offered me a job as chief purser, with a possible upgrade to hotel manager. I thought it best not to tell my new employer what had happened on the *Azure Seas*.

My first assignment with Bermuda Star was on a smaller ship called the *SS Vera Cruz*. Although it was primarily built for day cruises, it wasn't unusual for us to go on three- and four-day cruises. I had plenty of interaction with passengers on that ship, but most of it was unpleasant. The passengers targeted the pursers when they had complaints, and boy, did they have complaints. The ship had the tiniest rooms I have ever seen, and passengers let us know they were unhappy about it. I agreed with them, though there wasn't anything I could do about it. But at least I had a job, and I was still in the cruise industry.

Then I was transferred to the *Queen of Bermuda*. Our home port was in New York City and we sailed to Bermuda. We had a no-nonsense German captain, Jens W. Thorn, who was quite the character. When I say "character," I'm trying to politely say that he was not exactly a people person. We also had a staff captain who ate onions like they were apples. That makes some sense, I suppose, since I understand that onions were used by both sides during the Civil War to prevent scurvy, a disease caused by a deficiency of Vitamin C. Scurvy was common on ships even into the nineteenth century. Union general and eighteenth president of the United States Ulysses S. Grant once famously said during the war, "I will not move my army without onions."[2]

One of the perks was that I got to go to Bermuda quite a bit, particularly to Hamilton and St. George. I also took one cruise up the Hudson River for a reunion of sorts for a West Point graduating class from the late 1940s. As you can imagine, there were a lot of generals on board.

When the company desperately needed a chief purser for the West Coast, it transferred me to the *Bermuda Star*, cruising out of Vancouver into Alaska. We needed some refitting so, in late 1989, we went to Swan Island, Oregon, downriver on the Willamette River from Portland. On December 7, while using blow torches to remove tables in the dining room, which are welded to the floor so they don't move while the ship is at sea, shoreside welders somehow caught the older asbestos between the decks, which had been mixed with chemicals and other additives, on fire. It looked like a firefighters' convention before it was finally put out. According to *The Oregonian* newspaper, it was a five-alarm fire that engaged one hundred firefighters and thirty pieces of equipment.

I managed to salvage the ship's payroll and all our visas, which made me a bit of a hero. I was even quoted in *The Oregonian*, advising that all crew members were accounted for. One of the crew, identified in the newspaper as Julian Calidonio, had been trapped aboard. He smashed through a porthole with a fire extinguisher and "poked his head through, gasping for breath." Firefighters broke out the rest of the glass in the porthole, and he was able to climb out to safety. That scene was depicted in a picture in the article, which includes me in uniform, back to the camera, giving Julian a thumbs up.[3]

Because of the fire, we couldn't sail, so the company sent everyone home except for essential personnel. I stayed as the temporary hotel manager instead of chief purser. The steel-hulled ship wasn't designed for cold weather and, because of a lack of insulation, I ended up spending the coldest winter of my life aboard that vessel. To make things worse, the Coast Guard found that our forepeak hull (the forwardmost area in a ship) was rusted out. In places, it was as little as one-sixteenth of an inch thick. All it would take was one good hit from a floating log to pierce the hull of the vessel.

We managed to limp to the boatyards in San Diego to replace the whole forepeak. Everything in front of the bridge had to be cut off and all new steel attached. We were docked in a barrio area in San Diego that wasn't exactly the safest place to go wandering about. As a result, I spent most of my time on board the ship. I had already lost one job due to drinking and drugging, so I promised myself that I would get straight. I even wrote a letter to my parents explaining my situation. I can't remember what I said, but I poured out my heart about the loss of my unborn child and my despair at my own condition, both physically and psychologically, and my desire to heal myself.

There were only two telephone lines from the shore to the ship. One was to the bridge and the other was to my cabin. I had a lot of traffic to and from my cabin with crewmembers making and taking phone calls. One day, I got a call from Hollywood.

CHAPTER TWENTY-THREE

The Secret City in the Secret War

"We are not about to send American boys nine or ten thousand miles away from home to do what Asian boys ought to be doing for themselves."

Lyndon B. Johnson

By all accounts, John Kearns was an exceptional paramilitary operations officer at Nam Yu. According to reports from superiors in his personnel file, John "showed a genuine respect for the Laotian people and a concern for their well-being. Early on, he demonstrated a leadership ability that enabled him to motivate his men to undertake difficult and dangerous assignments. From all indications, he wrote clear reports, worked hard, and established good relationships with colleagues."[1] John Kearns was going places.

Tony Poe may have considered his move from Long Tieng to Nam Yu as a demotion of sorts. If so, then going the other way would be a promotion. John Kearns was reassigned from Nam Yu to the CIA subsection at Long Tieng (or Long Cheng), where he was made the Commando Raider Officer. When he arrived in Long Tieng, he must have felt like Jed Clampett arriving in Beverly Hills. In 1970, Long Tieng was a thriving area of somewhere between thirty and fifty thousand civilians (depending upon which source you accept as valid), many of whom provided support to the cadres of Hmong fighters and CIA advisors who resided there.

Much as Nam Yu had been built by one man, Bill Young, Long Tieng was the brainchild of CIA officer William Lair. Lair had been recruited by the CIA in 1951 during his senior year at Texas A&M, where he was studying for a career in oil engineering. He accepted the CIA's offer almost immediately and, upon graduation, was assigned to Thailand. There, he educated himself on the Hmong peoples, their culture and history, and built his own file of information. His duties took him to Laos in 1961. He had been informed that only Vang Pao could raise sufficient forces to fight the communist Pathet Lao, so he met with Pao in January. In a telephone interview with historian Joshua Kurlantzick, Lair said that Pao promised that he could raise a force of ten thousand Hmongs to be armed and trained by the United States. "Either we fight, or leave," Lair said Pao told him. "If you give me weapons, we fight."[2] So, when President Kennedy authorized the CIA to expand Operation Momentum, Lair used that authorization to obtain new weapons shipments to the Hmongs.

Long Tieng was selected as the spot for Pao's headquarters.

> The flat valley would prove perfect for a runway, though foggy in rainy season, and the surrounding mountains made it challenging for an enemy army to attack it. New fighters and their families were hastily putting up wooden homes with thatched roofs and holes in the middle for Hmong clay stoves. Across the runway from the village of thatched houses, the CIA and Vang Pao's lieutenants erected more mod-

ern concrete buildings with iron roofs that had communications technology, rooms for food and ammunition, strategy rooms with safes for CIA documents, and beds for pilots who needed to rest before their next flight.[3]

Airfield at Long Tieng, Laos (Lima Site 20A). *Public domain.*

In 1964, a runway was built that, at 1,260 meters (4,134 feet; almost four-fifths of a mile), could accommodate just about any aircraft. By the end of the decade, that runway helped Long Tieng, also known as Lima Site 20A or Lima Site 98, become one of the busiest airports in the world. With nearly five hundred flights daily—including Laos Air Force, US Raven pilots, and Air America aircraft—it rivaled Chicago's O'Hare Airport for takeoffs and landings. Of course, that included multiple takeoffs and landings by the same aircraft, but the number was still remarkable.

Long Tieng and its neighbor, Sam Thong (about nineteen miles from Long Tieng), "rapidly grew into large bustling towns, populated by refugees and the families of Vang Pao's soldiers." Long Tieng would "become the focal point of America's secret war in Laos."[4] British journalist Christopher Robbins offered this description:

> The CIA base of Long Tieng became one of the most secret spots on earth and developed into the largest Agency field HQ in the world. It was second in size only to the Agency's

> urban mission in Saigon and, after Vientiane, was the largest city in Laos. From the air its thousands of aluminum roofs gave it the look of an American urban sprawl, while on the ground it was crammed with sophisticated electronic gear. A macadam airfield was built, the only one in Northeastern Laos capable of handling jet aircraft in trouble, and the USAF conducted secret bombing missions into North Vietnam and eventually all over Laos itself. CIA men, posing as assistant military attaches from the embassy in Vientiane and working in the field with Army units, were directed by the base. Journalists called it Spook Heaven.[5]

When media interest in the not-so-secret-anymore war in Laos began to crest in 1971–1972, the United States government decided to give select reporters an inside look at the goings-on at Long Tieng in an effort to appear transparent. Tammy Arbuckle of *The Washington Star* reported that a press group was invited to the base on January 19, 1972, following a North Vietnamese attack on December 31. There were ground rules, which Arbuckle termed "quite sensible," including one that "U.S. personnel supporting irregular troops are not to be filmed, photographed, or otherwise identified by name or function. They may, however, be quoted or referred to as U.S. officials."[6]

But not all was open and aboveboard. Arbuckle complained that she had been given permission to remain overnight but that permission was then revoked without explanation. Additionally,

> The fact that all newsmen wanting to go to the Long Cheng area were made to go together on the same day picked well in advance, and that a single newsman is not allowed to go to

the area on U.S. transport traveling constantly between Long Cheng and Vientiane, can only give rise to suspicion that the U.S. is sanitizing the area on specified days for the purpose of press junkets aimed at showing secrecy has stopped.[7]

The New York Times reported on the same press junket and described the base at Long Tieng this way: "The base consists of a mile-long paved runway, with reloading facilities and stores of bombs for the small Laotian T-28 bombers, a complex of communications buildings at either end and a large cluster of villages that housed 30,000 civilians before the [December 31] attack began and they fled."[8]

John Kearns arrived at Long Tieng in 1970 as the Commando Raider Officer in charge of the force of Lao irregulars who had been first organized by the CIA's paramilitary personnel in 1968.

> These enhanced guerrillas—coined Commando Raiders—were in theory to be on call for the most challenging of raids, ambushes, prisoner snatches, bomb damage assessments, airborne pathfinder duties, and cross-border missions. And unlike the earlier Savannakhet teams, which served local, tactical objectives, the new commandos were to have a strategic dimension. "The difference between the old teams and the new Commando Raiders," noted an advisor, "was the difference between seduction and rape."[9]

As the officer in charge, John had supervisory and operational responsibility for all aspects of the Commando Raiders at Long Tieng.

> . . . he was deeply involved in high-priority special operations to send action teams against North Vietnamese installations deep in enemy-held territory. He oversaw all phases of these operations—planning, training, team leadership and motivation, command and control, and post-mission debriefing and analysis. According to his supervisor, he was decisive in his leadership and command functions, and directed his Laotian assets with quiet self-confidence.[10]

★ ★ ★ ★ ★

During the Laotian Civil War, CIA-backed Royalist forces launched multiple offensives from Bouam Long (sometimes spelled Bouamlong or Boaum Lung) in northern Laos, northeast of the Plain of Jars, against communist forces. They included Operation Raindance in March and April of 1969, which included air support from the United States Air Force; *Kou Kiet* (which translates to "Redeem Honor"), or Operation About Face, in September of 1969, backed by air strikes from The Ravens;[11] Operation Counterpunch III, under the leadership of Vang Pao from late November 1970 to early January 1972; and Operation Strength in February and March of 1972, also under Vang Pao, but against advice from the Americans.

There were also counteroperations against Bouam Long by the People's Army of Vietnam, including as part of Campaign 139, a major military offensive between September 1969 and late April 1970, and Campaign 74B in February through April of 1971. Although Campaign 74B officially ended with the withdrawal of a portion of the communist forces, the People's Army of Vietnam continued artillery and mortar attacks on Bouam Long and left three Pathet Lao battalions behind as monitors.[12]

Writing in 2013, John McBeth of *The Straits Times* compared Bouam Long to Long Tieng, which he called the "CIA's secret city":

> Similar sensitivity prevails around LS32, Colonel Cher Pao Moua's former command and the only outpost never to fall, and LS85, where sappers scaled sheer cliffs in March 1968 to overrun a US Air Force radar site directing the air war over North Vietnam. It could simply be lasting paranoia—or it may well be because of unexploded ordnance and scores of minefields that still litter the most heavily bombed piece of real estate in the world.
>
> At LS32, for example, where soldiers made it clear outsiders were unwelcome, dozens of unspent 37mm anti-aircraft rounds lay in the grass beneath one of the series of hills surrounding the now barely recognisable [sic] earthen airstrip.
>
> Better known as Bouam Long, LS32 is 100km south-west of Phou Pha Thi (LS85), a towering 1,750m massif reachable from the west today by a deeply rutted four-wheel-drive track and approachable only along a series of trails.
>
> Foreign trail-bikers received a hostile reception some years ago when they sought to scale the marginally accessible eastern side of the giant limestone slab, which lies just 40km east of the Pathet Lao's old Sam Neua-Vieng Xay cave complex.
>
> Again, that might be because of the mines that guarded the edifice, albeit ineffectively, and the tonnes [sic] of bombs

dropped around it as a crack Vietnamese regiment began its offensive against a target Hanoi couldn't ignore.

Eleven Americans died in the assault, the highest single death toll the US Air Force suffered during the war. The remains of only three of them have been recovered in the years since, the last in July last year.[13]

Shortly after noon on June 2, 1971, an Air America C-46, call letters XW-PFL, took off from its base in the capital city of Vientiane, Laos, headed for LS-32, a strategic Hmong outpost in the vicinity of Bouam Long. Piloted by Captain Herbert W. Clark, the fateful flight into hostile territory was actually XW-PFL's second run of the day, having already dropped supplies earlier that morning in a different drop zone. XW-PFL, which operated pursuant to Contract 439-342 with USAID, had been loaded with food supplies, primarily rice, to drop to Laotians below. Joining Clark on the flight were First Officer Trikit Thuttanon and three air freight dispatchers (AFD), a fancy term for the men who would provide muscle in dispensing the pallets of rice. More commonly called "kickers" because their job was to kick cargo from the plane, their names were Hatsady Khambong, Sousakaly Khmouth, and Oudomvilay Thayanh.

Records from a subsequent Air America accident investigation reflect that each of the AFDs checked out backpack parachutes from the Air America equipment room at Vientiane, while Air America emergency personnel placed two chest-pack parachutes onboard on the left side of the main cabin. Captain Clark checked out three parachute harnesses for use with chest-packs and placed them on board, along with one survival vest. Records show that the plane had been loaded with 10,660 pounds of cargo, including 112 sacks of rice placed on pallets, eighteen sacks to a pallet.

Upon reaching the drop zone, Captain Clark brought the plane beneath the cloud cover at about 1300 hours, or 1:00 p.m., for an initial "observation pass." As the plane swept over the drop zone, the AFDs later reported they heard gunfire from the jungle below, similar in sound to the firing of AK-47s or 12.7s. The latter is a heavy machine gun associated with Warsaw Pact countries, a defense treaty signed in 1955 that included the former Soviet Union and Soviet satellite Eastern European states during the Cold War. AFD Khamouth said he reported the sounds of firing to Captain Clark.

After making an observation pass to scope out the drop zone, and now alerted to groundfire, Clark commenced a second pass, this time to make an actual food drop. The AFDs kicked out one pallet on that pass and, again, reported sounds of firing to Captain Clark. The pattern was repeated uneventfully on a third pass, but the fourth raised the stakes considerably. At least two projectiles of unknown size struck the C-46. One hit the left wing near the engine, which set off an explosion and triggered a fire on the wing. Captain Clark made a left turn to evade the barrage. But, according to the accident investigation report, "On this pass as the aircraft apparently was observed from the ground to be in trouble, the AFDs report that everybody began firing at them." The AFDs continued to kick pallets out the cargo doors, but Captain Clark sounded the bail-out bell. First Officer Thuttanon entered the cargo hold from the cockpit and yelled, "Jump out! Jump out!"[14]

AFD Khambong attempted to exit via the left cargo door but was forced back by flames from the left wing. Instead, he opened the right aft emergency exit and bailed out. The other two AFDs later reported seeing his parachute deploy. They, however, lacked Khambong's confidence in bailing out. "AFDs Khamouth and Thavanh hesitated on bailing out either on basic fear of jumping or of fear of jumping in proximity of hostile forces."[15] Either fear seems legitimate.

After a delay estimated to be one to two minutes, both men finally jumped. Their chutes deployed and they safely reached the ground. AFD Thavanh said that while descending, he saw that the C-46's right wing was also burning. They both reported that the plane continued flying for a short period before disappearing from sight. "Afterward a sound similar to a bombing was heard." The accident report noted that "the aircraft remained airborne for an extremely long time (estimated 4 ½ minutes) with a generalized burning wing fire." AFD Khamouth also reported that, on his last visit to the cockpit before bailing out, Captain Clark was still flying the plane, and neither he nor the first officer showed any signs of injury.[16]

AFDs Khamouth and Thavanh were rescued later after fleeing into the jungle and then setting a small signal fire in a semi-open area, using paper from Thavanh's personal briefcase, which he carried with him when he bailed out. The two men set the paper on fire then used it to burn scraps of their Air America uniforms. That smoke attracted the attention of an Air America captain of an S-58T aircraft, which rescued the two men. AFD Khamong was listed as missing.

The following day, on June 3, an investigative team flew over the crash site in a helicopter and snapped photographs of the wreckage. They made no attempt to land or lower any team members to the plane, for two reasons: a malfunction of the S-58 horse collar and lowering winch and "the probable presence of hostile forces in this, a known hostile territory."[17] The latter seems highly likely, not merely probable, given that weapons fired from the ground in this territory had brought down the plane in the first place.

Reconnaissance photos listed damage seen to the C-46:

> a. Left Wing: Severly [sic] damaged, primarily by an intense fire, located and identified by the patterned walk way on its upper surface.
>
> b. Left Engine: Not located in any of the areas of the localized wreckage, but is reported by the one witness to be in the wreckage area.
>
> c. Empennage [tail section] and Tail Cone: Lying on its left side, tail gear attached, less wheel well doors, broken from the main cabin by the impact, the vertical stabilizer and rudder components burned and melted on its upper portions.
>
> d. Aft Main Cabin: As noted separated from the tail cone, lying on its tail side with the cabin floor generally intact. Severe impact cracking of the upper fuselage and left side as a result of the impact forces. Minor burn damages.
>
> e. Forward Main Cabin: Generally undistinguishable but appears to be the same as aft main cabin with some circumferential cracking.

f. Cockpit: Undistinguishable, but reported by one statement to be a mass of wreckage lying on its left side.[18]

The accident report has an account of possible "human factors" in the downing of the plane but dismissed them as causes. It noted that Captain Clark was a "skilled" C-46 pilot who was known for flying drop patterns "closer than the average pilot." His records reflected "several minor incidents" on delayed flights where he "appeared to loose [sic] his temper at the ground crew." However, that did not appear to be the case on this particular day, given "reports he was happy."[19]

At the time of the reconnaissance flight, the two AFDs had already been rescued. The accident report stated that "[l]ate on 28 June 1971, a report was received at Vientiane, Laos that AFD Khambong (the missing AFD) was on an aircraft returning to LS20A."[20] That left only the pilot and copilot unaccounted for.

★ ★ ★ ★ ★

On June 5, 1971, three days after the downing of Captain Clark's C-46, an oral statement was made to Air America's Jerry Connors, later transcribed to memorandum form and signed by investigator J. D. Anthony. According to the written document, the statement came from "Customer"—no name was given, but that was a generally used reference to the CIA. The statement detailed, albeit briefly, a helicopter trip to the crash site just a few hours after the C-46 was shot down in an attempt to recover survivors or at least the bodies of the pilot and copilot. Flight Watch records show that the C-46 reported first being over the drop zone at 1300 (1:00 p.m.) and was shot down shortly thereafter, while the recovery attempt was made at 1640 hours (4:40 p.m.) that same day. The hostile forces that brought down the C-46 were likely still in the area.

"Customer" stated he was lowered approximately 125 feet by hoist from helicopter H-73. He estimated, visually, that wreckage was strewn over an area of about fifteen meters by thirty-five meters, with some of the sections broken off from the fuselage and still burning. Rice sacks and other metal debris were scattered about.

On first examination of the fuselage, "Customer" discovered the body of the copilot, First Officer Trikit Thuttanon, buried beneath the front part of the fuselage. Digging for about three minutes, he was able to extricate the body. He then scanned the area for evidence of Captain Clark's body but didn't see anything. His search time was limited, though, to a total of approximately ten minutes on the ground "due to lack of fuel [in the helicopter], enemy situation, and lateness of the time of day." It's clear that "Customer" regretted not being able to search more diligently for Captain Clark, whose body was never found.

> Two parachute back packs and one reserve parachute were observed by me at the crash site. I can not state for sure if the pilot was or was not in the aircraft wreckage. It would have taken a four-man team a good thirty minutes to accurately check the crash site. It is my opinion however that the pilot of "PFL"[21] was killed and buried beneath the fuselage of "PFL." Extensive low level VR [visual reconnaissance] by an aircraft at the crash site [the following day] did not reveal any opened parachutes in the area nor was any body observed around the crash site. I called out for survivors the whole ten minutes I was on the ground at the crash site and I received no response.[22]

A note at the bottom of the statement indicates that it is "Certified to be a copy of a verbal statement," and was signed by investigator J. D. Anthony.

The narrator, or Customer, was almost certainly John Kearns. Kenneth Michael Absher's article "John Kearns and Winning the Cold War in Laos," approved for release by the CIA in 2015, describes acts of "personal courage" by Kearns based on classified CIA documents, besides the event that resulted in his death. One of them included "overflying dangerous terrain to support one of his teams in securing a helicopter landing zone for a major troop infiltration behind enemy lines, despite suffering a high fever from malaria." On another occasion,

> . . . in June 1971, Kearns volunteered to try a cable landing from a helicopter to search for the missing crew of a crashed C-46 aircraft. Dense ground foliage had prohibited a ground search. He made it down, but only had ten minutes on the ground due to his helicopter's shortage of fuel. During that time he extracted the copilot's body, inspected the part of the fuselage that could be entered, and called out in vain for survivors.[23]

This description by Absher matches, blow-by-blow, the account of "Customer" in the June 5, 1971, statement. Former CIA director Richard Helms refers to this event in his memoir and credits it to John Kearns. However, he confuses some of the key facts and appears to conflate Captain Clark's death with the death of a CIA paramilitary operator named John Peterson.[24] It makes one wonder about the possibility of other factual inaccuracies in Helms's memoir.

What is not inaccurate, though, was the heroism of John Kearns.

CHAPTER TWENTY-FOUR
A Time to Heal

"Addiction, at its worst, is akin to having Stockholm Syndrome. You're like a hostage who has developed an irrational affection for your captor."

Anne Clendening

It was December 1989 and the *Bermuda Star* was in drydock under the Coronado Bridge in San Diego. The forepeak had been completely removed from the bow of the ship. Hammers, drills, and all sorts of other power tools seemed to be in constant use, all day every day. The landline in my cabin rang, and I answered.

"Paul, this is Thomas Henderson."

Yeah, right! I knew who Thomas Henderson, better known as Hollywood Henderson, was. I primarily remembered him from his days with the Dallas Cowboys from 1975 to 1979. I remembered him dunking a football over the goalpost after returning a kickoff ninety-seven yards against the St. Louis Cardinals during his rookie season. There was also his feud with Pittsburgh Steelers quarterback Terry Bradshaw prior to Super Bowl XIII when Henderson said Bradshaw "couldn't spell cat if you spotted him the C and A."[1] His career continued after the Cowboys, including stints with the San Francisco 49ers, Houston Oilers, and Miami Dolphins. I also knew about his well-publicized battles with drug addiction and his time in prison. And I had personally known him in my days at the Playboy Club in Dallas, where his ex-wife Wyetta was a Bunny. It was far less likely that he would remember me after so many years. And he was highly unlikely to be calling me on a cruise ship in San Diego. I was skeptical, and I said so.

"Tell you what," he said. "I'll give you my number and you can call me back."

I called the number and the same voice answered. Thomas has a distinctive voice that I remembered from those earlier years, and it sure sounded like him. We carried on a brief conversation as I tried to probe for proof. We talked about the Playboy Club, Wyetta (he had been through more than one wife by the time we spoke), and the Cowboys, of course. By now, he had convinced me. He explained that, after they received my letter, my parents had contacted him for help. They knew I had known him in the past and, from articles in newspapers, knew that he had built a reputation helping addicts kick the habit, working for a sober living facility in Arizona called Sierra Tucson. I don't know what they had in mind when they contacted him, or how they were able to track down his contact information in the first place, but they were determined to find help for me.

Thomas told me that, if I wanted to check in, he would let me know when a bed opened at the facility. I wasn't too sure about it, at first. I mean, did I really want to give up this great job, making good money and going to all these cool ports, and trade that in for no money, just a room, with no guarantee of success and no promise of employment? On the other hand, I knew I had to do something.

Thomas didn't put a hard sell on me, but he invited me to visit him at his condo in Costa Mesa, a little over an hour up the road from San Diego, just south of Los Angeles. I figured I didn't have anything to lose. Besides, it would be good to renew an old acquaintance, so I took him up on the offer. After getting permission to take off for a couple of days, I rented a car and drove up the coast. Thomas and I spent an afternoon reminiscing for a while about Dallas, then the talk turned serious. He told me his story of addiction and recovery, and how he had been doing since he turned sober a few years earlier. That pretty much sold me. I left with his promise to get me into Sierra when a bed opened up.

The cruise line transferred me to another ship, which was also in dry dock. It was a little odd to work on cruise ships that didn't cruise. I was pretty good in all facets of the purser's job, from visas and passports to handling the money (if you overlook that little glitch that once got me fired), so I became, in effect, a one-man purser's office. That worked quite well in dry dock, and it allowed the other pursers to take much-needed vacations.

Paul Heckmann and Thomas "Hollywood" Henderson at Costa Mesa, California. *Photo courtesy of Paul Heckmann.*

Then one day I got a call from Sierra Tucson. A bed had opened up and they could admit me for a thirty-day stay. It was short notice, and it took a couple of days to make sure my job duties were caught up and a replacement arranged. I didn't want to leave the ship in a lurch. When the first purser returned, he took over my job. I packed a few things and headed out to Arizona, unsure what to expect when I got there. Little did I know my cruising days had come to an end.

I had about an eighth of an ounce of cocaine with me on the flight to Tucson, and I decided this might be my last time, so why not go out swinging? Periodic trips to the restroom and I managed to snort it all on the flight. By the time I arrived in Tucson, I was pretty much wired out of my gourd. The date was January 30, 1990, which I now consider my "birthday" because it marked the first day of a new life. But I first had to bury the old life. The folks at Sierra knew I was high when I got there—my guess is that I wasn't the first resident to show up high—so they put me in their hospital to let all the drugs get out of my system. That took about three days. Then came the rehab.

Sierra Tucson is still in operation today. Its website calls it the "Premier Residential Treatment Center for Drug & Alcohol Addiction & Behavioral Health." Its mission statement is "to provide a safe place for emotional, physical, and spiritual healing with a collaborative community of professionals who provide insight, understanding, and empowerment enhanced by a lifetime of alumni support."[2]

The facility was nice, but it was a far cry from a resort. Rooms were spartan, at best. Showers didn't have doors. I guess they were worried about what might go on in seclusion and wanted as much openness as possible. It also seemed that Sierra Tucson was the place of choice for many celebrities. One website lists the following who have rehabbed there over the years: Nicole Richie, Whitney Houston, Ringo Starr, Rob Lowe, Michael Douglas, and Rush Limbaugh.[3] Add Paul Heckmann to that list.

I brushed shoulders with the famous right off the bat. My first roommate was Malcolm John Rebennack Jr. That name might not mean much to you, nor did it to me at first. But consider his stage name and the recognition sets in: Dr. John, the New Orleans–born and –influenced singer, songwriter, and pianist, who played and sang everything from blues to jazz to R&B to funk. His biggest hit was probably "Right Place Wrong Time," with its classic title and lyrics that, in some respects, bespoke my life. Or maybe wrong place, wrong time. We overlapped for only a couple of days and then I got a new roommate who worked crew on Hollywood film sets, which gave us some things in common to talk about. He was also the father of a well-known actor. Since his son is still working in the film industry, I am not going to name names.

Almost immediately, the counselors made me wear a sign that said, "Ladies, don't talk to him except in class." Literally. The counselor put a placard around my neck with those words on it. I guess he thought I was talking up the women, as if trying to put a move on them. I didn't see it that way. I had been shy my whole life, although drugs and drink can remove those inhibitions. But here, I was straight, so that wasn't the problem. Besides, I felt like it was the other way around. The women were talking me up, and I was just being friendly. After all, my prior jobs involved being nice to customers and passengers.

One of the things that struck me about the counseling was a warning against "people, places and things" from your old life. I never considered that a problem or that I needed to be warned about it, but they explained how familiar things can trigger addiction urges. For example, if you see a razor blade, you might think of using it to cut lines of coke. If you pass a park where you used to buy drugs, it can trigger the memory. If you pass a liquor store, it might be where you used to buy gin and create an urge to enter.

Therapy and group sessions were pretty much all talk. I don't mean that in a negative way. It was just that we needed to talk stuff out. The idea was to find solutions. Everyone in the sessions was invited to discuss and help advise, not just the counselors. It was amazing how much I learned about myself and my weaknesses just by talking. I began to hear things like, "You shouldn't go back to the cruise ships." Actually, I heard that one quite a lot. It started to sink (no pun intended) in on me that, regardless of how much I had enjoyed cruising, my near-decade of working on cruise ships was over. At least if I really wanted to stay sober. I told the cruise line that I would not be coming back, so to please pack up all the stuff in my locker and send it to me.

After thirty days, I committed to going to a halfway facility, Prescott House in Prescott, Arizona. On its current website, Prescott House touts itself as "a beacon of hope for men facing addiction and behavioral health challenges" and states that, since it was established in 1988, it has "earned a reputation for success by offering individuals a positive environment and the time needed to heal."[4]

There were absolutely stunning landscapes around Prescott, but there were not a lot of part-time jobs available there. That might not ordinarily present a problem except we were required to do some kind of paying work, or at least to apply for work. That was usually a dead end from the start, even if work was available, because no one wanted to hire someone who was already planning to leave in ninety days. Then I had an idea. I had noticed some things at the facility that needed repairs, and I convinced the owners that they needed my help fixing them. I must have been pretty convincing because they put me right to work. It was hard work, but it was great work. It humbled me after a decade of being

"The Man" on cruise ships. I never anticipated it at the start, but I actually enjoyed my time there. I even enjoyed the manual labor.

While I was at Prescott, my grandmother on my dad's side passed away. She and I had a special bond, and I desperately wanted to go to her funeral. After I spoke with my family, though, we all agreed it was best that I finish my three months uninterrupted.

As I neared the end of my stay, it dawned on me that I had no idea what was next in my life. Maybe I could trace my drug problems back to high school, drinking and smoking pot, with an acid trip or two thrown in, but it had been the nightclubs, with free-flowing cocaine, that opened a dark door for me. Clubs were out. Cruising also seemed out of the question. Drugs were way too accessible there, particularly in some of those exotic ports-of-call. I hadn't been able to make a full-time living in Dallas as an actor or model, so that was out. What was I going to do? I didn't even have a place to stay.

I made some calls and found out one of my old drinking and drugging buddies, "Warren," had gone straight while I was on the high seas. I guess he had seen the light long before I did. He lived in a house in Richardson, a suburb just north of Dallas, with his girlfriend and a roommate, but they were looking for another. So I moved to Richardson! With no job in sight! But at least I had a place to stay. I also had a chance to further my sobriety, which I was determined to do.

I regularly met Warren for noon meetings at the Central Alcoholics Anonymous group and attended Narcotics Anonymous meetings as well. I told the AA group that I was new and they provided me with great support. I got my six-month sobriety chip there. One young guy—must have been in his mid-thirties—came over to congratulate me after a meeting. We sat and talked for a while. He looked vaguely familiar, but I had no idea who he was. He had long, stringy hair and wore a lot of turquoise jewelry, which seemed out of place, but he was very knowledgeable about the program. He told me that he had made an AA video for the group. I thought that was nice and even a bit innovative, though I never got a chance to see it.

Warren had waited on me while I talked with this guy. As he and I walked to our cars afterward, he asked, "What did you and Stevie Ray talk about?" And it clicked. I had been talking to Stevie Ray Vaughan, sans his trademark flat-brimmed hat. Without the pervasiveness of the Internet in those days, face recognition, particularly of musicians, was pretty much based on whether you recognized them either from a concert or from an album cover. Stevie Ray was one of those Dallas ISD high schoolers who made it big. He attended Kimball High School, although he didn't graduate. Instead, he dropped out and moved to Austin to pursue his music. He was already, at thirty-five, one of the best and most influential blues guitarists of all time. But like me, he struggled with drug and alcohol addiction. Once I realized who he was, I raced back inside to get his autograph, but he was already gone.

Just a few months later, on August 27, 1990, he and four others, including three from Eric Clapton's entourage, were killed in a helicopter crash in Wisconsin. I will always remember that sit-down that we had following an AA meeting and Stevie Ray's kindness to me.

CHAPTER TWENTY-FIVE
The Papers: Publish or Perish

"The history of things that didn't happen has never been written."

Henry Kissinger

Less than two weeks after John Kearns descended to a crashed C-46 in hostile territory in Bouam Long, Laos, to search for the bodies of crewmembers, President Richard Nixon's daughter Tricia married Edward F. Cox in a ceremony in the White House Rose Garden. The next day, on June 13, 1971, *The New York Times* published the first in a series of what would become known as the Pentagon Papers ("Papers"). An initial excerpt of the Papers was also published five days later by *The Washington Post*, followed by *The Boston Globe* on June 22. Because the Vietnam War was still raging, publication of the Papers created a firestorm of controversy from Main Street to the Oval Office. It didn't stop even when the issue of whether the government could prevent publication of the Papers reached the United States Supreme Court.

After the Supreme Court ruled that the government was powerless to stop further publication, the man who leaked the Papers to the media in the first place, Daniel Ellsberg, was indicted for alleged violations of the Espionage Act of 1917, as well as for theft and conspiracy. President Nixon, in an act that would come back to haunt him during the Watergate scandal, authorized the creation of a team to investigate the leak. That team burglarized Ellsberg's psychiatrist's office in search of dirt to discredit the patient, and the charges against Ellsberg were ultimately dismissed because of prosecutorial misconduct.

The controversy hasn't fully abated today.

So how did the Papers come into being in the first place, and how did they end up in the hands of prominent newspapers? Moreover, how did they relate to the "secret war" in Laos and, ultimately, to the death of John Kearns?

In June of 1967, LBJ's Secretary of Defense Robert McNamara commissioned a top-secret study of US involvement and decision-making in Indochina, including the reasons for going to war in the first place and maintaining an ongoing military presence in Vietnam. The study resulted in about three thousand pages of narrative and more than four thousand pages of appended documents, spanning forty-seven volumes.

In his memoir, McNamara attributed the inception of the project to altruism. He wanted some kind of record to be left for historians, he said, and as a cautionary guide for future administrations.

Secretary of Defense Robert McNamara. Photo by Yoichi R. Okamoto, White House Press Office. *Public domain.*

> By now it was clear to me that our policies and programs in Indochina had evolved in ways we had neither anticipated nor intended, and that the costs—human, political, social, and economic—had grown far greater than anyone had imagined. We had failed. Why this failure? Could it have

been prevented? What lessons could be drawn from our experiences that would enable others to avoid similar failures? The thought that scholars would surely wish to explore these questions once the war had ended was increasingly on my mind.

Honesty and completeness were the watchwords. Or at least so he said. He claimed he told his assistant secretary John McNaughton to "cast his net wide," gathering relevant documents from not only the Defense Department but other departments as well. "'Tell your researchers not to hold back . . . . Let the chips fall where they may.'"[1] One suspects that McNamara never expected the chips to end up on the front pages of the nation's leading newspapers.

McNamara designated Leslie Gelb, Director of Policy Planning and Arms Control for International Security Affairs at the Department of Defense, to head the study and charged him with putting together a team of researchers and analysts. The number of people on the team is unclear—Gelb later said he had a team of six while other sources, including McNamara, said it was as many as thirty-six.[2] The latter number may be attributable to the fact that, according to *The New York Times*, "The majority of the approximately 36 authors who wrote the narrative-analysis sections of the Pentagon papers were career military and civilian officials who were promised anonymity," and so "only a relatively small number of authors' names have so far emerged."[3]

Names that did emerge, in addition to Gelb's, included Colonel Paul F. Gorman, who later commanded a brigade of the 101st Airborne Division in Vietnam; Richard Moorstein, who was a staff member at the Pentagon's Office of International Security

Affairs; Richard Holbrooke, assistant to Under Secretary of State Nicholas Katzenbach; Melvin Gurtov, of the think tank RAND Corporation; and Daniel Ellsberg, a former RAND member who had served as assistant for pacification to the deputy United States ambassador in Saigon in 1966 and 1967. In hindsight, McNamara may have regretted that last name. His sole reference to Ellsberg in his memoir states, "the effort to assist scholars was also a lesson in unintended consequences" due to Ellsberg's leak that resulted in "intense embarrassment of officials from both the Johnson and Nixon administrations."[4]

Gelb later disputed the purity of McNamara's motive, which he asserted was an after-the-fact invention by McNamara to justify authorizing something that caused so much governmental embarrassment. In a segment of *On the Media*, Brooke Gladstone interviewed Gelb, who said that "almost everybody in the government felt that the war was not going well but a number felt there were ways to fight it better." The study originated with a list of one hundred questions presented to him by McNamara.

> Eight of the hundred questions were historical. I was given six people to work on these questions and we were given two months to get 'em done. I collected the people. By the way, we were told not to tell anybody about this. We stared at the questions and we all started laughing. They said, well, why are we doing this? This is the kind of stuff we send up to the press secretary when we're preparing him to answer questions, and we're not going to be able to add anything to what we're doing on a daily basis.[5]

Gelb's team assembled a collection of documents and what

he called "monographs," which he sent to McNamara, who approved them. Although Gelb acknowledged that McNamara told him to "let it be encyclopedic," his team was prohibited at the time from telling even such persons as CIA Director Richard Helms, Secretary of State Dean Rusk, National Security Advisor Walt Rostow, or even the president. "The notion that this was a definitive history is just plain wrong," Gelb said. "I think that's an explanation that Bob McNamara came up with after the fact. And he told some people that he was doing this to save future leaders from making the same mistakes and he told others, who didn't like it, for example, he told Dean Rusk that he never asked for these studies, he just wanted a collection of documents."[6]

Gelb noted that very few people who wrote about the Papers had ever read them, and even McNamara, when presented with boxes of documents, took one of the monographs, "flipped through it like you flip through a deck of cards, with his thumb, and he threw it back into the box and he said, and I quote, 'Take them back to the Pentagon.'" When asked if he thought McNamara ever read them, Gelb said, "I have no idea. I spoke to him many times over the years and I never asked him and he never said."[7]

Daniel Ellsberg speaking at a press conference in New York, 1972. Photo by Gotfryd Bernard. *Public domain.*

Daniel Ellsberg, one of the Papers' authors, is either the hero or the villain in the narrative, depending upon whom you ask. It was he who leaked the report to Neil Sheehan of *The New York Times*, and publication, along with public dissemination, followed. Ellsberg had an interesting background that, while certainly qualifying him to be involved in the creation of the Papers, also likely informed his decision to leak them. A graduate of Harvard University in 1952, with a B.A. in economics, he next studied at King's College in Cambridge for a year, earning credits toward a Ph.D. before returning to Harvard. Without completing his doctorate, he enlisted in the US Marine Corps, where he earned a commission and was discharged in 1957 as a first lieutenant. He returned to Harvard for two years before going to work at RAND Corporation, a nonprofit think tank, where he concentrated on nuclear strategy while completing his Ph.D. at Harvard.

Following his studies at Harvard, Ellsberg worked in the Pentagon for Secretary of Defense McNamara and as special assistant to Assistant Secretary of Defense for International Security Affairs John McNaughton. He also spent two years back in Vietnam as a member of the State Department. Beginning in 1964, he worked for General Edward Lansdale, who had been an air force officer before retiring in 1963 and joining the CIA. After Ellsberg's second homecoming from Vietnam, he returned to RAND.

Despite being part of McNamara's team putting together the Papers, Ellsberg, like many other Americans, had become disaffected with the Vietnam War. Sanford J. Ungar, a reporter for *The Washington Post*, wrote that Ellsberg said, "his intense exposure to the Pentagon Papers was the final step in his turning completely against the war." According to Ungar, Ellsberg "wanted to have a personal hand in helping to end the war, and—unrealistic as the notion may have been—he thought that disclosure of the Pentagon Papers would have that effect."[8]

In 1969, Ellsberg secretly made copies of the Papers as part of a plan to make them public. He urged US Senators J. William

Fulbright and George McGovern to release the Papers on the Senate floor. Ellsberg believed this could be done without jeopardy, at least as far as the senators were concerned, because of the speech and debate clause, found in Article I Section 6 of the United States Constitution,[9] which effectively immunized senators and representatives from their activities on the respective floors of Congress.[10]

When the two senators declined, Ellsberg provided copies of the Papers to both *The New York Times* and *The Washington Post*, which began publishing the Papers as a series. White House Chief of Staff Alexander Haig reported the leak to Nixon the first day of publication by the *Times*, referring to it as this "goddamned *New York Times* exposé of the most highly classified documents of the war." Calling it a "devastating security breach of the greatest magnitude of anything I've ever seen," Haig described it as "a tough attack on Kennedy. It shows that the genesis of the war really occurred during '61." He added that "it's brutal on President Johnson," but Nixon homed in on the real issue.

NIXON: But also massive against the war?

HAIG: Against the war.[11]

Nixon managed, at least initially, to look on the bright side—the political side. This was not an indictment of his administration but rather that of prior, Democratic administrations. In a phone conversation with Secretary of State Henry Kissinger, Nixon sought confirmation of what Haig had told him, that it "all relates to the two previous administrations, is that correct?" Kissinger responded, "That is right . . . . In public opinion, it actually, if anything, will help us a little bit, because this is a gold mine of showing how the previous administration got us in there." In response to a laughing Nixon, Kissinger added, "What this proves is that, if it's anybody's war, it's Kennedy's and Johnson's."[12]

But Leslie Gelb believed that there was a bigger issue than simply which administration was most at fault. "Ellsberg created the myth that what the Papers show is that it all was a bunch of lies. But the truth is people actually believed in the war and were ignorant about what could and could not actually be done to do well in that war. That's what you see when you actually read the Papers, as opposed to talk about the Papers."[13]

Nixon's Chief of Staff, H. R. Haldeman, wasn't nearly so sanguine as Haig and Kissinger. In an Oval Office discussion on June 14, he pointed out that the Papers could still reflect poorly on the office of the president, regardless of its particular occupant at the time.

> [Secretary of Defense] Rumsfeld was making this point this morning. . . . To the ordinary guy, all this is a bunch of gobbledygook. But out of the gobbledygook comes a very clear thing . . . . You can't trust the government; you can't believe what they say and you can't rely on their judgment; and the—the implicit infallibility of presidents, which has been an accepted thing in America is badly hurt by this, because it shows that people do things the president wants to do even though it's wrong, and the president can be wrong.[14]

That same day, Attorney General John N. Mitchell convinced Nixon to proceed with legal action lest the government waive any rights. If the government failed to act, he said, "we will look a little foolish in not following through on our, uh, legal obligations." And Nixon already had a perfect target: the hated *New York Times*. "Well look, look, as far as the *Times* is concerned, hell, they're our enemies—I think we just ought to do it."[15] So the government sued both the *Times* and the *Post* for injunctions to prevent both papers from publishing any more of what were already being publicly called the "Pentagon Papers."

On further reflection, Nixon began to worry that Ellsberg might have other documents that showed his duplicity, such as whether he lied about bombing in Cambodia. Notwithstanding Ellsberg's personal role in putting the Papers together, the paranoid Nixon believed Ellsberg had inside help, and he wanted to ferret those others out. Nixon also wanted to, in effect, blackmail Ellsberg into silence, so he took a step that would ultimately help to fuel his own downfall: he authorized creation of the White House Special Investigations Unit—the "Plumbers"—to investigate leaks to the media. The result of that unit's work, which included the burglary of Ellsberg's psychiatrist's office in search of blackmail material on Ellsberg, can be better studied in Watergate history.

The trial court in the *New York Times* case denied an injunction, but the Second Circuit Court of Appeals disagreed, at least for the moment, and entered an injunction that would expire June 25. In the *Washington Post* case, both the trial court and the Court of Appeals for the D.C. Circuit denied injunctions, although the D.C. Circuit stayed the matter until it could be heard by the Supreme Court.

The government took the position in the litigations that releasing the Papers endangered national security—that the United States was attempting to enter into peace talks and that the information contained in the Papers merely emboldened the enemy. The lower courts, though, believed that it was more a matter of embarrassment than anything, which wasn't enough to impose a prior restraint. In denying an injunction in the *New York Times* case, the federal court for the Southern District of New York said,

> This Court does not doubt the right of the Government to injunctive relief against a newspaper that is about to publish information or documents absolutely vital to current national security. But it does not find that to be the case here . . . . It is true that the Court has not been able to read through the many volumes of documents on the history of Vietnam, but it did give the Government an opportunity to pinpoint what it believed to be vital breaches of our national security of sufficient impact to controvert the right of a free press. Without revealing the content of the testimony, suffice it to say that no cogent reasons were advanced as to why these documents except in the general framework of embarrassment previously mentioned, would vitally affect the security of the Nation.[16]

The court went on to say,

> If there be some embarrassment to the Government in security aspects as remote as the general embarrassment that flows from any security breach, we must learn to live with it. The security of the Nation is not at the ramparts alone. Security also lies in the value of our free institutions. A cantankerous press, an obstinate press, a ubiquitous press must be suffered by those in authority in order to preserve the even greater values of freedom of expression and the right of the people to know.[17]

The cases were consolidated for a final appeal to the US Supreme Court. On the eve of resolution in the high court, another effort to make the Papers public was playing out. Ben

Bagdikian, the editor at *The Washington Post* to whom Ellsberg had given the Papers, passed along a copy to Alaska Senator Mike Gravel. Gravel snuck them into his Senate office in suitcases, then enlisted his congressional staff to aid in analyzing the Papers. On the evening of June 29, prior to the high court's ruling the next day on the *Times* and *Post* cases, Gravel attempted to read the Papers into the Congressional Record, only to be thwarted by the lack of a quorum, which prevented the Senate from convening a session. After failing to call a full meeting of the Senate, Gravel used his role as chairman of the Senate Subcommittee on Public Buildings and Grounds to call a subcommittee meeting. He then read a portion of the Papers before entering the entire set into the record.

On June 30, 1971, the Supreme Court issued its ruling in *New York Times Co. v. United States*.[18] Relying upon a prior decision in *Near v. Minnesota*,[19] the Supreme Court held the injunction halting publication represented a classic prior restraint and that the government was trying, unsuccessfully, to take advantage of the national security loophole from the *Near* case. Although the government argued that release of the Papers constituted a threat to national security, the Court, by a vote of 6-3, didn't buy its argument. The brief, unsigned opinion read,

> Any system of prior restraints of expression comes to this Court bearing a heavy presumption against its constitutional validity. . . . The Government "thus carries a heavy burden of showing justification for the imposition of such a restraint." . . . . The District Court for the Southern District of New York, in the New York Times case, and the District Court for the District of Columbia and the Court of Appeals for the District of Columbia Circuit, in the Washington Post case,

held that the Government had not met that burden. We agree.[20] [citations omitted]

Justice Hugo Black minced no words in rejecting the government's argument in his concurring opinion. "The injunction against *The New York Times* should have been vacated without oral argument when the cases were first presented. . . . [E]very moment's continuance of the injunctions against these newspapers amounts to a flagrant, indefensible, and continuing violation of the First Amendment." This wasn't about national security, Black said; the government simply was embarrassed about history and its deception of the American people. One of the purposes of a free press, he wrote, was to expose precisely this kind of thing.

> Only a free and unrestrained press can effectively expose deception in government. And paramount among the responsibilities of a free press is the duty to prevent any part of the Government from deceiving the people and sending them off to distant lands to die of foreign fevers and foreign shot and shell. In my view, far from deserving condemnation for their courageous reporting, *The New York Times, The Washington Post* and other newspapers should be commended for serving the purpose that the Founding Fathers saw so clearly. In revealing the workings of the government that led to the Vietnam war, the newspapers nobly did precisely that which the founders hoped and trusted they would do.[21]

Following the decision, Alaska Senator Gravel arranged for the Papers to be published by Beacon Press, a left-wing nonprofit publisher associated with the Unitarian Universalist Association, a liberal religious group. In addition to publishing the Papers, Beacon had also served as publisher for such notables as James Baldwin (*Notes of a Native Son* in 1955), Martin Luther King Jr. (*Where Do We Go From Here: Chaos or Community?* in 1967), and Viktor E. Frankl (*Man's Search for Meaning* in 1959; this was the English translation of *Ein Psychologe erlebt das Konzentrationslager*, first published in Austria in 1946). Publication of the Papers by Beacon in October of 1971, however, was nearly its downfall. Reverend Robert West, then president of the Unitarian Universalist Association, said that publishing the Papers "led to two and a half years of harassment and legal difficulties."[22]

An issue was raised regarding an aide to Gravel, Leonard Rodberg, who sought to quash a subpoena requiring him to testify about his role in arranging for publication of the Papers by Beacon.[23] In a 5-4 ruling, the Supreme Court found that, although the clause extended protection to aides, it was "confined to those services that would be immune legislative conduct if performed by the Senator himself. This view places beyond the Speech and Debate Clause a variety of services characteristically performed by aides for Members of Congress, even though within the scope of their employment." Furthermore, it said that the Clause does not "immunize Senator or aide from testifying at trials or grand jury proceedings involving third-party crimes where the questions do not require testimony about or impugn a legislative act."[24]

Furthermore, the Clause did not extend the privilege to a publisher. "[P]rivate publication by Senator Gravel through the cooperation of Beacon Press was in no way essential to the deliberations of the Senate, nor does questioning as to private publication threaten the integrity or independence of the Senate by impermissibly exposing its deliberations to executive influence."[25]

As it turned out, the Papers caused enough embarrassment to spread around. Not only, as Haig and Nixon had discussed, for the Kennedy and Johnson administrations, which had escalated the Vietnam War in the first place, but also for Richard Nixon and his own administration. In addition to embarrassment, the Papers threatened to confirm one of the worst-kept secrets the government had been hiding—the action in Laos, which would ensnare John Kearns and lead to his death—and also threatened to expose just exactly how long that secret had been going on. It was one thing to learn a secret; it was another entirely to learn how long you had been deceived.

There had been snippets of information about Laos made public over the years, ranging from the October 1969 articles in *Time* magazine, *U.S. News & World Report*, and *The New York Times* to Senator Stuart Symington's "surprise, shock and anger" in 1970 at his "recent discovery" of CIA activity in Laos. Two months prior to the first of the Papers series in *The New York Times*, Ellsberg wrote an article that not only addressed the secret war in Laos but also implicated Nixon in an escalation of activities in Laos (notwithstanding Nixon's apparent later glee that the real victims of the Papers were Kennedy and Johnson). Nixon seemed determined, Ellsberg wrote, to create "many Vietnams" in Southeast Asia, including one in Laos. A new offensive in Laos "linked the past, present, and future of a fundamentally unchanging US strategy in Indochina."[26] In other words, Nixon was not innocent in Laos and, by extension, in Vietnam.

To Ellsberg, the fact that on February 9, 1971, US bombers were for the first time accompanying South Vietnamese forces into Laos marked a widening of the war, despite protestations of Secretary of Defense Melvin Laird. "We have not widened the war," Laird said. "To the contrary, we have shortened it." Ellsberg argued that expanded bombing in Laos and bombing raids into North Vietnam represented a dismantling of "Johnson's 'understanding' which had strictly limited the justification for such raids." As for Laos in particular, he wrote, "By expanding the war, the US commanders are multiplying their risks and committing themselves to protracted war in three countries, for only limited gains." But, as Nixon saw in Cambodia, "the war can be reduced in visibility while expanding geographically, so long as US ground units are not involved."[27]

The Papers were the crowning blow to the secret and Nixon's role in it. One analysis concluded, "It was not until the publication of the Pentagon Papers in 1971 (thank you Daniel Ellsberg!) that the U.S. public was made aware of the extent of U.S. atrocities [in Laos], and not until two years later that the campaign formally ended."[28]

The Papers contained considerable discussion of Laos and the covert, and overt, activities there, going back to the first half of the 1960s. In fact, the gradual uptick of the secret war in Laos can be traced throughout the '60s by the progression of documents released in the Papers. On January 19, 1961, Robert McNamara, incoming Secretary of Defense for incoming President John F. Kennedy, met with outgoing President Eisenhower and some of his cabinet members, as well as some of Kennedy's other incoming cabinet members, to discuss Indochina. According to McNamara, "Eisenhower's focus in that part of the discussion was actually on Laos, not Vietnam."[29] According to transition advisor Clark Clifford, "Laos is the present key to the entire area of South East Asia. If Laos were lost to the Communists, it would bring an unbelievable pressure to bear on Thailand, Cambodia and South Vietnam."[30]

In a memorandum to LBJ dated December 21, 1963, McNamara described the continued infiltration of men and equipment into South Vietnam from the North, via Laos and Cambodia, the Mekong River, and possibly from the sea. To counter that, he reviewed proposed plans including "cross-border operations into Laos." However, he conceded that "these would not be politically acceptable or even militarily effective." Hence, the need for secrecy.

Another segment of the covert war discussed in the Papers was surveillance operations, including in Laos, "manned by pilots of Air America (a pseudo-private airline run by the C.I.A.)." That focus on surveillance would soon turn to bombing of the Ho Chi Minh Trail. The December 21, 1963, memo from McNamara to LBJ described the infiltration problem, and first steps for solution, this way:

> Infiltration of men and equipment from North Vietnam continues using (a) land corridors through Laos and Cambodia; (b) the Mekong River waterways from Cambodia; (c) some possible entry from the sea and the tip of the Delta. The best guess is that 1000-1500 Viet Cong cadres entered South Vietnam from Laos in the first nine months of 1963. The Mekong route (and also the possible sea entry) is apparently used for heavier weapons and ammunition and raw materials which have been turning up in increasing numbers in the south and of which we have captured a few shipments.
>
> To counter this infiltration, we reviewed in Saigon various plans providing for cross-border operations into Laos. On the scale proposed, I am quite clear that these would not be politically

> acceptable or even militarily effective. Our first need would be immediate U-2 mapping of the whole Laos and Cambodian border, and this we are preparing on an urgent basis.
>
> One other step we can take is to expand the existing limited but remarkably effective operations on the Laos side, the so-called Operation Hardnose, so that it at least provides reasonable intelligence on movements all the way along the Laos corridor; plans to expand this will be prepared and presented for approval in about two weeks.[31]

Operation Hardnose was a CIA espionage operation on the Ho Chi Minh Trail that began in the summer of 1963 during the Laotian Civil War. The operation had been approved by John F. Kennedy and was commanded by General William Westmoreland, Secretary of Defense Robert McNamara, and CIA case agent Mike Deuel. Deuel was later killed when the Air America Sikorsky H-34 helicopter in which he was riding lost its engine and crashed in October of 1965. He was awarded the CIA's Intelligence Star.

In a memo to McNamara on January 22, 1964, Maxwell Taylor, Chairman of the Joint Chiefs, said that "the United States must be prepared to put aside many of the self-imposed restrictions which now limit our efforts, and to undertake bolder actions which may embody greater risks." He warned that Laos existed "on a most fragile foundation," and would likely not be able to stand up to a communist nation to its east. Thailand, he warned, would be the next to fall, likely followed by Cambodia. Taylor suggested that the Joint Chiefs consider overflights of Laos and Cambodia "to whatever extent is necessary for acquisition of operational intelligence" and that they should "[i]nduce the Government of

Vietnam to conduct overt ground operations in Laos of sufficient scope to impede the flow of personnel and material southward."[32]

Neil Sheehan, who composed narrative for the Papers in *The New York Times*, noted that throughout 1964, the United States conducted air operations in Laos as a "second major segment" of the "covert war" against North Vietnam, gradually stepping them up over the spring and summer.[33]

> A force of propeller driven T-28 fighter-bombers, varying from about 25 to 40 aircraft, had been organized there. The planes bore Laotian Air Force markings, but only some belonged to that air force. The rest were manned by pilots of Air America (a pseudo-private airline run by the C.I.A.) and by Thai pilots under the control of Ambassador Leonard Unger.[34]

Sheehan said the Papers disclosed that for six months prior to the Tonkin Gulf Incident in August of 1964, the US military had engaged in "clandestine" attacks against North Vietnam. The Papers indicated that covert operations began on February 1, 1964, and by August, Thai pilots flying the aforementioned American T-28 fighter planes were strafing North Vietnamese villages near the border with Laos.[35]

In a memorandum dated March 16, 1964, Secretary McNamara recommended to the president that he "authorize continued high-level U.S. overflights of South Vietnam's borders and to authorize 'hot pursuit' and South Vietnamese ground operations over the Laotian line for the purpose of border control." He cautioned that "more ambitious operations . . . involving units beyond battalion size" should only be conducted after first obtaining the approval of Laotian Prime Minister Souvanna Phouma.[36]

A March 17 National Security Action Memorandum recited US policy to "prepare immediately to be in a position on 72 hours' notice to initiate the full range of Laotian and 'Cambodian Border Control actions' . . . and the 'Retaliatory Actions' against North Vietnam." By August, the month of the Tonkin Gulf Incident, William Bundy, Assistant Secretary of State for East Asian and Pacific Affairs under LBJ, was advocating "action against infiltration routes and facilities." In November, an outline was prepared for Bundy, apparently by Deputy Assistant Secretary Marshall Green.[37] Part VIII of the outline was titled "Immediate Actions in the Period Prior to Decision," and stated that the "working group is agreed that our aim should be to maintain present signal strength and level of harassment, showing no signs of lessening of determination, but also avoiding actions that would tend to prejudge the basic decision." The outline advocated overt actions in Laos, such as building an inventory of "40 T-28 aircraft for which a pilot capability, including Thai, is present in Laos," "[g]eneral harassing activities against Pathet Lao military installations and movement," "[t]actical support missions for Operation Anniversary Victory No. 2 (Saleumsay), the FAR[38]-Meo clearing operation up Route 4," and "[t]actical support for Operation Victorious Arrow (Sone Sai), a FAR clearing operations [sic] in southern Laos."[39]

Plans were not only made for overt actions, but also for covert actions. One section of the outline unambiguously outlines

> F. COVERT OPERATIONS IN LAOS
>
> Consideration is being given to improving Hardnose (including greater Thai involvement) and getting Hardnose to operate more effectively in the corridor infiltration areas.[40]

According to narrative in the Papers, the documents refer to "an elaborate program of covert military operations against the state of North Vietnam" under the code name Operation Plan 34A. Plan 34A began on February 1, 1964, and involved commando raids and inserting agents to act as spies and to spread disinformation and anticommunist propaganda.[41] According to the Military Assistance Command, Vietnam-Studies and Observation Group (MACV-SOG) website, "The organization propose [sic] under OPLAN 34A was the conduct of covert operations that would convince Hanoi that its support and direction of conflict in the South and its violation of Laotian neutrality needs to be reexamined and halted."[42]

Plan 34A's execution was predated by Secretary McNamara's December 21, 1963, memo, which referenced plans drawn for it by the CIA as an "excellent job." LBJ ordered the plan into effect on McNamara's recommendation and the CIA's hope that placing "progressively escalating pressure" might "eventually force the Vietcong guerrillas in Vietnam and the Pathet Lao in Laos to halt their insurrections."[43]

The Papers were replete with discussion of the "secret war," and the secret was spilled across the country by the *Times* and the *Post*. The government may have been following the philosophy once espoused by novelist Margaret Atwood: "The best way of keeping a secret is to pretend there isn't one." But, as Benjamin Franklin wrote in *Poor Richard's Almanack* [sic], "Three may keep a secret, if two of them are dead."[44]

Though Leslie Gelb believed the Papers could have provided a cautionary tale, whether that was McNamara's true intention or not, they failed to do so. Years later, when asked how he felt when he first learned that the Papers were about to be published by *The New York Times*, Gelb said,

> . . . my first instinct was that if they just hit the papers, people would think this was the definitive history of the war, which they were not, and that people would think, would think it was all about lying, rather than beliefs. And look, because we'd never learned that darn lesson about believing our way into these wars, we went into Afghanistan and we went into Iraq. . . . You know, we get involved in these wars and we don't know a damn thing about those countries, the culture, the history, the politics, people on top and even down below. And, my heavens, these are not wars like World War II and World War I, where you have battalions fighting battalions. These are wars that depend on knowledge of who the people are, what the culture is like. And we jumped into them without knowing.[45]

Gelb's primary takeaway from the Papers? "[W]hile the Papers show some lies, the main message is that our leaders, from Truman onwards, didn't know hardly anything about Vietnam and Indochina. They were ignorant. And it also shows that the foreign policy community believed that if we lost Vietnam the rest of Asia would fall. And that was kind of a given."[46]

Daniel Ellsberg had hoped publication of the Pentagon Papers in June of 1971would help quickly end the Vietnam War.[47] In that respect, it was a failure. If it had succeeded, subsequent history would have been different. For example, there might not have been a Watergate break-in with a subsequent scandal that brought down a president. And history certainly would have been different for John Kearns. Slightly more than eighteen months after the first installment of the Papers was published by *The New York Times*, he lay mortally wounded on the floor of a helicopter in Laos.

CHAPTER TWENTY-SIX
Broken

Humpty Dumpty had a great fall. All the king's horses and all the king's men couldn't put Humpty together again.

Origins obscure

In the 1990s, I spent time in the corporate world, drawing on my experience from the cruise industry. For a while, I was head of marketing for a company called Hotel Express, but I got laid off after a couple of years. I next took a job in the film and television world in Dallas again, this time calling on my prior experience in that industry. Linda McAlister, who ran her own talent agency, represented me, and I got a few jobs, though not enough to earn a full-time living. My roles included playing President Theodore Roosevelt in a live performance at the Morton Myerson Symphony Center in Dallas. With my addictive nature, but no longer drinking, food became my indulgence. I was so fat, they barely needed to add any padding—although they did, anyway—to make me fit the image of the overweight Roosevelt. That's not exactly something I wanted to put on my resume.

Because acting wasn't a full-time job, I took other employment—regular jobs. I was manager at the Gold Club in Dallas, then, when that operation moved, the Health and Tennis Corporation of America, also known as Bally Total Fitness. After that, I moved to the east Texas city of Longview for a position as vice president of marketing for a company there. Longview was where I injured my back for the first time, doing leg presses at a gym. I don't know if I was simply pushing too much weight or if I somehow twisted or contorted my back, but the result was a diskectomy to remove part of a disk in my spine. When I returned to Dallas, I began experiencing those incidents of road rage and fighting that led me to a psychiatrist and, ultimately, to finding my birth mother. So, maybe that wasn't all bad.

While working at Bally, I met a guy named Mark Williams, for whom I worked at several companies after I returned to Dallas. I even learned the information technology end of the business and worked for a number of years as an IT manager. It wasn't glamorous and nowhere near as exciting as sailing to remote, tropical destinations, but it paid the bills. By the time you reach your forties and roll into your fifties, that becomes important.

But I had other issues, besides finances, to consider as I aged. Years of abusing my body with drugs and alcohol left me with an acute awareness of how finite my time on earth might be and fueled a desire to get back into shape. Maybe not the same shape I was in working with Allen Stanford, or even the shape I was in at A&I after rehabbing my knees multiple times. Still, as I grew older, I realized that my quality of life might very well be connected to my health and physical fitness. So, I started doing Brazilian jiu-jitsu (sometimes abbreviated as BJJ) with Professor Carlos Machado.

BJJ is very different from the taekwondo I studied with Luther Duffy in Waco in my younger days. It is a martial arts self-defense system that, like judo, involves taking your opponent to the ground. Once you have them down, the goal is to force them into submission by using a variety of holds or locks. BJJ has been around since the early part of the twentieth century, developed by a quartet of Brazilian brothers, Carlos, Oswaldo, Gastão Jr., and Hélio Gracie. On his website, Carlos Machado touts himself as the "founder and president of the Carlos Machado Jiu Jitsu Association" with "familial ties with the Gracie family, the creators of this art form."[1] That was a fancy way of saying that Carlos is a nephew of Carlos Gracie.

Life seemed to settle down for a bit. I was making decent money as an IT manager for several companies run by Mark Williams. I was also acting again, mostly stand-in work, on films and television shows, like the reboot of *Dallas.* One day, I got a call about a shoot for the ABC television show *Good Christian Belles,* or *GCB,* scheduled to debut in the spring of 2012. The show was based on a 2008 novel by Kim Harmon Gatlin (married at the time to Rudy Gatlin, one of the singing Gatlin Brothers) titled *Good Christian Bitches,* published by Dallas's Brown Books Publishing Group. The novel was ostensibly a semiautobiographical tale of life in Highland Park, an affluent city-within-a-city in Dallas, near the SMU campus. My take on the novel's storyline is that it was not a slam on Christianity, although it received plenty of criticism as such, but rather a slam on a little group of hypocrites that many, if not all, churches have at least to some degree. The "holier than thou" group that, in the end, isn't really very holy at all. The show starred Leslie Bibb (who had had roles in such television shows as *ER* and *Crossing Jordan*), Marisol Nichols (*24* and *The Gates*), David James Elliott (best known for *JAG*), Annie Potts (*Joan of Arcadia* and *Any Day Now*), and Kristin Chenoweth (*Pushing Daisies*). Even with that great cast, it ran for only one season—ten episodes—in 2012.

With a friend named Steve Kerr, who was also an actor, I arrived for the shoot at Munger Methodist Church, at the lowest part of Greenville Avenue where it turns into Munger Avenue in the Swiss Avenue historic district. The scene required us to go in and out of the church building, which had broad concrete, or cement, steps outside, but carpeted stairs on the inside. The carpeting had come loose on the inside stairs and, even though I had already made multiple trips up and down the stairs, on one pass, I lost my footing when the carpet gave way. As I fell, I bounced off the wall along the staircase, spun in a turn, and continued down the stairs until I hit the concrete floor at the foot of the stairs.

I was able to get back up and continue, though I had twisted a knee pretty bad. I had some pain and numbness as well, but nothing debilitating. I thought that I just had a stinger in my back and hip. Stingers occur when nerves are compressed after an impact, which creates a stinging or burning pain that shoots down your arm or other extremities, almost as if you have received an electric shock. It's a common injury in football, and I'd had them before, so I wasn't worried.

It wasn't until we moved to another church to shoot another scene that I first got an inkling that my injury was more than simply a stinger. My knee was starting to bother me, but I also felt sharp pains in my lower back that came and went, almost as if someone were repeatedly plunging a knife into me. My left leg also started to experience some numbness. I knew right away that I needed to see a doctor, so I told the production assistant that I had to leave and why. We filled out some incident paperwork for insurance purposes and then I left.

I didn't go immediately to a doctor, though. Like a typical football player, I thought maybe I could "play through the pain," or, as my coaches always used to say, "Shake it off." The swimming pool at my apartment had pretty powerful jets, so I got in and sat in front of them, trying to get some relief. It didn't work. I don't remember exactly how long I waited but the pain got so bad that I couldn't deal with it on my own. No shaking it off this time. I went to a doctor, who took X-rays and, after reviewing them, told me the bad news.

"There are bone chips and fragments, as well as breaks, in the spine."

It didn't take a medical degree to interpret what he said: I had broken my back. And those stabbing pains? Probably the result of bone shards stabbing nerves in my spine. I needed surgery right away, so he referred me to a specialist. That was not something I expected when I had gotten up in the morning a few days earlier to go to a film shoot, something I had done many times before without incident.

As much as I hated that visit to the doctor and his diagnosis, it was nothing compared to the next doctor I saw. Not the back specialist, but the guy who reviewed worker's compensation claims. I had filed one with the production and, as part of that, I had to be examined by the Worker Compensation (WC) carrier's doctor, then be subjected to an examination by a "judge," who would make the final call on the claim. He had me lie on an examining table, then began poking, prodding, and pushing. At one point, he poked in the wrong place. The pain was so intense and sudden that I screamed. Like a girl. I so startled the nurse, who was holding a wooden clipboard, that she threw it straight up. It hit the cork ceiling and stuck for a moment, before falling. Not to brag, but I believe I set a record for the quickest workers compensation acceptance ever. The scream might have helped.

Then I found out the worst part of the injury. Of course, it was financial. The way workers comp worked, calculating a payment to the claimant included, in addition to the degree of physical impairment, an analysis of your average weekly wage. I had been making mid-to-high five figures as an IT manager, but Mark's company had shut down a few weeks prior to my fall. Since then, I had been solely receiving unemployment compensation. For purposes of WC, then, my numbers included only the minimal amount I received as a daily rate for working on the TV show plus the amount I received from unemployment. Workers comp was going to pay me about $200/week.

After my initial back surgery, funded by workers comp, and lots of therapy, comp dropped off and I went on Social Security Disability Insurance (SSDI). I knew nothing about it, so it was a learning experience. Much of my job as an IT manager had involved crawling around inside walls and ceilings, tracing wires and connections, and sitting at desks in front of computers for long periods of time. With my back issues, which had not improved much even with surgery and therapy, my working days were over. And I was only fifty-eight at that time. Depressing! I really like to work. At least it gave me something to do.

The amount you receive from SSDI is what you would receive at your retirement age of sixty-five under Social Security. That, of course, depends upon how many quarters you worked over how many years, and how much you paid into Social Security. More bad news for me. I worked overseas for much of the 1980s, and even before that I'd had jobs in clubs where you survived mainly on tips. Combine that with the fact that I was "retiring" seven years early, so seven years in which I would not pay any amount into my Social Security account, and I was not at the full rate I otherwise might have been. My "retirement" would have to support me on about $1,200 a month. That wouldn't go very far in

Dallas, Texas, in the twenty-first century.

Since I was used to working, sitting at home didn't exactly suit me. I took several jobs over the years trying to get back into the work force, but my back issues ended all of them. I got involved in my church quite a bit more. I took on a "job" as a teacher for the Prince of Peace Lutheran Church Special Needs group in Dallas, something I did for a decade. I put "job" in quotation marks because I wasn't paid for doing that, but I got more benefit out of it than any other job I ever had.

As a result of that fall, I have now had twenty procedures on my back, with the possibility of more in the future. But even with all that, over the next few years as I dug deeper into the story of John Kearns, the brother I never knew, I came to realize how lucky I was. At least I was still here.

CHAPTER TWENTY-SEVEN

The Death of Lone Star

We regret to inform you that Mr. John W. Kearns III was killed by incoming artillery fire in the Paksong area . . . .

On October 3, 1971, the CIA selected John Kearns for the Clandestine Service Career Staff. Up until then, he had been a contractor with the CIA, which solved several problems for the Agency but created problems for the contractor. Working on a contract basis, contractors were not actual employees of the company. They were vetted, just like employees, and did jobs that employees might do, but they worked under contract, much like a homeowner might contract with a builder to construct a home. That meant, among other things, the contractor was not entitled to employee benefits, so contracting could be cost-saving for the CIA, eliminating the need to pay for health insurance or retirement benefits, or even a way of insulating it from legal liability for the actions of its contractors. But, as far as the CIA was concerned in Laos, it could also be a way of maintaining plausible deniability. It would also help politicians hedge their bets, such as President Richard Nixon's statement on March 6, 1970, reiterating prior statements at press conferences, that "the United States has no ground combat forces in Laos."[1]

The "Clandestine Service" was actually an informal appellation for what, at the time, was known as the Directorate of Plans, so named from 1951 to 1973, then changed to Directorate of Operations (from 1973 to 2004), then the National Clandestine Service. The CIA described the Clandestine Service this way:

> . . . the National Clandestine Service (NCS), operates as the clandestine arm of the CIA, and serves as the national authority for the coordination, deconfliction, and evaluation of clandestine operations across the Intelligence Community. The NCS supports our country's security and foreign policy interests by conducting clandestine activities to collect information that is not obtainable through other means. The NCS also conducts counterintelligence and special activities as authorized by the President.[2]

Becoming a member of the Clandestine Service Career Staff moved John from contractor status to employee of the CIA. Here is how one source defines the role:

> The CIA's Clandestine Service is the front-line source of clandestine information on critical international developments, from terrorism and weapons of mass destruction to military and political issues. The mission often requires clandestine service officers to live and work overseas, making a true commitment to the Agency. This is more than just a job—it's a way of life that challenges the deepest resources of personal intelligence, self-reliance and responsibility. National Clandestine Service Officers are individuals with varied backgrounds and life experiences, professional and educa-

tional histories, language capabilities, and other elements that allow us to meet our mission critical objectives.[3]

There were various clandestine service positions. One was Paramilitary Operations Officer—Specialized Skills Officer, with this job description: "Specialized Skills Officers focus on intelligence operations for US policymakers in hazardous and austere overseas environments. Military special operations or combat arms experience (ground, air, or maritime), previous foreign travel, combat service and foreign language proficiency are highly valued."[4]

Easy to see how John Kearns, formerly with the Army Security Agency, fit the bill. For his new role, he was sent from Long Tieng to CIA headquarters in Langley, Virginia, to immerse in a full-time Thai language training course, which would facilitate his work with Thai irregulars. After that, he took the basic clandestine operations course at the CIA. But he also managed to do something else of great importance while temporarily back in the United States: he got engaged to be married. He had first met Kathy Mains at North Texas State University while he was completing his degree. He encouraged her to finish her degree, which she did in December of 1971, obtaining a BA in History and English. They were married on Christmas Eve of 1971.

★ ★ ★ ★ ★

In August of 1972, following completion of his training for clandestine service, John returned to Laos, this time with his bride, Kathy. His initial posting was right back where he came from, at Long Tieng, but he had been replaced as the Commando Raider Officer when he left for training at Langley. He found it difficult to serve merely as someone's assistant to a job he had previously held and excelled in, so he requested a transfer. His request was granted and he was transferred to Pakse in southern Laos. Pakse was the third of four CIA subsections in Laos that John was assigned to. It would be the last.

In Pakse, he was tasked with working with Thai irregulars who made up Task Force Phasouk, named after Laotian General Somly Rasphakdi Phasouk. There was one other case officer in Pakse besides John, Leon Williamson, and both of them reported to Paul Payne, who ran Task Force Phasouk for the CIA. The task force was made up of seven infantry battalions and one artillery battalion. The battalions, called Battalion Commandos, or BCs, consisted of five hundred Thai irregulars each, plus fifty regular Thai personnel, for a total of forty-four hundred at Pakse. There were an additional thirty-six hundred irregulars, mostly Laotian, making up three *groupements mobiles* (GMs) who were in Pakse under direction of the CIA officers but were not part of Task Force Phasouk.

There was no sharp division of BCs among the CIA case officers at Pakse. Instead, each case officer was equally responsible for all of the Thai troops, traveling with and advising them on an ad hoc basis. An operational assistant, called a "forward air guide," was assigned to each case officer and each BC. Their purpose was to assist in communication between case officers and the troops. This was, of course, why John's clandestine training started with full-time Thai language training, as he would be working with Thai irregulars whether assigned to Long Tieng or Pakse.

Case officers stayed busy, even when there was no active combat. Typically, at least one of the officers would be in the field with the irregulars, while the other officers remained in Pakse. Some travel was involved but usually only in daylight hours. Case officers were expected to return to Pakse at the end of each day to brief station chief Paul Payne and prepare operational cables and intelligence reports to send to the CIA station in Udorn.

> All of Kearns's supervisors describe him as a highly capable, reliable case officer, who exercised good judgment and got along well with everyone. He loved his work. He tended to be quiet and unassuming, but was definitely aggressive in leading the Thai irregulars against the NVA. The task force chief recalls that one of the case officers had a family emergency in Udorn, which caused him to spend time away from Pakse. At times, this resulted in Kearns being assigned to the field almost every day. According to his supervisor he preferred the field to staying behind in Pakse. Kearns was considered fearless. A case officer who shared living quarters with Kearns in Pakse described him as one of the "Young Turks" in Laos who wanted to take the fight directly to the enemy, the NVA.[5]

While John was in Pakse, his new bride Kathy lived in Vientiane where she taught at the American school. John's schedule was nine days on followed by three days off, and they had to squeeze in time together during those off days. Either she would visit him in Pakse or John would go to Vientiane. Their house in Vientiane was on a street without a name, so Kathy came up with her own name: Kearns Boulevard. She even put up a street sign with that name on it.

Kathy was shuttled from Vientiane to Pakse on her visits. The first leg took her, via fixed-wing aircraft, to Udorn. From there, it was on to Pakse via helicopter. Both modes of transportation were most likely compliments of Air America. According to Kathy, avoiding ground fire was a constant concern on that second leg, so the chopper pilots typically flew at tree top level. The house in Pakse where the CIA case officers lived was certainly no mansion, but it was a large, multibedroom structure on stilts that had to accommodate all the officers. There was a tennis court next to the house, but a sandbag-reinforced bunker that housed the kitchen was a sober reminder of the dangers of living there.[6]

By the time John arrived in Pakse in late summer of 1972, action had already been heating up in southern Laos. In Vietnam, the North Vietnamese had earlier undertaken one of their most extensive offensive efforts in the war. Known as the Easter Offensive, it marked North Vietnam's first attempted invasion of the South since the Tet Offensive in January 1968. Things had already taken a turn for the worse in Laos in the first few months of 1972, when the North Vietnamese launched an effort to take Skyline Ridge.

The ridge was a series of limestone mountain peaks that provided a natural protective buffer for Long Tieng, which, in turn, guarded the entry to Vientiane. Following a series of battles from late 1971 into early 1972, during which time John was back in the United States training for clandestine service, the North Vietnamese claimed they had taken the ridge and captured Long Tieng, although they were later forced to withdraw. Well, maybe "forced" isn't the right word, because much of the troop withdrawal was voluntary, in order to send them into South Vietnam as part of the Easter Offensive. Besides, it was the rainy season and their forces were needed elsewhere. But once the rainy season ended, the North Vietnamese went back on the offensive in Laos, with much of the fighting in and around Pakse.

★ ★ ★ ★ ★

Following the Easter Offensive, 1972 saw a series of operations in Laos under variations of the moniker Black Lion. The Savannakhet station of the CIA planned the first operation, simply called Black Lion. Khong Sedone, which sat between Pakse and Savannakhet, had fallen to the communists, who had rebuffed a couple of efforts to retake it. In June of 1972, two *groupements mobiles* of the Royal Lao Army, GMs 32 and 33, succeeded in recapturing the area but, in the process, the town of Khong Sedone had been virtually destroyed.[7]

Black Lion III aimed to retake the town of Saravane, about 70 miles north of Paksong, from the communists. With the aid of Air America Twin Otters, CH-53s, and H-34s, along with Royal Laos Air Force aircraft to handle the infiltration of Commando Raiders, the operation was a success. But not without a cost. Christopher Robbins wrote:

> On the very first day a helicopter was shot down, killing a CIA man and two Laotian aides. A Lao general who was on board survived, but the chopper that picked him up took several hits and the copilot was seriously wounded. Air Force doctors, who were not surgeons, had to perform a botched emergency operation to save his life. The word went around AA that the Saravane Operation was a dangerous mission to draw. There began to be friction between the pilots and CIA case officers.[8]

According to Robbins, a later fight occurred between a pilot and a case officer "who was a close friend of the killed CIA man." Blows were exchanged and "the case officer lost two front teeth."[9]

Though Robbins does not name any names, the timeline of the downed helicopter and loss of the "CIA man" matches with the death of John Peterson. Kenneth Michael Absher's article records Peterson's death as occurring east of Pakse on October 19, 1972, during an airlift of two GMs to a site southwest of Saravane. Peterson was killed on that date when the helicopter in which he was a passenger was hit by North Vietnamese Army ground fire and "crashed and burned." His duties had been "advising the field commanders and managing the deployment of GM, to include outfitting, paying, training and inserting irregular troops into the areas of operation." Peterson "often was present at the infil sites," as he was that October day. His helicopter, "rising above the tree line, was struck by enemy ground fire near Saravane, Laos." The chopper crashed. For two days, Peterson's troops carried his body through the jungle while searching for a safe landing zone for a helicopter to retrieve him. He was twenty-seven years old. Like John Kearns, Peterson was awarded the CIA's Intelligence Star.[10] There is no way to determine whether John Kearns was the CIA case officer who came to blows with the Air America pilot that Robbins writes about, nor whether John lost two front teeth. He was, however, a close friend of John Peterson.

As a follow-up to the prior Black Lion operations, another was launched in late October, aimed at resecuring the Bolovens Plateau. The operation started when a team of fifty Commando Raiders parachuted from Air America Twin Otter aircraft. The Commando Raiders were to secure a landing zone between Saravane and the retaken, but destroyed, Khong Sedone to enable infiltration of GM 33. In November, GM 33 was to link up with Thai mercenaries from GM 401, which was being advised by CIA paramilitary case officer John Kearns. The idea was to create a pincer movement with the rest of Task Force Phasouk, converging at Paksong. It was this convergence that was dubbed Operation Black Lion V.[11]

> Subject to light probes, GM 401 on 15 December was deployed along a defensive triangle around the town. That same day, the new Task Force Phasouk commander, Special Col. Panya Singsakda, call-sign Panharn, came for an orientation tour of the Paksong front. Landing in the town, he was receiving a briefing from his field commanders when a PAVN 85 mm round landed in their midst. Eight persons were killed, including the GM 401 deputy commander, the BC 613A commander, and Unity case officer John Kearns; Panharn was wounded.[12]

Previously classified CIA documents provide a bit more detail, albeit not much, about what happened. The area around Paksong "remained fluid" for the beginning half of December, with sporadic clashes between Thai irregulars and the North Vietnamese.[13] There were already about three thousand troops from GM 401 and GM 33 in the area and, on December 15, John arrived to supervise and assist in the infiltration of two hundred replacements for GM 401. Three H-34 and one CH-47 helicopters were en route with those replacements. No enemy activity had been reported and, after approximately two hours on the ground, John met with the commanders and staff of the two GM units to discuss the situation. A mortar round landed nearby.

Mortars are a particularly devilish weapon, launching explosive shells at high angles, allowing them to drop onto targets from almost directly overhead. The mortars themselves are lightweight tubes that are mounted to bi- or tripod mounts. Mortar rounds do their damage upon impact with the ground, detonating and ejecting shrapnel at high rates of speed. It's impossible to know for sure the type of mortar delivering incoming ordinance that day, but the typical North Vietnamese mortars during the Vietnam War were M-43s discharging 120 mm rockets. M-43s were Soviet mortars that were first introduced in 1943, known as the Samovar. Other mortar sizes often utilized by the North Vietnamese included the 82-PM-41 82 mm mortar, which was also a Soviet weapon.[14] Mortars firing 120 mm shells had a range of up to 5,700 meters, or three and a half miles, while those firing 82 mm shells had a range of 3,000 to 5,000 meters, or 1.8 miles to 3.1 miles. Either way, the source of the attack that day would have been out of sight.

The time of the mortar attack is unclear due to conflicting reports—the CIA notice of John's death is a bit blurred, but it appears to call it "1130 local time," which would have placed the meeting in the morning of December 15 at 11:30 a.m. Absher's account, however, called it "1930 hours," which would have placed it at about 7:30 p.m.

When the first mortar round exploded, everyone sought cover in nearby bunkers, but a second landed before all could reach safety. A metal fragment from the round struck John in the chest. He was then airlifted but died before reaching a hospital. It was not the size of the fragment that made it deadly; it was the damage it did, piercing his aorta. The aorta is the largest artery, carrying oxygenated blood from the heart to the rest of the body. When the aorta is punctured—known as a "traumatic aortic injury"—blood escapes through the outside aortic wall. Sometimes surrounding tissue of the aorta can contain the bleeding, at least for a short while, but the wound is life-threatening and requires almost immediate surgery to repair the tear. If the victim does not receive emergency care, he can quickly find himself having difficulty breathing, not to mention experiencing severe pain at the site of the injury. Soon, he will go in to shock. Absent immediate repairs to the puncture, death follows. Multiple medical websites, including the National Institute for Health, report that the death rate, in the absence of immediate treatment, approaches eighty to ninety percent.[15] John did not fall within the minority.

★ ★ ★ ★ ★

Christopher Robbins writes about an incident sometime in December—he calls it "the week before Christmas"—but does not identify individuals other than an Air America pilot named Mel Cooper.

> The CIA were also running another operation on a road that led out of the Ho Chi Minh trail to Saravane and were using helicopters and fixed-wing aircraft to supply the troops they had out there. They had clusters of two hundred troops on three small hills about a quarter of a mile apart from one another which formed a triangle. At night the enemy would probe the positions' perimeter, but it was generally considered that the area inside the triangle was safe in daylight.
>
> Cooper had gone out to the area to pick up some wounded and then headed for what was considered to be the most secure area, right in the middle of the triangle. The chopper was flying low when a wave of tracer bullets arced toward it. "It was another one of those heart stoppers," Cooper

said. "All of a sudden, right in front of us and coming right at us was .50 cal. tracers." They were so low that they ducked behind a tree where they could no longer see the tracers, but heard the unmistakable slow pump of the guns.[16]

Joe Leeker's *Aircraft of Air America* describes a Sikorsky UH-34 that was hit by ground fire on a medevac mission on December 22, 1972, near New Paksong.[17] That date fits better with the "week before Christmas" that Robbins describes than does the date of John's death on December 15. December 22 was a Friday, and Christmas was the following Tuesday, while December 15 was a week prior to this particular incident. But Leeker's December 22 incident does not name Mel Cooper as the pilot but R. Carpenter. It's possible that two, or even all three of these events, including John Kearns's death, have been conflated by the fog of war. Even if not, it is instructive in understanding the hazardous conditions for CIA operatives and Air America personnel at that time in southern Laos.

CHAPTER TWENTY-EIGHT

Uncontrollable

"[Heath Ledger's Joker] . . . keeps making involuntary, repetitive movements—flicking his tongue, smacking his mouth—which suggest tardive dyskinesia . . . ."

Travis Langley, *Batman and Psychology: A Dark and Stormy Knight*

Ever get the sense that you're the last person to know something about yourself? I had that distinct feeling some years back about something that ended up being devastating for me physically. And it's something that I am still dealing with today.

Starting in the early 2000s, I began experiencing unpleasant, at least visually to others, facial contortions, primarily involving my mouth. My doctors wrote it off as a temporomandibular joint (or TMJ) disorder. The TMJ is a joint in your face that connects the jawbone to the skull. TMJ disorders produce symptoms that run the gamut from headaches to neck and tooth pain to difficulty chewing and on to, in what appeared to be my case, the joint locking and thereby creating difficulty in opening or closing your mouth. My symptoms didn't fit precisely but at least it was an explanation I could understand.

Sometime in the 2010s, I was alerted to the fact that my feet wouldn't stop moving when I was sitting down. I know that sounds funny at first, and it wasn't something that I noticed. Other people told me that it almost appeared as if I were tap dancing while seated. My lower legs and feet seemed to be moving completely of their own accord. My hands started to take on a life of their own. Some thought I was joking, but I was alarmed when they brought it to my attention. As a former athlete, I was used to having control over my body, but I quickly discovered that I had no control over this. Somehow, some way, instructions from my brain ordering my feet to be still got waylaid, and there I would sit, tap dancing away.

I did some rudimentary research to see if I could figure out for myself what was happening. It was obvious to me that something neurologically wrong was causing these uncontrollable movements. The first thing that came to mind was Parkinson's Disease. But these weren't really tremors, like I had always associated with Parkinson's through celebrities like Michael J. Fox. Instead, they were more herky jerky. Almost like a tic. I thought Tourette syndrome might be a possibility, though at this point I wasn't experiencing any facial tics beyond the jaw movements nor any uncontrollable verbal outbursts. My mind tumbled from one thing to another as I tried to make sense of what was happening to my body.

At first, I put off going to a doctor in the unfounded belief that I could figure it out, and fix it, for myself. Just like I got stronger and ran faster getting ready for college football by working on it myself, I thought I simply had to concentrate and focus on the problem. Besides, sometimes things like that don't seem real until they are confirmed by a professional. If you haven't named it, it's not there.

It's called denial.

When I finally realized I wasn't going to be able to self-diagnose and self-repair, I went to see Dr. John Richmond in Dallas, who had been my regular doctor for about four or five years. He immediately recognized what I instinctively suspected, that the problem was neurological in nature. That confirmation alone was frightening. You can surgically repair ligaments and cartilage in your knees and ankles, but even in my rudimentary knowledge of the body, I knew that the central nervous system was on a different plane from bones, joints, and connective tissue. Those disorders and diseases ran the gamut from Parkinson's, which I had already dismissed, to Guillain-Barré syndrome to Huntington's disease to cerebral palsy to multiple sclerosis to ALS (Amyotrophic Lateral Sclerosis, commonly known as Lou Gehrig's Disease). It was a "pick your poison" dilemma, and I couldn't decide if I preferred one over the other. Most of them were life sentences and, in some cases, death sentences.

I was scared.

Dr. Richmond referred me to a neurologist in the Casa Linda area of East Dallas. He turned out to be a child neurologist, but he worked with me anyway. Maybe that was a commentary on my level of maturity, or maybe he was just being kind. I like to think it was the latter.

After grilling me with questions and running a battery of tests, he sat me down to share his conclusions. "You've got a condition known as tardive dyskinesia," he said.

"What the heck is that?" I asked.

He responded with some medical mumbo jumbo that I didn't fully understand, but as I have since dealt with the condition that some simply refer to as TD, I have come to learn more about it. I'm still not an expert, by any means, but I have developed a layman's working knowledge, particularly as it applies to me.

Though often mistaken for Parkinson's, tardive dyskinesia is actually a bastard cousin to that disorder. Just as Parkinson's can cause uncontrollable movements, so, too, does TD. With Parkinson's, though, the movements are tremorlike, almost a vibration of the limbs, while TD movements tend to be more jerky. It can include orofacial or oro-bucco-lingual dyskinesia, which is a fancy way to describe uncontrolled movements in your face. That manifests with fast eye-blinking, chewing and smacking motions with your lips, puffing your cheeks, sticking out your tongue, even frowning and emitting grunting sounds. It's not a pretty sight, nor is it limited to the face. It can also affect your limbs, resulting in arm-flapping, foot-tapping—the aforementioned chair-dancing—and swaying from side to side. It doesn't play favorites; it's a full body disorder.

One of the primary causes of TD is long term usage of antipsychotic medications, or neuroleptics, used in the treatment of schizophrenia, depression, and bipolar disorder. Does that ring a bell? Other medications, including anti-nausea and anti-seizure treatments, can also result in TD, as can decongestants and, ironically enough, medications for movement disorders. Think about that last one. Medication to control movement disorders can result in movement disorders.

Dopamine is a chemical component in the brain that helps control movement. The way these medications work is that they block dopamine receptors in the brain, which scientists believed would relieve the symptoms of psychological diseases. The problem is that, correspondingly, it reduces the brain's ability to control the movement of body parts. It's like disconnecting the connection to control.

Although TD as a disorder first appeared in medical literature in the 1950s, the term "tardive dyskinesia" was first used in 1964. "Tardive" is derived from the French term *tardif*, which means tardy, delayed, or late, and is primarily used to describe the progression or development of a disease. *Merriam-Webster* defines it as "tending to or characterized by lateness especially in development or maturity."[1] Dyskinesia is defined as "impairment of voluntary movements resulting in fragmented or jerky motions."[2] Combined, it refers to abnormal movement that doesn't manifest until after prolonged usage of certain medications. A delayed reaction, so to speak. By the way, it's not always delayed for a long time. It can develop within weeks, but onset is more common after extended periods of time.

There is no known cure, though symptoms may improve after stopping the medication that caused it, so early detection is crucial to treatment. It can even be managed through other medication but, as far as I know, there is no treatment to reverse it. According to a report published by Mad in America detailing two new drugs for the treatment of TD (Ingrezza and Austedo, at a price of as much as $7,000 per month), "Given that TD is a disorder caused by antipsychotics, there is an obvious outrageous element to this story: the pharmaceutical industry is now profiting by developing drugs to treat the harm caused by its own products."[3]

Statistics vary as to how common TD is, but medical websites vary between five to six hundred thousand people in the United States. Approximately 20 percent of people who take those medications are affected, and the risk increases for women and older adults. I was one of the unlucky minority. In my case, the culprit was a drug called Quetiapine, which I had been prescribed under its trade name Seroquel. It is what is known as an atypical antipsychotic, developed in 1985 and approved for medical use in the United States in 1997. I was first prescribed Seroquel in the late 1990s (which suggests I was a sort of guinea pig for early usage after its USDA approval) for treatment of bipolar disorder and other issues relating to obsessive-compulsive disorder and manic episodes. During the course of years over which I was prescribed Seroquel, I went through three general practitioners, each of whom renewed my prescriptions but none of whom ever mentioned tardive dyskinesia as a side effect. I suppose it could have been included in the fine print in literature that accompanied the drug, and maybe it was my fault for not having read it closely and asking enough questions at the start. Still, it seems like the kind of thing a doctor might have mentioned at some point, at least in passing, before I started sit-down tap-dancing.

The neurologist took me off Seroquel and prescribed a different drug, whose name I don't recall, to treat TD. He later changed the treatment prescription to Ingrezza, whose generic name is Valbenazine. Its official website touts it as effective in treating the "persistent, uncontrollable movements" of TD.[4] Side effects include allergic reactions, sleepiness and tiredness, heart rhythm problems, neuroleptic malignant syndrome (a reaction that can occur with drugs that block the effects of dopamine, including high fever, stiff muscles, problems thinking, fast or uneven heartbeat, or increased sweating), and Parkinson-like symptoms. I learned that there was another side effect: lack of balance. At first it was merely inconvenient, but it took a bicycle accident—a one-bicycle crash—at White Rock Lake in East Dallas, in which I shattered my right arm, to realize how serious it was. Fortunately, several other bike riders witnessed the accident and called 9-1-1. I don't remember much about the immediate aftermath of the wipeout, but I do recall insisting to the ambulance attendants that they bring my bike along. They agreed and attached it to their vehicle for the trip to the hospital. After an operation to embed titanium rods and a new metal elbow in my right arm, followed by six months of rehab, I straightened out the front wheel and frame of my bicycle and hopped right back on.

By then, I also had a new prescription, this one for a medication called Austedo (generic name deutetrabenazine), which is most commonly used to treat involuntary movements in Huntington's disease as well as the involuntary, uncontrollable movements indicative of TD. According to the drug's official website, side effects include irregular heartbeat, neuroleptic malignant syndrome, akathisia (restlessness or a strong urge to move), Parkinsonism, and sleepiness.[5] The most common side effects for people suffering from TD are inflammation of the nose and throat, and insomnia. But even the switch to Austedo didn't totally resolve my balance issue.

In August of 2022, I was rushed to Baylor Hospital Emergency Room for a very nasty urinary tract infection, which graduated to sepsis and sidelined me for two weeks in the intensive care unit. That was followed by a couple more weeks in a hospital room, culminating in a month in a nursing home before finally being able to return home. But I was determined to get back on my feet. The problem was that I found myself constantly off balance. A series of falls followed in rapid succession. The first was on the concrete front porch of the house where I rented a room on Swiss Avenue in East Dallas. The most severe, though, was a face-first fall in my bathroom right by the kitty litter. The indignity was bad enough, but in falling, I landed with one arm beneath me, re-tearing my rotator cuff that had been surgically repaired a couple of years earlier. I lay there for five hours without being able to get up.

I was not yet seventy years old and I found myself looking at the prospects of full-time care in a nursing home for the rest of my life. But before I could find one to take me, I inadvertently allowed my medication prescription to run out and was unable to pick up a refill at the pharmacy. A simple miscalculation, but one of the best mistakes I ever made. My balance issues started to improve!

At the suggestion of a new physician, Dr. Mazen Elkard at Baylor Hospital, we decided to go with a new, and lower level of, Austedo called Austedo 12XR. I also now make it a practice to take the dosage at bedtime, so its adverse effects, at their highest potency, come while I am asleep. So far, that strategy works. Stay tuned.

Chapter Twenty-Nine

What Really Happened to Lone Star?

"No event in American history is more misunderstood than the Vietnam War. It was misreported then, and it is misremembered now."

Richard M. Nixon

The *Oxford Dictionary of Phrase and Fable* defines "fog of war" as "a phrase now much used to describe the complexity of military conflicts."[1] Its origins are not entirely clear. Many attribute it to the nineteenth-century Prussian General Carl Philipp Gottlieb von Clausewitz, although he never actually used the phrase. In his 1832 treatise *Vom Kreige*, translated into English as *On War*, von Clausewitz wrote, "War is the realm of uncertainty; three quarters of the factors on which action in war is based are wrapped in a fog of greater or lesser uncertainty. A sensitive and discriminating judgment is called for; a skilled intelligence to scent out the truth."[2]

In 1836, poet McDonald Clarke wrote "The Battle of Bunker Hill," which included the phrase:

Will they dare a third attack?
Is a question seen in every eye;
Old Put across the neck and back,

Rides slowly, their vengeance to defy—
Wildly, in that deadly hour,
The Ramparts shove their bolted shower,
While mid the waving fog of war,
Thunders the Yankee's loud hurrah.[3]

In 1896, Sir Lonsdale Augustus Hale wrote of the "fog of war" as "the state of ignorance in which commanders frequently find themselves as regards the real strength and position, not only of their foes, but also of their friends."[4]

In short, the phrase refers to that "fog" of uncertainty on the battlefield resulting from lack of information, misinformation, and conflicting information. It is often difficult, if not impossible, to know the facts during an active battle, much less make informed decisions. The same is true when trying to piece together facts from years, decades, and even centuries earlier. Conflicts and contradictions abound.

Historians relish primary sources, which are original documents or firsthand accounts of an event. Secondary sources typically involve analyses or summarizations, often well after-the-fact, of primary sources and, often, of earlier secondary sources. Arguably, primary sources are inherently more accurate, particularly if contemporaneous with the event. However, accuracy can be tainted by the motive behind an account, particularly if that motive appears, or even seemingly appears, to color the account. Eyewitness accounts may not be contemporaneous but, instead, may be based upon memories of a witnessed event. Memories fade with time, and even multiple contemporaneous accounts from primary sources can contradict one another. Different people can, and often do, view the same event differently through the prism of their own biases and perspectives. Or maybe each saw one aspect of an event while others operated from a different viewpoint, leaving the historian to fit the ill-fitting puzzle pieces together.

The fog of war.

The events of December 15, 1972, involving the death of John "Lone Star" Kearns are not crystal clear. CIA documents, formerly classified, including some created at or near the time of death, provide the initial pieces of the puzzle. These include a message issued by the CIA, dated December 16, 1972, advising, "MR. JOHN W. KEARNS III WAS KILLED BY INCOMING ARTILLERY FIRE IN THE PAKSONG AREA AT APPROXIMATELY 1130 LOCAL 15 DECEMBER"; a "Recommendation for Honor or Merit Award," undated, with an attached narrative, recommending John Kearns for the CIA's Intelligence Star; and a March 27, 1973, "Report of Honor and Merit Awards Board" posthumously awarding the Intelligence Star to John Kearns.[5] CIA Director George Tenet, in his remarks at the annual Memorial Ceremony on June 2, 2000, added additional puzzle pieces but, unfortunately, planted the seeds of inconsistency.

Other valuable pieces have been supplied to the author by Thai "Forward Air Guides" who served with John in southern Laos at the time of his death. Unsung heroes in a secret war, tagged with code names to conceal their identifies, they were collectively given the unfortunate acronym FAG in order to distinguish them from FACs, "Forward Air Controllers." FACs were airborne spotters who helped direct fighters and bombers to pinpoint targets. FAGs accomplished a similar purpose but were ground-based, working with CIA paramilitary operators. They assisted attack aircraft in identifying targets, assessed the results of air strikes, and helped to coordinate medical evacuations. Following a "friendly

Cover of *The Unknown Warriors: Secret War in Laos*, by Charlie Khachen, aka Chalermchai Thammawetin. *Photo courtesy of Chalermchai Thammawetin.*

fire" incident in April of 1971, in which an American pilot erroneously bombed Thai troops, killing sixteen, including two Thai commanders, the CIA "institutionalized" the FAG concept.[6]

Among FAGs stationed at Pakse during John's tenure were those code-named Space (real name Chalermchai Thammawetin), Sparkplug (real name Weera Star), Ringer (real name Therdsak Phothilak), and LollyPop (real name Supradit Kanthawanij). Space was John's operations assistant, and the two of them worked closely, albeit only briefly, together. Space described his role as a FAG this way: "My role is to coordinate with the air attack units called 'ABCCC' (night time) and 'Raven' (day time)." ABCCC stands for US Airborne Command, Communication & Control Center. The Ravens were a group of US Air Force fighter pilots who were part of what was called the Steve Canyon Program, named after the Milton Caniff–created comic strip. Getting down to more specifics, Space said that, when coordinating with Ravens during the daytime, "a FAG gives information and adjusts distance." At night, FAGs would provide reports on targets to C-130 ABCCC reconnaissance aircraft and then coordinate with gunships to attack the targets.[7]

In addition to a series of email communications with me, in which he patiently and fully answered a seemingly endless supply of questions, Space has written about the FAG program, including a discussion of John's death, in a book titled *The Unknown Warriors: Secret War in Laos*, under the Americanized version of his name,

Charlie Khachen.[8] He first printed it in 1995, then again in 2002, and a third time in 2018. Space was not present at the site in Paksong when John's life was taken by a mortar attack, but he witnessed the event from the air.

Weera Star, code name Sparkplug.
Photo courtesy of Weera Star.

I also engaged in extensive communications, via Facebook Messenger and by telephone, with Sparkplug, who, like Space, patiently answered my questions. Sparkplug provided a photo of a contemporaneous note of the December 15 mortar attack that he entered in his memoranda pad. At the time of the attack, he was "in the field a few clicks [kilometers] away," so he was not an eyewitness. He reported what he had been told about the attack by FAG Ringer, who was physically present with John at the attack, in a story he posted on the Internet on September 24, 2021.[9]

One of the first references to the fatal mortar attack, if not *the* first, outside of the CIA documents mentioned above was in a series of "Indochina Monographs" published by the US Army Center of Military History.[10] Brigadier General James L. Collins Jr. described the monographs as "written by officers who held responsible positions in the Cambodian, Laotian, and South Vietnamese armed forces during the war in Indochina" and said that the "authors were not attempting to write definitive accounts but to set down how they saw the war in Southeast Asia."[11] One of those, titled *RLG* [Royal Lao Government] *Military Operations and Activities in the Laotian Panhandle*, was written by Lao Brigadier General Soutchay Vongsavanh, who was commanding general at the time of Region 4 in Laos, which encompassed southern Laos and the Ho Chi Minh Trail.

Vongsavanh, who dated his acknowledgements as of February 21, 1978, scarcely five years after the death of John Kearns, succinctly summarized the event this way, though he did not mention John by name:

> The [North Vietnamese] counteroffensive began to materialize in late November 1972 when the NVA 9th Infantry Regiment was deployed north from the Paksong area and committed against GMs 41 and 42 at Saravane. Despite this move, the GMs held their ground. In one attack, GM 41 headquarters suffered a direct hit by a 122-mm field gun round which completely demolished the command post, killing all except the GM commander who escaped unscathed.[12]

Houmphanh Rattanakhom, code name Red Lion, commander of GM 41 of Thai Battalion 408. *Courtesy of Joe Rattanakhom.*

Later books mention John by name and make cursory references to his death, but they fail to provide much detail. One of the earliest is *Shadow War: The CIA's Secret War in Laos,* published in 1995. In *Shadow War,* Kenneth Conboy, writing with James Morrison, references the mortar attack near Paksong on December 15, 1972. "Eight persons were killed, including the GM 401 deputy commander, the BC 613A commander, and Unity case officer John Kearns; Panharn [call sign for Special Colonel Panya Singsakda] was wounded."[13]

Ted Gup's *The Book of Honor* asserts simply

that John Kearns, along with John Peterson, are "still nameless stars from the long-ago secret war in Laos" on the CIA's Memorial Wall.[14] Gup's book was published on May 16, 2000, predating by less than a month the Memorial Ceremony at which Director Tenet first publicly revealed John's name—at least officially. Gup doesn't mention how he came to have knowledge of these "still nameless stars."

In 2002, Kenneth Michael Absher wrote his article for *Studies in Intelligence* called "John Kearns and the Cold War in Laos: Recalling a CIA Officer's Sacrifice." Absher writes that he relied upon "research in CIA personnel files, review of daily combat intelligence reports from Laos, and interviews with 12 people knowledgeable about John Kearns's career and Agency activities in Laos in the late 1960s and early 1970s." He states that he also reviewed 219 daily Situation Reports from Pakse between June 1972 and March 1973, as well as information that John's "Thai operations assistant reported." Another of Absher's sources was Leon Williamson, a fellow CIA caseworker and John's roommate at Pakse, who, after John's death, "arrived on the scene by helicopter."[15]

In 2003, in *Top Secret Missions: Performed by Elite Commo & Intel Specialists*, John E. Malone devoted a short chapter to John Kearns and his role in Vietnam and Laos. He summarily stated that John was "Killed-In-Action (KIA) on 12 December 1972, during his third tour to Laos."[16] The date is incorrect; it was actually December 15.

In his 2003 memoir, *A Look Over My Shoulder*, former CIA Director Richard Helms erroneously described John Kearns's descent to recover a downed pilot's body. He mistakenly identified the pilot as John P., presumably a reference to John Peterson, although the actual pilot was Herbert W. Clark.[17] In *Safe for Democracy: The Secret Wars of the CIA*, published in 2006, John Prados writes of more than two hundred deaths in Laos—at least that was the number the Nixon administration "admitted to," and "about that number" was also missing. "The CIA's deaths now included Louis Ojibway, Wilbur Greene, Wayne McNulty, John Kearns, and John Peterson, one of them in North Vietnam."[18]

In 2018, Paul T. Carter challenged some of the specifics of Director Tenet's and Absher's versions of John's death with *CIA Secret Warriors: Thai Forward Air Guides in the US War in Laos: The Untold Story.*[19] Carter relied upon the recitations of FAGs Space and Sparkplug, which the authors have also relied upon in *Searching for Lone Star.*

Putting together all the puzzle pieces from these various sources creates a more complete, but sometimes fuzzy and contradictory picture. And there are still pieces missing.

The fog of war.

★ ★ ★ ★ ★

As the fighting in southern Laos grew more intense in late 1972, additional battalions of Thai irregulars were sent to the area: BCs (Commando Battalion) 610, 621, 627, and BA (Artillery Battalion) 635. Fifteen additional FAGs were sent there as well, including Sparkplug and a FAG called Knife. Paul Payne, code name Electric, who ran Task Force Phasouk out of Pakse for the CIA, divided the FAGs into three teams under the command of Space, Ringer, and Office. They were housed in rented quarters near the Pakse airport.

In August of 1972, John and his bride Kathy returned to Laos following John's CIA training in the United States. They were initially stationed at Long Tieng but transferred shortly afterward, specific date unknown, to the CIA substation at Pakse in southern Laos. When John arrived at Pakse, Payne introduced him to Space, who would be John's operations assistant. Space said his best estimate was that John arrived at the end of September. He described John as "short and stocky" and said he spoke clearly. John told him, "he would rather be my friend than my boss." In recent email correspondence, Space wrote, "John and I [were] very close buddies. But sadly, he had to leave me [after] such a short time. He was a warrior with a strong spirit and he remains my favorite hero to this day."[20]

Others concur with Space's assessment of John. Absher wrote that John was considered "fearless" and "definitely aggressive in leading the Thai irregulars against the NVA." A "case officer who shared living quarters with Kearns in Pakse," presumably Leon Williamson, described him as "one of the 'Young Turks' in Laos who wanted to take the fight directly to the enemy, the NVA."[21] The narrative accompanying the recommendation for the Intelligence Star stated,

> Mr. Kearns' professionalism and personal dedication to Agency objectives were repeatedly demonstrated in his field service prior to his death. He was a strongly motivated young officer who consistently displayed courage, leadership and resourcefulness. Throughout his brief career with the Agency Mr. Kearns was consistently given strong performance ratings and his enthusiasm and dedication were repeatedly recognized by his superiors.[22]

Sparkplug, who didn't work as closely with John as did Space, also concurred, saying that John was a "very good fighter." He described John as "a hot-blooded American from Texas who was arrogant."[23] He is not the only one to cite John's apparent quick temper. Space said that, when he was first assigned to work with John, Paul Payne aka Electric told him that John was "a brave and hot-tempered person, speaking frankly and working diligently."[24] Space described an incident in which John berated FAG Knife for security violations and for failing to respond to radio calls. John threatened to fire Knife, but Space talked him out of it. "He finally agreed with me and told me that he would send him as far away as possible. His words puzzled me quite a bit."[25] Space also wrote that John's wife Kathy, who, for security reasons, was known to everyone by the pseudonym Anita, said that "her husband was a hot-tempered person."[26]

John Kearns, center, and team at Pakse in December 1972. Front right, with back toward camera, is Therdsak Phothilak, code name Ringer. *Photo courtesy of Weera Star and Supradit Kanthawanij, code name LollyPop.*

John's arrival at Pakse gives rise to one of the inconsistencies in some reports. Paul Carter says that John Kearns arrived in Pakse with his three-month pregnant wife "Anita" at an unspecified date in 1972. As noted above, John probably arrived in Pakse in September. John and Kathy/Anita's son, John Douglas Kearns, was born August 21, 1973, so Kathy/Anita could not have been three months pregnant, or even pregnant at all, when they first arrived at Pakse. In fact, when John was killed on December 15, she was likely less than a month pregnant.

While stationed at Pakse, John spent much of his time in the field, which, according to his CIA supervisor, he "preferred" to staying behind in Pakse.[27] His normal practice, with Space as his ops assistant, was to travel by Jeep to visit the Thai units in the area, with an M60 machine gun mounted on the vehicle and a tall radio antenna attached. On one occasion, while returning to base, John and Space unexpectedly encountered the enemy. Carter wrote that these people were attempting to lay booby traps on the road, while Space simply said he and John spotted a group of armed people "running across the road." Carter wrote that John fired first, drawing return fire, while Space said it was the opposite. "Lone Star stopped the jeep, jumped out into the machine gun . . . . Minutes later they fired AK-47s. [S]everal bullets hit the jeep body and shattered the windshield. He countered fire with several machine gun rounds."[28]

It's unclear when this skirmish occurred. Space reported that John cautioned him not to tell Kathy/Anita because she might be upset and it could affect her "two-month pregnancy." In his emails with the author, Space amended the timeline. He reiterated that John asked him not to tell Kathy/Anita because she might be "emotionally affected" during her pregnancy, but said, "I think she

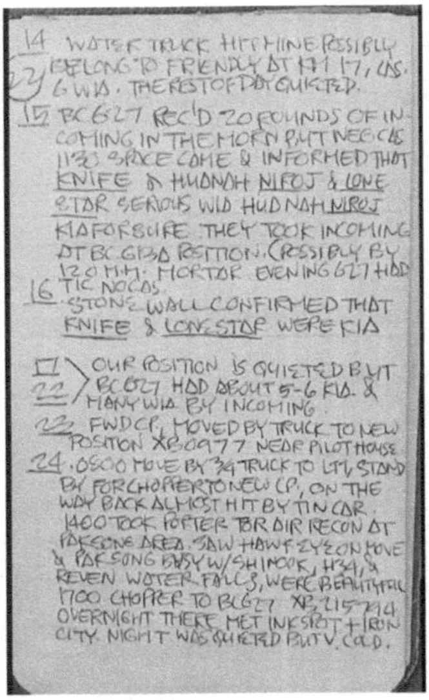
14 WATER TRUCK HIT MINE POSSIBLY BELONG TO FRIENDLY AT KM 17, CAS. 6 WIA. THE REST OF DAY QUIETED.
15 BC 627 REC'D 20 ROUNDS OF INCOMING IN THE MORN BUT NEG CAS
1130 SPACE CAME & INFORMED THAT KNIFE & HUDNAH NIFOJ & LONE STAR SERIOUS WIA HUDNAH NIROJ KIA FOR SURE THEY TOOK INCOMING AT BC 613A POSITION. (POSSIBLY BY 120 MM. MORTAR EVENING 627 HAD TIC NO CAS.
16 STONE WALL CONFIRMED THAT KNIFE & LONE STAR WERE KIA
17 22 OUR POSITION IS QUIETED BUT BC 627 HAD ABOUT 5-6 KIA. & MANY WIA BY INCOMING.
23 FWD CP. MOVED BY TRUCK TO NEW POSITION XB 09777 NEAR PILOT HOUSE
24 . 0800 MOVE BY 3/4 TRUCK TO LTT, STAND BY FOR CHOPPER TO NEW CP., ON THE WAY BACK ALMOST HIT BY TIN CAR.
1400 TOOK PORTER FOR AIR RECON AT PAKSONG AREA. SAW HAWKEYE ON MOVE & PAKSONG BUSY W/SHINOOK, H34, & SEVEN WATER FALLS, WERE BEAUTIFUL
1700 CHOPPER TO BC 627 XB 215 714 OVERNIGHT THERE MET INKSPOT + IRON CITY. NIGHT WAS QUIETED BUT V. COLD.

Sparkplug's "sitrep" memo for December 15, 1972. *Photo courtesy of Weera Star.*

was about a month pregnant." As noted, Kathy/Anita was likely less than a month pregnant on the day John was killed, but if he at least suspected she was pregnant, that would place this ambush incident very close to December 15.

On the fateful morning of the 15th, John ordered Space to fly reconnaissance in an Air America plane over Route 23, between Pakse and Paksong, and to monitor enemy activity around Paksong. John then left in his Jeep, accompanied by FAG Ringer, for Paksong for a strategic meeting at what was called Forward Headquarters. Backward Headquarters was in Pakse, while Headquarter 333 was in Udon Thani, in northeast Thailand, the location of a US airbase. Others in attendance at the Paksong meeting were Thai Colonel Panya Singsadka (whose call sign was "Panharn"), commander of Task Force Phasouk, along with GM 401's deputy commander, BC 613A's commander, and FAG Knife, whom John had once threatened to fire.

The men were standing under a large tree in front of headquarters when, around 11:30 a.m., a mortar round landed nearby. As reported to Sparkplug by Ringer, John was in an argument with one of the officers at the time, but they seemed unconcerned by the explosion. It was, as Sparkplug said, "a sloppy shot."[29] Space, who saw the meeting from the air, heard the first explosion. He radioed to John, who assured him there was nothing to worry about and ordered him to continue his surveillance.

In Sparkplug's recounting of what Ringer told him, a second mortar round followed, closer but still not on target. At that point, just as Ringer and others decided to go for coffee, a third round landed. Other reports don't mention a second missed shot but state that the second shot hit the jackpot. Space wrote, "Suddenly, another shot was fired, that time it exploded in the middle of the meeting, seeing fire and smoke rising and people fled in panic."[30] In an email, he confirmed that it was the second round that "reached the middle of the meeting."[31]

In his Indochina monograph, Laotian General Vongsavanh simply stated, without counting mortar rounds, that the Paksong headquarters suffered a "direct hit" that "quickly demolished the command post."[32] Conboy writes of Special Colonel Singsakda receiving a briefing from field commanders when, again without counting rounds, a mortar round "landed in their midst."[33] The CIA notice of John's death, sent the day after the attack, said that John was discussing matters with commanders and staff when "a second round landed in the proximity of the group killing John and GM 401 commander."[34] The Recommendation for Honor or Merit Award nominating John for the CIA Intelligence Star places blame on a second round. "Before Mr. Kearns and the local commanders could disperse into bunkers, a second round landed near the group, killing Mr. Kearns and the regimental commander."[35]

Whether it was the second or third shot is not a significant disagreement. What happened next, though, is subject to a higher level of controversy. The 1973 recommendation for the Intelligence Star states that the fatal attack occurred while John was "assisting in the helicopter insertion of 200 replacements for his unit and for tactical discussion with his unit commanders."[36] But in 2000, we see the first account of a mortally-wounded John

Kearns directing counter-battery fire and supervising evacuation in Director Tenet's remarks at the Annual Memorial Ceremony.

> On December 15, 1972, John Kearns and his group were hit by a sudden barrage of North Vietnamese mortar fire. Lonestar radioed for help, reporting that he had men seriously injured. What he did not say was that he, too, had been wounded. A thumbnail-sized mortar fragment had struck him in the chest.
>
> John directed counter-battery fire, helped the others to safety, and, refusing medical attention for himself, supervised as much of the emergency evacuation as he could until he became too weak to stand. He died in the rescue helicopter en route to the hospital.[37]

In 2002, Absher, taking his cue from Tenet's remarks, wrote that John's "Thai operations assistant reported" that, although seriously wounded, John "directed counter-battery fire, led others to safety, and supervised as much of the evacuation of the wounded by helicopter as he could before being evacuated himself."[38] It's unclear how Absher could have obtained this detail from John's operations assistant, since Space was not present, although he witnessed the mortar attack or at least evidence of the attack from the air. It's possible, if not probable, that Absher was referring to Ringer who, although not assigned as John's operations assistant, had accompanied John to Paksong and was physically present at the time of the attack.

Sparkplug reported that Ringer, who was headed to get coffee, told him that he "turned to see the people falling in a pile like fallen leaves." When he ran over, "he was shocked to find the bodies of both John and [FAG] Knife lying in a pool of blood." He makes no mention of John radioing for help, directing counter-battery fire, or supervising evacuation. Ringer then assisted in loading their "still breathing bodies" onboard an aircraft—he said it was a "plane," though Tenet stated in his remarks that it was a helicopter.[39] The CIA advisement of John's death, dated the following day, reported there were about three thousand friendly troops around Paksong and that replacements were on the way via three H-34s and one CH-47, all helicopters—the H-34s were Sikorsky and the CH-47 a Chinook.[40] Sparkplug reported that John was placed on an H-34.

Carter dismisses Absher's article, accusing him of giving "an erroneous account" of John's death. Carter then quotes a portion of a paragraph from Absher, omitting some language without identifying the language he has omitted, and states, "None of this is true, according to FAGS in the area."[41]

The following provides a comparison between Absher's and Carter's versions, with the differences noted in brackets:

> At 1930 hours *on 15 December, [Carter omitted the date]* eight rounds of 82mm mortar fire impacted near a battalion of Thai irregulars; hours later, 15 more rounds slammed in. A C-47 "Spooky" gunship silenced the suspected mortar positions, *but there had been casualties [Carter wrote "not before there were casualties"].* Among them, John Kearns.
>
> *Kearns was on the ground near Paksong supervising the infiltration of several hundred replacement troops for a Thai irregular battalion exhausted by combat, according to Leon*

> *Williamson, a fellow case officer who was Kearns's roommate at Pakse and who had arrived on the scene by helicopter. [Carter omitted the prior sentence in its entirety with no ellipsis or other indication that language had been omitted]* Although Kearns was seriously wounded in the mortar attack, he directed counter-battery fire, led others to safety, and supervised as much of the evacuation of the wounded by helicopter as he could before being evacuated himself, his *Thai [Carter used the letters CIA within parentheses, (CIA), rather than Thai] operations assistant [Carter used upper case O and A]* reported. Kearns died *en [Carter wrote in]* route to the hospital. A mortar fragment had pierced his aorta.[42]

Notwithstanding Carter's blanket "none of this" assertion, he does not specifically dispute all the specifics of the account, but simply disputes the time of the attack—Carter says it didn't occur at 1930 hours but rather in the morning—and claims that there was no C-47 gunship in the area.[43]

Carter is correct as to the time of the attack. The CIA notice of John's death places it at 1130 hours, as does the Recommendation for Honor or Merit Award. Sparkplug's note in his memo book, which he calls his "sitrep memo," similarly places the event at 1130. Carter's sources, the FAGs, also suggest that Absher's statement that a "C-47 'Spooky' gunship silenced the suspected mortar positions" was incorrect.[44] Space told me that, upon getting word of the attack and casualties in Paksong, he contacted the Raven base in Pakse to coordinate an air attack on the location using F-104/105 aircraft, not Spooky gunships, which he said were used only at night. He wrote that the "C-47 Laos Spooky was not involved in the incident."[45]

The Douglas AC-47 "Spooky" gunship, sometimes known as "Puff the Magic Dragon," was a side-firing aircraft with three M134 Miniguns mounted to fire through openings on the side of the fuselage. This side mounting allowed the craft to loop around an enemy position in a circular pattern. One report says that it would

> light up an incoming enemy invasion, both with flares and fire, which not only stripped away the defense of darkness but provided fast, accurate close air support shooting 8,000 rounds a minute on targets 8,000 feet away. Because of the glowing red tracers across darkened skies, the AC-47 had a psychological effect on those it flew against, and took on a mythical identity, living up to the names "Spooky" and "Puff the Magic Dragon."[46]

The Lockheed F-104 "Starfighter" frequently escorted the F-105, which was also known as the "Thunderchief." Both were utilized in Vietnam and Laos, heavily along the Ho Chi Minh Trail. But calling for F-104/105 strikes does not mean there not might have been a Spooky gunship in the area. Although the Spooky was primarily used, and attained near-mythic, almost legendary status, during nighttime, it was utilized for daytime missions as well. Neither Space nor Sparkplug saw any Spooky gunship, but Space had returned to Pakse and Sparkplug had been stationed in the field a few kilometers away, so it's unlikely either would have actually seen attacks on the mortar positions. Absher does not cite his specific source for saying a Spooky took out the position. While the type of aircraft remains a little unclear, it was probably not a Spooky. Apparently there is no dispute, however, that the mortar positions were silenced.

But it was too late.

★ ★ ★ ★ ★

Carter could have specifically challenged the idea of John supervising counter-battery fire, etc., but for some reason he didn't—other than, one supposes, lumping it generically under the "none of this" catch-all. It's unclear what sources Tenet relied upon for his description of John's actions after being wounded, which Absher parroted in his article. Maybe Tenet relied on other CIA documents that have not yet seen the declassified light of day. Maybe Absher's review of situation reports and interviews with knowledgeable persons confirmed Tenet's account. That account, though, seems at odds with Ringer's observation of seeing bodies fall and running over to find John lying in a pool of blood, then loading his still-breathing body on board an aircraft. Unfortunately, Ringer is now deceased, so there is no way to follow up on his eyewitness observation as he related it to Sparkplug.

Sparkplug confirmed in a telephone interview that Ringer did not mention the actions Tenet and Absher related.[47] Space told the author in an email, "All I know was that mortar later fired a shot into the middle of the meeting, the situation was very confusing."[48] That doesn't mean they didn't happen. Omission is not contradiction. It just means there is no crystal clarity. The fog of war.

But regardless of whether Tenet and Absher relied upon other reports, or whether they were simply resorting to heroic hyperbole, John's mere presence in Laos, and in Paksong that fateful morning, was an act of heroism and self-sacrifice.

★ ★ ★ ★ ★

Once aboard the H-34, first aid was administered to John and Knife. John died en route to headquarters in Pakse. According to Ringer's account, both were in bad shape when loaded onto the helicopter. John had lost a lot of blood from a "gaping abdominal wound," which is consistent with Space's statement that "Lone Star's body was torn apart."[49] Although Space was not present on the ground at the attack, he witnessed the body when it was returned to Pakse. According to Sparkplug, John's eyes remained open after he died but "Ringer rubbed his hand over John's drooping eyelids to put him to a deep sleep."[50]

As the helicopter drew closer to Pakse, the pilot was notified that both John and Knife had died. No longer worried about needing emergency medical treatment for his passengers, he dropped down over the Mekong River, flying low enough that the craft was barely above the surface of the water, and weaved from side to side across the water. According to Sparkplug, the gesture was meant to salute and honor the lost lives on board. According to the death notice, "John was pronounced dead upon arrival at PS-18 and it was doctor's opinion that shrapnel had severed the aorta."[51]

When Sparkplug returned to Pakse, he saw Space parking John's Jeep, but saw no sign of John. When he asked where Lone Star was, Space "shook his head slowly before collapsing into his seat." He didn't, as yet, know that John's and Knife's injuries had been fatal, just that they had been severely hit. Sparkplug wrote, "Everyone was speechless. I myself was shocked, and my whole body was goosebumps." It was not until later in the afternoon that they received word that the injuries had been fatal.[52]

★ ★ ★ ★ ★

Thailand is, and was at the time, an overwhelmingly Buddhist country. One of the time-honored death ceremonies in Buddhism is the bathing ceremony. Traditionally, the ceremony begins with family members or other loved ones gently washing the body with cloths and warm water, paying particular attention to arms, legs, and torso. Sometimes aromatic herbs are used. The cleansing is intended as an act of purification and love, symbolizing that "maintaining a mind as pure as coconut water will lead one to the path of nirvana upon death."[53]

The deceased is then dressed in simple clothing to help guide the spirit to reincarnation. In Theravada Buddhism, a water-pouring ceremony may be involved, in which water is poured into the deceased's hand and allowed to flow into a bowl. This symbolizes merit transfer of the soul. The ceremony, accompanied by chanting by monks, is highly symbolic, illustrating purification by wiping away worldly attachments and sins, a final act of care to symbolize love and respect, and ultimately to help the consciousness detach and move on to the next world.

According to Space, when John's body was delivered to Pakse, along with that of four others killed in the attack, "We then went to the ritual of washing Lone Star's body." It started at approximately 4:00 p.m. and was witnessed and participated in by FAGs and American case officers. First, the medic team washed the bodies, which were then dressed in plain clothing. A water-pouring ceremony followed, using perfume instead of water. After the bodies were placed in coffins, they were sprinkled with sage and lavender. Monks continually chanted prayers throughout. Once the ceremony had ended, the bodies of Thais were sent to Thailand, where they would be picked up by relatives for their funerals. John's body was taken to the Air Operations base in Pakse for transport back home to Texas, accompanied by his friend Douglas Hardy, after whom his son would be named.[54]

John was laid to rest in a small cemetery at Cahill Methodist Church in Alvarado, Texas, with a simple grave marker. Kathy went on to a career of her own in the CIA before joining John in death on August 3, 2016. She was laid to rest beside her husband. A joint headstone was placed opposite John's grave marker. Above each of their names, the reference to a Bible verse was etched.

For Kathy, it is Matthew 25:21: "His lord said unto him, Well done, thou good and faithful servant: thou has been faithful over a few things, I will make thee ruler over many things: enter thou into the joy of the lord."

For John, it is John 15:13: "Greater love hath no man than this, that a man lay down his life for his friends."

Fitting.

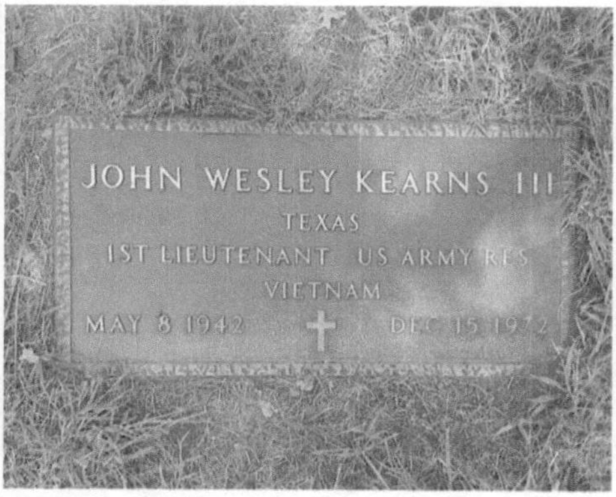

Grave marker for John Kearns at Cahill Methodist Church in Alvarado, Texas. *Photo courtesy of Mike Farris.*

Headstone for John Kearns and Kathleen Main Kearns at Cahill Methodist Church in Alvarado, Texas. *Photo courtesy of Mike Farris.*

Epilogue

Finding Lone Star

"All the wrong people remember Vietnam. I think all the people who remember it should forget it, and all the people who forget it should remember it."

Michael Herr, Vietnam War correspondent for *Esquire*

I wasn't present in Langley, Virginia, that June day in 2000 when CIA Director George Tenet stood in front of the CIA's Wall of Honor and first revealed John Kearns's name publicly as a recipient of the Intelligence Star. I had first learned of my half-brother's existence in the mid-1990s, a time when I was angrily storming the walls of middle age. As I grew to know my birth mother and her other children, there was a gap in my knowledge about John. After all, he had already been gone for more than twenty years. I became fixated on knowing more about this larger-than-life, almost mythical, figure in Kearns family lore. Johnny, they called him. Lone Star, they said he was called by the CIA. A hero, I was told.

Even so, I didn't really begin my search for him for another nearly twenty years, when I decided to send a Freedom of Information Act request to the CIA on June 4, 2014. I wanted to know more about him. I had heard how he lived, but I wanted to know how he died. And I wanted to know more about myself.

Maybe, a blood brother might help me fill in some of those blanks in my own life. It took about four and a half years, and the assistance of Texas Senator John Cornyn, to finally receive partial documentation. Other documentation was withheld based upon FOIA exemptions related to the Central Intelligence Agency Act of 1949 and the National Security Act of 1947. But enough was provided to give me insights into just exactly who Lone Star was. Insights into who my brother was.

My brother whom I never met, who died before I even knew that he existed. Who died before he could even meet his own son, who was born eight months after his death.

Obviously, John Kearns's upbringing and life experience, shortened though it might have been, were not the same as mine. But the same blood courses through my veins that spilled from his onto the floor of a helicopter in Laos. Yet we are radically different. He was a hero; I am not. What made the difference? Was it nature or nurture? How would I have turned out if I had been raised in the same family he was? Timing certainly had something to do with it, of course. I was born more than a decade after John, and the Vietnam War was winding down when I came of draft age. Still, I dreaded the possibility of being drafted to be sent to a war where friends had died. John, on the other hand, had volunteered for service in that war, not once but twice. So yes, timing was a factor. But the real difference was the choices we made. Choices that had consequences. Any time someone tells you that they have no regrets with the choices they made in life, keep a close watch on your wallet. Everyone has regrets. I certainly do.

Life is a stern and unforgiving taskmaster. Many of the lessons it teaches are hard-learned, and they often leave scars, both physical and emotional. It has been humbling to learn about John and the choices he made, especially the unselfish choices that led to an early death. His was a life of service to his country. My history, on the other hand, is uneven, full of self-serving choices and regrets. Scars. There are also questions. Well, at least one question in particular. The "what if" question. But there are also things to be grateful for.

Here are my regrets:

Love and relationships: I regret not holding on to the women who were good for me. Too often I looked over the fence instead of staying where I was and building something lasting. That fear of settling down cost me real companionship. I lost two sons along the way, and today I have no one to take care of me in my old age. Those are my deepest regrets.

Service and duty: I regret not serving in the military. In 1972, when I turned eighteen, I expected to be drafted. I had no job, no high school diploma, and no direction. Instead of stepping forward, I let the experience slip past me. I'll always wonder what lessons I might have learned there. Could I have been a Lone Star? I'll never know.

Family and home: I regret not appreciating my adoptive mother more—the meals she cooked, the house she kept, the sacrifices she made. I regret not helping her more. I regret not listening to my father as he came home from long days running the rental store and gas station. He had a sharp mind for planning and investing, and I missed the chance to learn from him.

Finances: I regret spending too much on wine, women, and cocaine, instead of saving and building for the future.

Here is what I wonder about—the big "what if?":

A different life with my birth family: I wonder what life would have been like if my biological mother and father had stayed together, and I had not been put up for adoption. I would have grown up with four blood siblings: two brothers and two sisters. My birth father, a Fort Worth cop, might have given me a different path. Maybe I would have stayed out of jail in Ohio—or anywhere else. I'll always wonder why my birth mother turned him down when he proposed, and how different my life might have been.

Here is what I'm grateful for:

Adoptive family: I'm grateful I was adopted by good people, even though we had our struggles. I have a sister, also adopted, and through her, I have a nephew, James; a niece-in-law, Ashley Ann; and now a baseball-playing phenom grandnephew, Cooper. I have a family.

Opportunities to know my past: You can't know where you're going unless you know where you've been. I'm grateful for the woman, whose name I can't recall, who connected me with a judge who was willing to open my birth records. I'm grateful that I live in an age where the Internet made it possible to track down my family. I'm grateful that I found my birth sisters and that they turned out to be wonderful people. And I'm grateful that I found Lone Star.

John's legacy is reflected in a star carved on a wall. And mine? Maybe a part of it will be the 501(c)(3) I started, called Memories, Inc., where we explore remembrances of the past.[1] The jury is still out on that. I wonder whether this book is simply my personal Pentagon Papers, ostensibly a guide to others about mistakes to avoid, but in reality, nothing more than an embarrassing exposure of poor choices. I can't erase the mistakes of my past, so I've decided, instead, to embrace the lessons I have learned from them. My life, after all, is a cautionary tale. Maybe, just maybe, I can use my life to teach others. Maybe, just maybe, that can be my legacy.

Acknowledgments

Paul Heckmann:

I have been working on this book for fifteen years or so, though I had thought about it long before that. Finding a family you never knew you had can be exhilarating, especially when you learn about a hero in the family you'll never be able to know. When I decided to move forward, I was initially focused solely on the story of that hero, John "Lone Star" Kearns. As I tried to learn more, my newly found family pointed me in the right direction over and over: Frances Kearns, Sandy Kearns Bonaventure, Sharon Kearns Jackson, and John Douglas Kearns.

I spoke with John E. Malone, who had been a friend of John's since their days together as part of the Four Hundredth Army Security Agency and who wrote about John in his book *Top Secret Missions: Performed by Elite Commo & Intel Specialists.* Needless to say, his stories piqued my interest about my half-brother, but I still wasn't sure how to proceed. I finally got a jumpstart with the assistance of Texas Senator John Cornyn and his office. They led me through the Freedom of Information request process to the Central Intelligence Agency, which provided me with precious information about my half-brother. Thank you.

This book is also about my life, and my struggles, over the years. It's hard to sum up your life in a book without relying on friends and family who have been there for you at every bump in the road. It's even harder to thank all those without the fear of leaving out someone. Here's my best shot at it.

I have to start with my adoptive family, Joyce and Fred Heckmann (Mom and Dad) and sister Kathi Heckmann Quinn.

I would be remiss if I didn't mention those institutions of higher learning that tried their hardest to educate me, despite my seeming resistance at the time. They include Texas A&M-Kingsville (formerly known as Texas A&I University) and Baylor University.

Of course, I owe a huge debt of gratitude to friends and acquaintances who supported me, including during some very trying times: Bill Bronstad, Gene Cook, Rick Marshall, Fred Neusche, George Sanchez, Larry and Jan Mumford Hirt, Maryanne Brignac, Rod Keishnick, Fran Lucchesi Waslaski, Lenny Licht, Kelley Reese, Chuck Wilson, Dennis Dearborn, John and Carmen Malone, Mike Kapoustin, Thomas "Hollywood" Henderson, and my friends and cohorts at Memories Incorporated.

When it finally came time to put words and thoughts to paper, I wasn't sure how to proceed until I came across Mike Farris, a retired attorney and current adjunct professor at the University of Texas at Arlington. Mike had already written multiple books and knew how to put everything together. There would be no book without him

And finally, to the staff at TCU Press—Dan Williams, Adrienne Martinez, Paige Gulley, and Marco Roc—thank you for believing in this project. It is my fervent hope that others can learn from my mistakes.

Mike Farris:

When Paul Heckmann first approached me about helping him with a project about his half-brother, who had been killed during the Vietnam War, I was intrigued. The more we talked and the more I learned, the more I realized that Paul had a personal story of his own to tell. So we decided to move forward along two tracks, one track telling Paul's story and the second telling the story of John Kearns. I, of course, relied heavily upon Paul for the former, but the latter was a bit more challenging, and at times even a little frustrating.

For example, we had a start with declassified CIA documents that Paul had obtained, with the assistance of Texas Senator John Cornyn, through a Freedom of Information request. On June 26, 2025, I submitted a FOIA request of my own, this time seeking John Kearns's personnel file and his death certificate. Hurry up and wait, of course. I heard nothing until I received a letter, dated February 10, 2026, telling me that during a "shelf review," they discovered that they had not responded to my FOIA request. The letter assured me, however, that the request was placed in its queue "in the order in which it was received" and that it was "currently being processed . . . ." Stay tuned.

In researching the history of the so-called "secret war" in Laos, I received assistance from the good folks at the History of Aviation Archives in the Special Collections and Archives Division at the Eugene McDermott Library at the University of Texas at Dallas, which included an archive specifically related to Air America. Patricia Nava, Senior Curator of Aviation Archives, with the assistance of Henry Ortiz, facilitated my research in the archives. It was there that I discovered the transcription of a verbal statement from "Customer" given to an Air America investigator looking into the deaths of a pilot and copilot of a downed C-46 in June of 1971—a statement that, in all certainty, was the statement of John Kearns.

I also paid a visit to the Vietnam Center and Archive at Texas Tech University in Lubbock, where Sheon Montgomery, Reference Archivist, gave me a personal tour of the archives and answered a lot of questions.

Thank you, also, to Larry Ashmun, Distinguished Southeast Asian & Hmong Studies Bibliographer at the University of Wisconsin-Madison. Larry directed me to, and assisted me with finding, relevant photos in the Ernest and Phaythoune Kuhn Image Collection that is part of the university's Southeast Asian Images & Texts Project.

I want to thank Douglas Bonner III, an attorney in Washington, D.C. In my research into the CIA station at Nam Yu in northwest Laos, I came across an article in the Bucknell University alumni magazine that Doug had written about a visit he made to Nam Yu as a boy living in Vientiane, Laos, where his father was stationed with the CIA during the "secret war." I contacted Doug, who provided me with a full copy of the article that had been excerpted in the magazine, as well as additional information about his visit to Nam Yu. He also provided me with some family photographs, including the photo of his father and Vang Pao that is included in the book.

My study of Nam Yu and Tony Poe, who had been stationed there, led me to newspaper articles written by journalist Michael Morrow for the *Dispatch News Service* in late 1970 and early 1971. It's been more than fifty years, but I searched and found that Morrow is living in, of all places, Mongolia. I even found an email address for him and, on a hunch, sent an email that started a correspondence with him. He provided invaluable information about CIA activities in Nam Yu and his reporting on Tony Poe, who, he learned, had put a $10,000 bounty on his head. Thank you, Michael, for e-talking with me.

Just when I thought I had finished the manuscript and was ready to submit it to TCU Press, I made connections that caused me to totally rewrite the penultimate chapter, titled "What Really Happened to Lone Star." Again acting on a hunch, I posted on a Facebook group I found called "The Secret War – Laos List." In my post, I briefly described the subject matter of this book and sought to connect with anyone who might have known, or known of, John Kearns. I got several responses and ultimately connected with Weera Star, a Thai forward air guide (a group known by the unfortunate acronym FAGs) whose code name was Sparkplug and who actually worked with John during those final few months. He, in turn, connected me with Chalermchai Thammawetin, whose code name was Space. Space was John Kearns's operations assistant at Pakse, Laos, in the time leading up to John's death. I was in regular contact with both men for weeks—even speaking by phone with Sparkplug on several occasions—who both patiently answered my seemingly endless list of questions.

They also provided me with photographs and their own written recollections of John Kearns. That included Space's book *The Unknown Warriors: Secret War in Laos,* which he graciously sent to me, and an article by Sparkplug, which I had to have translated from Thai to English—thank you, Google Translate. Sparkplug informed me early on in our correspondence that I needed to move quickly because "we don't have much time left." Truer words were never spoken. When my text message to another FAG named Supradit Kanthawanij, whose code name was LollyPop, went unanswered, I asked Sparkplug to see if he could make contact on my behalf. In a message I received on the evening of January 23, 2026, Sparkplug wrote, "Sorry to inform you that LollyPop is gone. His son confirmed his death yesterday." Of LollyPop, Sparkplug said that he proved himself in "several daring actions." I am extremely grateful for the invaluable assistance these men provided to me—and for their courage during the "secret war" in Laos.

Through that Facebook group, I also made contact with a gentleman named Joe Rattanakhom, whose father, Houmphanh Rattanakhom, was commander of GM 41 of 408 Battalion of Thai forces in southern Laos. John Kearns's friend and roommate at Pakse, Leon Williamson, was advisor to GM 41. Houmphanh went by the code name Singh Dang, meaning Red Lion, while Leon was "Singh Kham," or Golden Lion. Thank you, Joe, for providing the photo of your father.

I also want to thank Dan Williams, Adrienne Martinez, Paige Gulley, and Marco Roc at TCU Press for helping to make this a reality. Thank you for believing this project to be worthy of publication.

Last, but not least, I want to thank my wife Susan for her constant and continued support. I couldn't do it without her.

APPENDIX A

SECRET
Remarks of the Director of Central Intelligence
George J. Tenet
at the
Annual Memorial Ceremony
June 2, 2000

Another year has passed since we last gathered here as an extended CIA family to honor the extraordinary men and women behind the stars on this wall. For those who visit our Headquarters Building, these silent stars symbolize the depth of the Central Intelligence Agency's commitment to our Mission and to our Country.

To us, the men and women of CIA, they are more than just inspiring symbols. They are fallen colleagues and cherished friends who profoundly touched the life of this Agency. And to you, their wives and husbands and fiancees, their mothers and fathers, sisters and brothers, children and grandchildren, nieces and nephews, they are loved ones forever lost, families forever fractured.

Each of the seventy-seven irreplaceable individuals had places to go, goals to reach and people to love. None of them would have wanted the distinction of being on this Wall of Honor. But now, they are eternally joined in quiet constellation.

Some might say that cruel Destiny drew them together. But I say that the magnificent men and women behind these stars were united in spirit long before each of them arrived on the Wall. As uniquely human as each of them was—all were patriotic Americans who dedicated their lives to their Intelligence Mission and to their Country. They did not choose their fate, but they did choose their calling and they gave their fellow Americans their last full measure of devotion.

On behalf of the men and women of CIA, I want you to know that we, too, hold your loved ones in our hearts and in our thoughts, for we serve the same intelligence mission and we were privileged to know them as others did not—as others could not. We are thankful for the portion of their lives that they spent with us, and for the precious legacy of service and sacrifice that they have passed on to us, from one generation to the next, from one century to the next. And we are thankful to you, their families, for sharing them with us.

As those of you who have attended before know, at this annual memorial ceremony we make a special point of telling the stories behind any stars that have been added to our Wall during the previous year. Since last year's ceremony, no new stars have been carved into the wall. By the grace of God, we have not lost anyone in the past year. And we pray that when we next gather, no new families will have suffered the heartache that you have known.

Every family here remembers the time when grief was fresh. For some, it came a half century ago. For others, much more recently. Whenever it came, it changed your lives forever. Ever since, a face has been missing from the family pictures. From that time on, you no longer heard that familiar voice on the other end of the phone, or the laugh you could pick out of a noisy crowd. A loving touch was felt no more.

The passage of time only makes your memories—and this ceremony—all the more important to you—and to us.

We are also very aware of the fact that many of you still bear the burden of secrecy. We realize that this annual ceremony is not just an opportunity for us, on behalf of our nation, to express our lasting gratitude for the contributions of your loved ones. We also know that this private gathering—here among other families and Agency employees—may be the only opportunity that many families have to freely acknowledge how your loved ones lived and died.

For some among you today, the heavy burden of secrecy has been lifted. Each year at our memorial ceremony we recognize the men and women whose stars have long been on the wall, but whose names can only now be revealed. The three names newly listed in our Book of Honor are: John W. Kearns, Norman A. Schwartz and Robert C. Snoddy.

Special Operations Officer John Kearns's callsign was "Lonestar," befitting a proud Texan with shining blue eyes. On the first day of her freshman year, the young woman who was to become John's wife walked into her geology class at North Texas State University, caught sight of those crystal blue eyes and knew that he was "The One." [redacted] says it took John a little longer than she did to figure that out. That's usually the way it works.

After graduating in 1968, John, a former Army special forces officer, joined the CIA on contract and was sent to Laos. John returned to the US in 1971 and converted to staff. Practically every weekend, John would drive—to Dallas and back—to see [redacted]. They were married on Christmas Eve in 1971. The newlyweds posted to Laos the next summer. [redacted] while John was running Special Operations [redacted] leading Lao forces against North Vietnamese regulars. John's mission was to tie down as many Vietcong as possible to prevent them from getting to South Vietnam and killing American forces there.

On December 15, 1972, John Kearns and his group were hit by a sudden barrage of North Vietnamese mortar fire. Lonestar [sic] radioed for help, reporting that he had men seriously injured. What he did not say was that he, too, had been wounded. A thumbnail-sized mortar fragment had struck him in the chest.

John directed counter battery fire, helped the others to safety and, refusing medical attention for himself, supervised as much of the emergency evacuation as he could until he became too weak to stand. He died in the rescue helicopter en route to the hospital. John Kearns was 30 when he gave his life on a lonely battlefield so that others might live. The following August [redacted] gave birth to a beautiful baby boy with curly blond hair, a winning smile and crystal blue eyes. She named him after the father he would never meet.

[redacted]

For those of you who attended last year's memorial ceremony, the stories of Norman Schwartz and Robert Snoddy will be familiar. Last year, their stars were added to the wall. This year, we have been able to inscribe their names.

Norm and Bob were pilots flying for a CIA proprietary company, Civil Air Transport, whose covert mission was to provide air support to anti-Chinese

Government guerrillas. Their plane was shot down by the Red Chinese over Manchuria in November 1952. Norm and Bob were killed in the crash. Norm was 30 and Bob was 31.

Their two passengers—CIA case officers Jack Downey and Dick Fecteau—survived and were captured. They each would endure two decades of imprisonment. In the low times, when all hope seemed futile, the two survivors must have thought that Norm and Bob had been the lucky ones. Jack and Dick could not then have known that they would be released in the early 1970s, and that they would go on to live happy, productive lives. When Jack and Dick were honored here a few years ago, they said that they felt so very blessed to have experienced the joys of long life that were so tragically denied to Norm and Bob. At the time Bob was killed, his wife Charlotte was expecting their first child. Their daughter Roberta was born three weeks after he died. Norm was a bachelor, but he left behind devoted parents and siblings.

[redacted]

At this, our first memorial gathering in the new century, I believe it is fitting that we now take a few moments to recall two early heroes of our Agency whose valor is undiminished by the passage of time: [redacted] and Douglas Mackiernan. Though their service and sacrifice date back over five decades, I regret that their work for this Agency still cannot be acknowledged outside our CIA family. [redacted]

[redacted]

[redacted]

[redacted]

[redacted]

Today, I also wish to recognize a large contingent from the Mackiernan family. Doug is often referred to as our "First Star" because he was the first of those honored here to be killed. [redacted]

The year 2000 marks the 50th anniversary of Doug's death at age 37. Doug and three others in his party were killed by mistake by a Tibetan military patrol at a remote crossing on the Chinese-Tibet border. It was on the final leg of their harrowing 7-month, 1,000 mile trek through some of the wildest, most austere, beautiful and unforgiving terrain on earth—across a desert known as White Death and over the Himalaya Mountains. The Tibetan patrol had not gotten word from Lhasa [a city in Tibet] that Doug and his party were to be given safe passage. We honor and remember Doug this morning, here within the circle of our Agency Family, not because he was the first among our stars to *die*—but because Doug was among the first to *serve.* [emphasis in original]

We have entered a new century. The world confronting us today is very different from the one that took [redacted], Doug, Bob and Norm to China, and John to Laos. But our history—the legacy of these 77 men and women—is the foundation of our future. We tell our young officers to stop at this wall—to say a prayer—to honor their fallen colleagues—not just out of respect—but so that they can be infused with a sense of service, honor, and devotion to country that simply cannot be taught.

And in the quietest of moments, I believe we can hear what the spirit of these stars might say to a young man or woman standing before this wall searching for a sense of purpose. And I think the message would be this:

"Our loss was for a noble cause. We await the day when we can be reunited with all those we love. Start your careers with pride—you are serving the greatest country in the world. Think of us in your most difficult moments—we will always be there to protect you from danger. There are 77 of us always covering your back. Remember, there is no greater honor than being known as an officer of the Central Intelligence Agency. May God always bless you."

Each year we pray that someone's beautiful son or daughter, husband or wife, mother or father, will not become the newest star on this wall—and each day I thank God for the seventy-seven men and women whose stars grace it now.

Their souls reside with the Lord. Their memories abide with us. May they rest in peace, secure in the knowledge that their service and sacrifice shall never be forgotten by this Agency and a grateful nation.

Now, I will ask representatives from each of our four Directorates to call the roll of honor. We are able to speak the names behind all seventy-seven stars only here within these walls among our extended CIA Family. Thank you for sharing your memories and this day with us. May God bless you all.

Appendix B

CIA Approved for Release: 2022/02/11 C06520612

SECRET

REPRODUCTION OF THIS COPY PROHIBITED

FE

DDP

1355

PRECEDENCE

FILE, VR.

S E C R E T 191228Z DEC 72 STAFF

CITE 64749 738617

(b)(1)
(b)(3)

IMMEDIATE DIRECTOR INFO PRIORITY UDORN.

RYBAT ADMIN PERS

1. REGRET TO ADVISE THAT MR. JOHN W. KEARNS III WAS KILLED BY INCOMING ARTILLERY FIRE IN THE PAKSONG AREA AT APPROXIMATELY 1137 LOCAL 15 DECEMBER. JOHN WAS IN AREA TO ASSIST IN INFIL OF 223 REPLACEMENTS FOR GM 401. HE HAD BEEN ON THE GROUND FOR APPROX TWO HOURS AND THERE WAS NO REPORTED ENEMY ACTIVITY IN AREA. APPROXIMATELY 3228 FRIENDLY TROOPS OF GM'S 401 AND 33 WERE SURROUNDING THE VICINITY OF PAKSONG. THREE H-34'S AND ONE CH-47 WITH REPLACEMENTS WERE EN ROUTE TO PAKSONG AT THE TIME. JOHN WAS DISCUSSING ACTIVITIES WITH GM COMMANDERS AND STAFF WHEN ONE MORTAR ROUND (82 MM OR 120 MM) LANDED SEVERAL METERS AWAY. BEFORE PERSONNEL COULD DISPERSE INTO BUNKERS A SECOND ROUND LANDED IN THE PROXIMITY OF THE GROUP KILLING JOHN AND GM 401 COMMANDER, AND WOUNDING APPROX 21 OTHERS. ADDITIONAL INCOMING FOLLOWED THIS TWO ROUND BARRAGE AND THE CH-47 WAS DIVERTED BACK TO PAKSE. THE THREE H-34'S WERE ORDERED TO STAND BY FOR MEDEVAC.

SECRET

Approved for Release: 2022/02/11 C06520612

CABLE SECRETARIAT DISSEMINATION | CLASSIFIED MESSAGE | TOTAL COPIES | ROUTING AND/OR INITIALS SEEN

SECRET (When Filled In)

REPRODUCTION OF THIS COPY PROHIBITED

ADVANCE COPY ☐ ISSUED ☐ SLOTTED

AT: Z

FILE, VR

PAGE 2 [redacted] 64749 S E C R E T (b)(1) (b)(3)

AFTER INCOMING CEASED H-34'S LANDED, DISCHARGED THEIR TROOPS AND EVACUATED KIA AND WIA TO PS-18, ARRIVING ABOUT 1318. JOHN WAS PRONOUNCED DEAD UPON ARRIVAL AT PS-18 AND IT WAS DOCTOR'S OPINION THAT SHRAPNEL HAD SEVERED THE AORTA. COU PAKSE ACCOMPANIED REMAINS TO UDORN AND THENCE TO [redacted] TO SEE [redacted] (b)(1) (b)(3) (b)(6)

2. DEATH CERTIFICATE EXECUTED BY MAJ BURT, MD, USAF, UDORN, WHICH STATES DEATH WAS ACCIDENTAL AND MEDICAL CAUSE INTERNAL BLEEDING. PLACE OF DEATH LISTED VICINITY OF PAKSE, LAOS. EMPLOYMENT LISTED U.S. GOVERNMENT CONTRACT CIVILIAN. WE DO NOT ANTICIPATE PRESS COVERAGE BUT WILL PREPARE STORY FOR USE BY EMBASSY PRESS OFFICER AND VIP AIR AMERICA LAOS IN EVENT PRESS QUERIES OCCUR LOCALLY. (b)(6)

3. [redacted] WHO SAFEHAVENED [redacted] HAS BEEN NOTIFIED BY COS. [redacted] REQUESTS RELATIVES LISTED BELOW BE NOTIFIED OF JOHN'S DEATH. [redacted] ADVISES ALL ARE WITTING OF JOHN'S TRUE EMPLOYMENT WITH EMERALD. NO KNOWN MEDICAL PROBLEMS INVOLVED IN CONTACT. [redacted] DESIRES FOLLOWING BE NOTIFIED BY PERSONAL CONTACT. PLEASE CONFIRM WHEN NOTIFICATION ACCOMPLISHED. (b)(1) (b)(3) (b)(6) (b)(6) (b)(1) (b)(3) (b)(6)

SECRET

CABLE SECRETARIAT DISSEMINATION

PERSON/UNIT NOTIFIED

ADVANCE COPY ☐ ISSUED ☐ SLOTTED

BY ______ AT ______ Z

DISSEM BY ______ PER ______ #

ACTION UNIT

FILE, VR

ACTION NO.

SECRET

(When filled in)

REPRODUCTION OF THIS COPY PROHIBITED

ROUTING AND/OR INITIALS-SEEN BY

1		5	
2		6	
3		7	
4		8	

PAGE 3 [redacted] 64779 ~~S E C R E T~~ (b)(1) (b)(3)

[redacted] OF JOHN'S DEATH. (b)(6)

ALSO NOTIFY [redacted] (b)(6)

ALSO ATTEMPT NOTIFY [redacted] US SPECIAL FORCES THAILAND OF (b)(6)

JOHN'S DEATH. IN NOTIFICATION, PLS ADVISE [redacted] (b)(6)

[redacted] (b)(6)

5. REQUEST HQS ADVISE [redacted] ETA IN (b)(6)

DALLAS. E2 IMPDET.

S E C R E T

SECRET

Appendix C

C06395113

Approved for Release: 2018/11/28 C06395113

SECRET

SECRET
(when Filled In)

RECOMMENDATION FOR HONOR OR MERIT AWARD
(Submit in triplicate - see HR 20-37)

SECTION A — PERSONAL DATA

1. EMP SER NO | 2. NAME OF PERSON RECOMMENDED (Last-First-Middle): Kearns, John W. III | 3. POSITION TITLE: Ops Officer | 4. GRADE: GS-10 | 5. SD (b)(3)

6. OFFICE OF ASSIGNMENT: FE/TBL/L | 7. OFFICE EXT. (Name): N.A. | 8. STATUS: X | (Specify location) (b)(1) (b)(3)

9. HOME ADDRESS (No., St., City, State, ZIP Code): 925 Chadwick, Richardson, Texas | 10. HOME PHONE: (214)235-8432 | 11. CITIZENSHIP: U.S.

12. RECOMMENDED AWARD: Intelligence Star | 13. IF RETIRING, DATE OF RETIREMENT: N.A. | 14. POSTHUMOUS: X YES | NO

15. NAME OF NEXT OF KIN | 16. RELATIONSHIP: Wife | 17. HOME ADDRESS (No., St., City, State, ZIP Code): 925 Chadwick, Richardson, Texas | 18. PHONE: (214) 235-8 (b)(6)

SECTION B — RECOMMENDATION FOR AWARD FOR HEROIC ACTION OR ACCEPTANCE OF HAZARD

19. WERE YOU AN EYEWITNESS TO THE ACT: YES | X NO [redacted]

PERSONNEL IN IMMEDIATE VICINITY OR WHO ASSISTED IN ACT OR SHARED IN SAME HAZARD:

20. FULL NAME	21. ORGN. TITLE	22. GRADE	23. OFFICE OF ASSIGNMENT
None	N.A.	N.A.	N.A.

LIST ANY OF THE ABOVE PERSONS GIVEN AN AWARD OR RECOMMENDED FOR AWARD FOR PARTICIPATING IN ACT:

24. FULL NAME	25. AWARD RECOMMENDED
None	N.A.

CONDITIONS UNDER WHICH ACT WAS PERFORMED

26. LOCATION: Paksong, Laos | 27. INCLUSIVE DATES: 15 December 1972 | 28. TIME OF DAY: 1130 (local)

29. PREVAILING GEOGRAPHIC CONDITIONS AND OBSTACLES ENCOUNTERED:
The geographic conditions included generally a flat plain with several mountains located to the east of Paksong. Mr. Kearns was being subjected to incoming enemy mortar fire which resulted in his death.

30. DATES FOR WHICH AWARD RECOMMENDED: 15 December 1972 | 31. ASSIGNMENT COMPLETED: X YES | NO | 32. NOW IN SAME OR RELATED ASSIGNMENT: N.A. YES | NO

SECTION C — RECOMMENDATION FOR AWARD FOR ACHIEVEMENT, SERVICE, OR PERFORMANCE

33. DO YOU HAVE PERSONAL KNOWLEDGE OF THE SERVICE OR PERFORMANCE: YES | NO [redacted]

34. OFFICIAL ASSIGNMENT OF PERSON RECOMMENDED AT TIME OF SERVICE OR PERFORMANCE

35. COMPONENT OR STATION (Designation and location)

36. DUTIES AND RESPONSIBILITIES OF ASSIGNED POSITION

37. INCLUSIVE DATES FOR WHICH RECOMMENDED | 38. ASSIGNMENT COMPLETED: YES | NO | 39. NOW IN SAME OR RELATED ASSIGNMENT: YES | NO

PERSONNEL WHO ASSISTED OR CONTRIBUTED SUBSTANTIALLY TO THE SERVICE OR PERFORMANCE:

40. FULL NAME	41. ORGN. TITLE	42. GRADE	43. OFFICE OF ASSIGNMENT
N.A.			

LIST ANY OF THE ABOVE PERSONS GIVEN AN AWARD OR RECOMMENDED FOR AWARD FOR PARTICIPATING IN THE PERFORMANCE

44. FULL NAME	45. TYPE OF AWARD

FORM 600 USE PREVIOUS EDITION — SECRET — (b)(3)

SECRET
Approved for Release: 2018/11/28 C06395113

SECRET

Mr. John W. Kearns III is recommended for the Intelligence Star in recognition of an act of courage, performed under hazardous conditions, which resulted in his untimely death from enemy fire on 15 December 1972.

In July 1969 Mr. Kearns was assigned to the Vientiane Station, as the Operations Support (b)(1) (b)(3) Officer. Mr. Kearns then assumed the duties of a (b)(1) (b)(3) paramilitary case officer. He was responsible for all phases of activity relating to irregular forces and intelligence teams. In performing these functions Mr. Kearns was rated as performing in a strong manner.

In November 1969, Mr. Kearns was assigned as the Commando Raider Officer with He (b)(1) (b)(3) became deeply involved with a special operations program to send action teams against installations deep in enemy-held territory. In this project, Mr. Kearns was involved in the operational planning, training and motivation of the indigenous personnel on these action teams. During this period these small units conducted several successful operations.

SECRET

Appendix D

C06395113

Approved for Release: 2018/11/28 C06395113
SECRET

(b)(3)

(b)(3)

REPORT OF HONOR AND MERIT AWARDS BOARD

DATE: 27 March 1973

The Honor and Merit Awards Board having considered a recommendation that:

SERIAL OR ID NO.	NAME (Last-First-Middle)	BIRTHYEAR	SEX	TYPE EMPLOYEE
	KEARNS, John W. III	1947	M	Staff

(b)(3)

OFFICE OF ASSIGNMENT	SD	SERVICE	GRADE	STATION
DO/FE	D	GS	10	Vientiane

BE AWARDED: Intelligence Star (Posthumous)

[X] FOR HEROIC ACTION ON 15 December 1972

[ ] FOR MERITORIOUS SERVICE OR ACHIEVEMENT DURING THE PERIOD

[X] RECOMMENDS APPROVAL   [ ] DOES NOT RECOMMEND APPROVAL

[ ] RECOMMENDS AWARD OF

UNCLASSIFIED CITATION

Mr. John W. Kearns III is posthumously awarded the Intelligence Star in recognition of his courageous performance under hazardous conditions. On 15 December 1972 Mr. Kearns lost his life while serving as an adviser to an irregular regiment in Southeast Asia. Although fully aware of the potential dangers faced daily by officers charged with such responsibility, Mr. Kearns accepted these dangers as a necessary part of his assignment. His courage, leadership and resourcefulness were abundantly clear to those with whom he was associated, and his record of accomplishment under adverse and trying conditions is a tribute to his ability and motivation. Throughout Mr. Kearns' career he consistently displayed a high degree of professionalism, reflecting great credit on him and the United States Government.

REMARKS

(Recommendation approved by ADD/O on 19 March 1973)

APPROVED

SIGNATURE

(b)(3)

13 April 1973
DATE

TYPED NAME OF CHAIRMAN, HONOR AND MERIT AWARDS BOARD: Harry B. Fisher

SIGNATURE: Signed Original

TYPED NAME OF RECORDER

(b)(3)

FORM 382 OBSOLETE PREVIOUS EDITIONS

SECRET
Approved for Release: 2018/11/28 C06395113

Appendix E
STATEMENT

05 June 1971

To: Jerry Connors, Air America, Inc.
From: Customer
Re: C-46, XW-PFL

On 02 June 1971 at 1640 hrs. I was lowered by hoist from H-73 approximately 125 ft. down to the crash site of PFL (VIC UG 165975).

The aircraft wreckage was scattered in an area approximately 15 meters by 35 meters. The wings, powerplants, and tail section were broken and separated from the fuselage with some sections still burning. Debris (Rice sacks, metal sections, etc.) covered most of the area.

The body of the co-pilot was under, what I assumed to be, the front part of the fuselage. It took about three minutes to dig the co-pilot's body out of the wreckage. I did not see the body of the pilot at the crash site but I was limited to only ten minutes on the ground due to lack of fuel, enemy situation and lateness of the time of day.

Two parachute back packs and one reserve parachute were observed by me at the crash site. I can not state for sure if the pilot was or was not in the aircraft wreckage. It would have taken a four-man team a good thirty minutes to accurately check the crash site. It is my opinion, however, that the pilot of "PFL" was killed and buried beneath the fuselage of "PFL". Extensive low level VR by an aircraft at the crash site did not reveal any opened parachutes in the area nor was any body observed around the crash site. I called out for any survivors the whole ten minutes I was on the ground at the crash site and I received no response.

NOTE: Certified to be a copy of verbal statement.

\S\
J.D. Anthony
MSAFE-VTE

ENDNOTES

Prologue: The Wall

1. Central Intelligence Agency, "About the CIA Memorial Wall," https://www.cia.gov/legacy/headquarters/cia-memorial-wall/.
2. Ian Shapira, "CIA's Memorial Wall for fallen operatives is shaped by a Northern Virginia stone carver," *Washington Post*, May 22, 2014.
3. "About the CIA Memorial Wall."
4. "Remarks of the Director of Central Intelligence George J. Tenet at the Annual Memorial Ceremony, June 2, 2000," CIA Document No. C05543218. See Appendix A.
5. Richard Helms with William Hood, *A Look Over My Shoulder: A Life in the Central Intelligence Agency* (Ballantine Books, 2003), 257, 261.
6. Ted Gup, *The Book of Honor: The Secret Lives and Deaths of CIA Operatives* (Anchor Books, 2001); John E. Malone, *Top Secret Missions Performed by Elite Commo & Intel Specialists* (Trafford Publishing, 2003).

Chapter One: Who Am I?

1. *Oxford Reference*, "baby boomers," accessed May 4, 2026, https://www.oxfordreference.com/display/10.1093/oi/authority.20110803095439163.
2. Leslie J. Nason, "Baby Boomers, Grown Up, Storm Ivy-Covered Walls," *Daily Press*, Newport, Virginia, January 28, 1963.
3. Cedric Doliger, "The Easterlin Hypothesis," *Historical Social Research / Historische Sozialforschung* 29, no. 3 (2004): 205–12.
4. "Report of Honors and Merit Awards Board," CIA Document No. C06395113. See Appendix D.

Chapter Three: Agreement on the Cessation of Hostilities—1954 Geneva Accords

1. Richard Helms with William Hood, *A Look Over My Shoulder: A Life in the Central Intelligence Agency* (Ballantine Books, 2003), 252.
2. "Editorial Note," *Foreign Relations of the United States [FRUS] 1952–1954, Volume XIII, Part 1*, Indochina, eds. Neil H. Petersen and John P. Glennon (Government Printing Office, 1982), Document 716.
3. "Notes of Conversation Between President-Elect Kennedy and President Eisenhower, January 19, 1961," *FRUS* 1961–1963, Vol. XXIV, Laos Crisis, eds. Edward C. Keefer and Glenn W. LaFantasie (Government Printing Office, 1994), Document 7.
4. Ho Chi Minh to Harry Truman, January 18, 1946, NAID: 28469393, Records of the

Foreign Service Posts of the Department of State, Record Group [RG] 484 US National Archives, https://catalog.archives.gov/id/28469393.

5. Ho Chi Minh to Harry Truman, February 16, 1946, https://vietnamwar.lib.umb.edu/enemy/docs/Ho_letter_to_Truman_Feb_46.html.
6. A "coup de main" is an "offensive operation that capitalizes on surprise and simultaneous execution of supporting operations to achieve success in one swift stroke." *DOD Dictionary of Military and Associated Terms*, "coup de main," updated August 2011.
7. Ho Chi Minh to Harry Truman, telegram, February 28, 1946, NAID 305263, Records of the Office of Strategic Services, RG 226, US National Archives, https://archives.gov/files/historical-docs/doc-content/images/ho-chi-minh-telegram-truman.pdf.
8. Civil Air Transport would later become better known as Air America.
9. For the various documents that make up the Geneva Accords of 1954, see "The Geneva Conference on Indochina May 8–July 21, 1954," *FRUS* 1952–1954, Vol. XVI, The Geneva Conference, eds. Allen H. Kitchens and Neal H. Petersen (Government Printing Office, 1981), Documents 455–1034.
10. "Final Declaration on Indochina," *FRUS 1952–1954, Vol. XVI, Document 1038.*

Chapter Four: Deep in the Heart of Texas

1. "15 Inspirational Adoption Quotes," American Adoptions News, American Adoptions Agency, August 12, 2016, https://www.americanadoptions.com/blog/15-inspirational-adoption-quotes.
2. Ale Russian, "All About Jamie Foxx's Family, Including His Mom Louise, Stepdad George and Late Grandma Estelle," *People, January 22, 2024, https://people.com/all-about-jamie-foxx-parents-8421883.*
3. *Ingraham v. Wright*, 430 U.S. 651 (1977).
4. "Texas Almanac: City Population History from 1850–2000," Texas Almanac, https://www.texasalmanac.com/drupal-backup/images/CityPopHist%20web.pdf.
5. "About Us," Marine Military Academy, 2021, https://mma-tx.org/about-us/.
6. "Lake Waco (Brazos River Basin)," Texas Water Development Board, https://www.twdb.texas.gov/surfacewater/rivers/reservoirs/waco/index.asp.

Chapter Five: 1962—It Was Not Quite as Good a Year

1. Pete Grathof, "Sixty years ago, Chiefs franchise won first championship game despite famous coin-flip gaffe," *Kansas City Star, December 20, 2022.*

Chapter Six: (Another) Agreement on the Cessation of Hostilities—1962 Geneva Accords

1. Christian A. Chapman, interview by Charles Stuart Kennedy, March 3, 1990, The Association for Diplomatic Studies and Training Foreign Affairs Oral History Project, 20, 21, https://adst.org/OH%20TOCs/Chapman,%20Christian%20A.toc.pdf.
2. "Laos," John F. Kennedy Presidential Library and Museum, https://www.jfklibrary.org/learn/about-jfk/jfk-in-history/laos.

3. Chapman, interview, 22, 25.
4. "Protocol to the Declaration on the Neutrality of Laos. Signed at Geneva, on 23 July 1962," No. 6564, United Nations, https://treaties.un.org/doc/Publication/UNTS/Volume%20456/volume-456-I-6564-English.pdf.
5. Joshua Kurlantzick, *A Great Place to Have a War: America in Laos and the Birth of a Military CIA* (Simon & Schuster, 2016), 12.
6. There is some debate as to whether Davis was actually the first killed, although he may have been the first killed in ground combat action. Air Force Technical Sergeant Richard B. Fitzgibbon Jr. was killed on June 8, 1956, but not in combat. Rather, he was shot and killed by a drunken fellow soldier in Saigon. Major Dale Ruis and Master Sergeant Chester Ovnand were killed on July 8, 1959, when the mess hall where the two men, along with others, were watching a movie (*The Tattered Dress*, starring Jeff Chandler and Jeanne Crain) was attacked by North Vietnamese forces. Other US personnel were wounded, and two South Vietnamese were killed. *Soldier of Fortune* magazine called it the "Massacre at Bien Hoa."
7. Mark D. Raab, "He was the First U.S. Soldier Killed in Ground Combat Action in Vietnam," HistoryNet, December 22, 2021, https://www.historynet.com/first-us-soldier-killed-vietnam/; "They Served in Silence: The Story of a Cryptologic Hero Specialist Four James T. Davis, USA," https://www.nsa.gov/Portals/75/documents/about/crypto-logic-heritage/cryptologic-memorial/davis.pdf.

Chapter Seven: We Weren't There

1. USAICoE History Office, "Army Security Agency Established, 15 September 1945," U.S. Army, September 6, 2013, https://www.army.mil/article/110544/army_security_agency_established-15-September_1945.
2. Brian Brehm, "Veterans of once-classified U.S. Army Security Agency finally able to swap stories," *Winchester Star*, November 10, 2023.
3. "An inside look at the Army Security Agency; a spooky world," Veterans Voices, DC News Now, November 19, 2020, https://www.dcnewsnow.com/news/veterans-voices/an-inside-look-at-the-army-security-agency-a-spooky-world/.
4. "An Imprecise History of the USASASODS," The U.S. Army Security Agency Special Operations Detachments, https://asalives.org/ASAONLINE/sodhist.htm.
5. David K. Shipler, "Slain U.S. Officer Had His Hands Up," *New York Times*, December 16, 1973.

Chapter Eight: Girls, Sports, Drugs, and Jail

1. Bill Minutaglio, interview by Ari Shapiro, "Nixon's Manhunt for the High Priest of LSD In 'The Most Dangerous Man in America,'" NPR, January 5, 2018, https://www.npr.org/2018/01/05/575392333/nixons-hunt-for-the-high-priest-of-lsd-in-the-most-dangerous-man-in-america.
2. Jonathan Gould, *Can't Buy Me Love: The Beatles, Britain, and America* (Three Rivers Press, 2007) 562, 574–75.

3. Timothy Leary, interview by *Playboy*, *PLAYBOY* magazine, September 1966.
4. *Merriam-Webster Dictionary*, "fracas," accessed April 14, 2026, https://www.merriam-webster.com/dictionary/fracas.
5. Kirby Warnock, "Remembering the Lee Park Massacre," *D Magazine*, April 13, 2020.
6. Warnock refers to Mattox in the story as a "young SMU law student," but Mattox received his law degree in 1968 and worked as a prosecutor for Dallas County District Attorney Henry Wade until going into private practice in 1970. Presumably, he had already left the DA's office and started his private practice by the time he made the offer to defend hippies arrested in the Massacre.
7. Warnock, "Remembering the Lee Park Massacre."

Chapter Ten: The (Not-So-Secret) War

1. Technically, the Korean War never ended. Rather, an armistice was signed ending hostilities but not terminating the police action.
2. Tonkin Gulf Resolution (1964), US National Archives, updated April 9, 2024, https://archives.gov/milestone-documents/tonkin-gulf-resolution.
3. Lieutenant Commander Pat Paterson, U.S. Navy, "The Truth About Tonkin," *Naval History* 22, no. 1, February 2008.
4. "Protocol to the Declaration on the Neutrality of Laos. Signed at Geneva, on 23 July 1962," No. 6564, United Nations, https://treaties.un.org/doc/Publication/UNTS/Volume%20456/volume-456-I-6564-English.pdf.
5. *American Heritage Dictionary*, "secret," accessed May 4, 2026, https://ahdictionary.com/word/search.html?q=secret.
6. *Merriam-Webster Dictionary*, "secret," accessed April 14, 2026, https://www.merriam-webster.com/dictionary/secret; *Merriam-Webster Dictionary*, "covert," accessed April 14, 2026, https://www.merriam-webster.com/dictionary/covert.
7. After the withdrawal of the US military from Vietnam and the CIA from Laos in the early '70s, the Hmongs (along with another indigenous people, the Montagnards) would be targeted by the Communists for eradication. On May 29, 1975, Pathet Lao troops opened fire on unarmed Hmong civilians attempting to cross a bridge on their way to Vientiane. Named the Hin Heup massacre after the bridge, fourteen were killed and more than one hundred wounded.
8. Roland A. Paul, "Laos: Anatomy of an American Involvement," *Foreign Affairs* 49, no. 3 (April 1971): 533–47.
9. Christopher Robbins, *The Ravens: The Men Who Flew in America's Secret War in Laos* (Crown Publishers, 1995), 1.
10. Dwight Jon Zimmerman, "The Ravens and the Secret Air War in Laos," Defense Media Network, October 15, 2015, https://defensemedianetwork.com/stories/the-ravens-and-the-secret-air-war-in-laos/; Robbins, *The Ravens*, 1.
11. Robbins, *The Ravens*, 49.
12. Joshua Kurlantzick, *A Great Place to Have a War: America in Laos and the Birth of a Military CIA* (Simon & Schuster, 2016), 101.
13. Richard Helms with William Hood, *A Look Over My Shoulder: A Life in the Central*

Intelligence Agency (Ballantine Books, 2003), 253, 254, 261.
14. "The War: Spillover into Laos," *Time*, January 26, 1968.
15. Helms, *A Look Over My Shoulder*, 261.
16. John Prados, *Safe for Democracy: The Secret Wars of the CIA* (Ivan R. Dee, 2006), 347.
17. John Hart Ely, *War and Responsibility: Constitutional Lessons of Vietnam and Its Aftermath* (Princeton University Press, 1993).
18. "Laos: The Unseen Presence," *Time*, October 17, 1969.
19. James M. Naughton, "Deaths of 27 Americans in Laos Disclosed by U.S.," *New York Times*, March 9, 1970.
20. Naughton, "Deaths of 27 Americans in Laos Disclosed by U.S."
21. Although Kearns had originally been a contractor with the CIA, at the time of his death he was an actual CIA employee.
22. Tammy Arbuckle, "U.S. Civilians Dying Unheralded in Laos," *Washington Star*, December 27, 1972.
23. Ely, *War and Responsibility*, 92.
24. "Laos: April, 1971, A Staff Report Prepared for the Use of the Subcommittee on U.S. Security Agreements and Commitments Abroad of the Committee on Foreign Relations United States Senate," August 3, 1971, https://www.cia.gov/readingroom/docs/CIA-RDP73B00296R000300080001-0.pdf.
25. Spencer Rich, "Senators Told CIA Aids Laos," *Washington Post*, May 22, 1971.
26. "Kennedy: Aid Goes to CIA Forces," *Washington Post*, February 7, 1971.
27. Symington, "Additional Statements, Laos—Further U.S. Military Operations in this Secret War," to Subcommittee on Criminal Laws and Procedures, July 12, 1971.
28. Symington, "Additional Statements, Laos."
29. Ely, *War and Responsibility*, 85.
30. The CIA described Phoenix as "a set of programs that sought to attack and destroy the political infrastructure" of the Viet Cong. Andrew R. Finlayson, "A Retrospective on Counterinsurgency Operations: The Tay Ninh Provincial Reconnaissance Unit and Its Role in the Phoenix Program, 1969–70," *Studies in Intelligence* 51, no. 2, p. 59, https://www.cia.gov/resources/csi/static/The-Tay-Ninh-PRU-Studies-51-2-2007.pdf.
31. Robbins, *The Ravens*, 121.
32. Memorandum, Briefing of Senate Armed Services Committee on Central Intelligence Agency Operations in Laos
33. U.S. Senator Stuart Symington, "Laos: The Furtive War," *World*, August 29, 1972.
34. Tammy Arbuckle, "Official U.S. Secrecy Persists in Laos, *Washington Star*, February 6, 1972; see also Craig R. Whitney, "CIA-Aided Laos Base Hit Hard," *New York Times*, January 20, 1972.
35. Peter Smith, "A Visit to a Secret American Base in Thailand," *Washington Post*, July 20, 1972.

Chapter Eleven: Keep On Keepin' On

1. Wendy Gamber, *The Notorious Mrs. Clem: Murder and Money in the Gilded Age* (Johns Hopkins University Press, 2016).

Chapter Twelve: A Walk-On Javelina

1. "Top 10 Largest Ranches in the World," WhiteClouds, https://www.whiteclouds.com/top-10/top-10-largest-ranches-in-the-world.
2. Daniel Wilco, "The 7 longest winning streaks in college football history," July 11, 2023, https://www.ncaa.com/news/football/article/2018-11-02/longest-winning-streaks-college-football-history.
3. Jason Dannelly, "The Top 25 NAIA Football Programs of All-Time," Victory Sports Network, March 4, 2024, https://victorysportsnetwork.com/2024/03/04/the-top-25-naia-football-programs-of-all-time-2/.
4. Jeff Pearlman, *Football for a Buck: The Crazy Rise and Crazier Demise of the USFL* (Houghton Mifflin Harcourt, 2018), 241, 242.
5. "Oilman Manges sentenced, fined for mail fraud," *Victoria Advocate*, August 26, 1995.
6. "Hall of Famers," Pro Football Hall of Fame, https://www.profootballhof.com/players.
7. Javelina Athletics, "Homecoming Reunion Rekindles Memories of 1976 European Tour," October 20, 2006, https://javelinaathletics.com/news/2006/10/20/GEN-83.aspx.

Chapter Thirteen: Anything, Anytime, Anywhere

1. This is the Air America Creed. "The Air America Creed," Air America, https://www.air-america.org/air-america-creed.html.
2. Mary Hamilton, "And the Enemy was in us: Vietnam War films and complicating visions of American Masculinity," (master's thesis, University of Texas at Arlington, 2024), https://mavmatrix.uta.edu/history_theses/1/.
3. These three were all made in the 1970s. The only other on the list from the '70s was *Apocalypse Now*.
4. The full title is *Air America: The Story of the CIA's Secret Airlines* (G.P. Putnam's Sons, 1979).
5. "Air America (1990)," Box Office Mojo, https://www.boxofficemojo.com/title/tt0099005/?ref_=bo_se_r_1.
6. Caryn James, "*Air America (1990): Review: Film, Gibson as C.I.A. Pilot,*" *New York Times*, August 10, 1990.
7. Alun Evans, *Brassey's Guide to War Films* (Potomac Books 2000), 8.
8. Christopher Robbins, "'*Air America*' doesn't fly right," *New York Times*, August 28, 1990.
9. Air America was a later iteration of Civil Air Transport, an airline created in China by General Claire Lee Chennault, leader of the "Flying Tigers" in World War II. "History," CAT Association, https:www.catassociation.org/history/.
10. William M. Leary, "CIA Air Operations in Laos, 1955–1974: Supporting the 'Secret War,'" https:biotech.law.lsu.edu/cases/nat-sec/Vietnam/air-america.htm#ft1.
11. CAT Association is a 501(c)(3) non-profit made up of CAT veterans, their families, and friends, dedicated to preserving the history of CAT. "History," CAT Association.
12. Air America Association, "Air America: A Historical Synopsis," https://air-america.org/air-america-history.html.

13. "Air America: A Historical Synopsis."
14. Joshua Kurlantzick, *A Great Place to Have a War: America in Laos and the Birth of a Military CIA* (Simon & Schuster, 2016), 9, 139.
15. Peter Dale Scott, "Air America: Flying the U.S. into Laos," *Ramparts*, February 1970.
16. "CIA Airliner Is Missing Over Laos," *Washington Post*, December 29, 1971.
17. Leary, "CIA Air Operations in Laos."
18. Richard Gough, *Tony Poe's CIA War: A Secret War Waged by his Paramilitary Army in Southeast Asia* (Knox Press, 2024), 193.
19. Alfred W. McCoy, with Cathleen B. Read and Leonard P. Adams II, *The Politics of Heroin in Southeast Asia* (Harper & Row, 1972), 385.
20. "A War to Help Sell Heroin?," review of *The Politics of Heroin in Southeast Asia*, by Alfred W. McCoy, with Cathleen B. Read and Leonard P. Adams II, *The Miami Herald, January 16, 1973.*
21. "Airline accused of shipping opium," *Rocky Mountain News, November 5, 1972;* "Politics and History of Heroin," *California Voice, September 21, 1972;* "Heroin Road In SE Asia," *Washington Star, September 10, 1972;* Jack Anderson, "U.S. Is Backbone of Laos Drug Trade," *Washington Post, September 9, 1972;* "Our Allies, Opium, and the CIA: When the Embarrassed Chuckling Stopped," *National Observer, September 2, 1972;* "Smuggling? Yes; collusion: No," *Houston Post, August 20, 1972;* "CIA Dope Tie in Charged," *Oakland Tribune, February 5, 1972;* "Uncle Sam—drug pusher," Torrington, CT *Register*, July 29, 1972.
22. "Nixon Warns of Aid Cut To Drug-Dealer Nations," *Washington Star*, September 18, 1972.
23. "The U.S. Heroin Problem and Southeast Asia Report of a Staff Survey Team of the Committee on Foreign Affairs House of Representatives," December 1972, https://archive.org/details/CIA-RDP74B00415R000100100002-4.
24. Seymour M. Hersh, *The Price of Power: Kissinger in the Nixon White House (Summit Books, 1983), 21.*
25. Anthony Summers, *Arrogance of Power: The Secret World of Richard Nixon* (Viking, 2000), 302–3; Robert "KC" Johnson, "Did Nixon Commit Treason in 1968? What the New LBJ Tapes Reveal," *History News Network*, January 26, 2009.

Chapter Fourteen: Big D-Little-A-Double L-A-S

1. Frank Loesser penned the song "Big D" about Dallas as part of his 1956 musical *The Most Happy Fella*, for which he wrote both lyrics and music, as well as a book. The play had a fourteen-month run on Broadway and was broadcast live on *The Ed Sullivan Show* on October 28, 1956. "Big D" was sung in the musical by actress Susan Johnson, playing the character of Cleo, and Shorty Long, playing Herman. Bing Crosby recorded it in 1956, but the most well-known performance might have been on *The Garry Moore Show* in 1961, where Carol Burnett and Julie Andrews sang it. The two performed it again on a CBS television special in 1962 called *Julie and Carol at Carnegie Hall.*
2. "Texas Almanac: City Population History from 1850–2000," Texas Almanac, https://www.texasalmanac.com/drupal-backup/images/CityPopHist%20web.pdf.

3. Mark Byrnes, "Dallas, 1963: 'City of Hate'?" *Bloomberg, November 22, 2013.*
4. Danny Gallagher, "*City of Hate Explores Dallas' Role in JFK's Assassination,*" *Dallas Observer, November 24, 2023,* https://www.dallasobserver.com/arts-culture/a-new-documentary-looks-at-dallas-as-a-city-of-hate-17947396/.
5. Darwin Payne, *Big D: Triumphs and Troubles of an American Supercity in the 20th Century* (Three Forks Press, 1994), 320–22.
6. Torn Peeler, "They built THIS CITY: Remembering the key players in downtown's first period of greatness," *D Magazine, October 1, 1996,* https://www.dmagazine.com/publications/d-magazine/1996/october/they-built-this-city.
7. Payne, *Big D, 326; "A City That Still Works," Time, https://time.com/archive/6858595/a-city-that-still-works.*
8. Steve Perkins, *Next Year's Champions: The Story of the Dallas Cowboys* (World Publishing, 1969).
9. Mike Shropshire, *Seasons in Hell: With Billy Martin, Whitey Herzog, and the Worst Baseball Team in History: The 1973–1975 Texas Rangers (Diversion Books, 2014).*
10. Randy Galloway, "Randle Frustration Explodes in Fistic Fury," *Sporting News,* April 16, 1977.
11. T. R. Sullivan, "Boys of Arlington: Lenny Randle vs. Frank Lucchesi," *Rangers Today,* June 27, 2024, https://rangerstoday.com/boys-of-arlington-lenny-randle-vs-frank-lucchesi.
12. Blackie Sherrod, "An Eyewitness to a mugging," *Dallas Morning News, March 29, 1977.*
13. Sullivan, "Boys of Arlington."
14. Adam Pockross, "Why are the NFL's Dallas Cowboys Called America's Team? The Nickname, Explained," NBC, September 3, 2025, https://www.nbc.com/nbc-insider/why-are-the-dallas-cowboys-known-as-americas-team.
15. "Texas International Pop Festival," City of Lewisville, https://www.cityoflewisville.com/about-lewisville/our-history/timeline/1969-texas-international-pop-festival.
16. Greta Bjornson, "Meat Loaf: The Many Origin Stories Behind the Late Singer's Name," *People,* January 21, 2022.
17. Paul Heckmann, "Michael Nesmith: 'Hey, Hey, He's a Texan,'" Memories, Inc., June 17, 2021, https://meminc.org/micheal-nesmith-hey-hey-hes-a-texan/.
18. "Perseverance, thy name is Bette," United States Patent and Trademark Office, https://www.uspto.gov/learning-and-resources/journeys-innovation/historical-stories/perseverance-thy-name-bette. See also Bette Graham interview by University of North Texas, University Libraries, "Oral history interview with Bette Graham," August 3, 1977, and April 2, 1980, https://discover.library.unt.edu/catalog/b2204263.
19. "Brief History of Michael Martin Murphey," Michael Martin Murphey, https://michaelmartinmurphey.com/about.
20. Tim Schuller, "A Prince at the King's Club," *D Magazine,* June 1, 1978.
21. *Squezze Play 1979,* IMDb, https://www.imdb.com/title/tt10950080/?ref_=fm_t_1.

Chapter Fifteen: Small Town Boy in the Big City

1. *Dallas Cowboys Cheerleaders, Inc. v. Pussycat Cinema, Ltd., Michael Zaffarano,* et al., 467 F.Supp. 366 (S.D.N.Y. 1979).

2. *Dallas Cowboys Cheerleaders, Inc. v. Pussycat Cinema, Ltd., Michael Zaffarano*, 604 F.2d 200 (2d Cir. 1979).
3. "Who We Are: Our Brand Story," 7-Eleven Corporate, https://corp.7-eleven.com/corp/our-brand-story.
4. Ryan Osborne, "How the 7-Eleven Slurpee was invented," WFAA News, July 11, 2024.

Chapter Sixteen: Oh, It Was a Scene, Man!

1. *Seinfeld*, season 6, episode 11, "The Switch," written by Bruce Kirschbaum and Sam Kass, directed by Andy Ackerman, aired January 5, 1995, on NBC.
2. The name "Frogtown" supposedly derives from the fact that frogs could be heard croaking from a small stream that fed the Trinity River. Peter Simek, "Lost Dallas; Uncovering secrets from the city's past buried by time, memory, and I-30," *D Magazine*, February 26, 2018.
3. Darwin Payne, *Big D: Triumphs and Troubles of an American Supercity in the 20th Century* (Three Forks Press, 1994), 48.
4. Doug J. Swanson, *Blood Aces: The Wild Ride of Benny Binion, the Texas Gangster Who Created Vegas Poker* (Viking, 2014), 39.
5. Rena Pederson, *The King of Diamonds: The Search for the Elusive Texas Jewel Thief* (Pegasus Crime, 2024), 121, 122.
6. Swanson, *Blood Aces, 41*, 123, 124.
7. "Low Moments in Dallas Bar History," *D Magazine*, June 1, 1988.
8. Helen Parmley, "Pakistani cowboy blazes money trail through stores, disco," *Dallas Morning News*, November 8, 1978.
9. Sarah Blaskovich, "50 Years Later: The wild, nearly unbelievable tales from 'unsavory' Dallas bar J. Alfred's," *Dallas Morning News, September 9, 2021; "Low Moments in Dallas Bar History," D Magazine, June 1, 1988.*
10. "Cowboy in Mishap," *New York Times*, October 17, 1984.
11. Hillary Juster, "The Village in '70s Dallas Was a Wild and Crazy Place (Proving Your Mom Partied Harder Than You)," KDAF CW 33, January 25, 2016, https://cw33.com/watercooler/wild-stories-from-the-village-in-70s-dallas-that-prove-your-mom-partied-harder-than-you/.
12. Kirby F. Warnock, "My Wild Ride Through the '70s Music Scene in Dallas, Thanks to 'Buddy Magazine,'" *D Magazine*, June 10, 2024, https://dmagazine.com/publications/d-magazine/2024/june/my-wild-ride-through-the-70s-music-scene-in dallas-thanks-to-buddy-magazine/.

Chapter Seventeen: Bombs Away

1. Fred Branfman, ed., *Voices from the Plain of Jars: Life Under an Air War*, 2nd ed. (Harper & Row, 1972; repr., University of Wisconsin Press, 2013), ix.
2. Joshua Kurlantzick, *A Great Place to Have a War: America in Laos and the Birth of a Military CIA* (Simon & Schuster, 2016), 177; see also Jessica Pearce Rotondi, "Why

Laos Has Been Bombed More Than Any Other Country," History, last updated May 28, 2025, https://www.history.com/articles/laos-most-bombed-country-vietnam-war.
3. "The Bombing of Laos: By the Numbers," *Laotian Times*, September 8, 2016.
4. Sarah Kolinovsky, "The Bombing of Laos: By the Numbers," ABC News, September 6, 2016, https://abcnews.go.com/international/bombing-laos-numbers/story?id=41890565.
5. Roger Warner, *Back Fire: The CIA's Secret War in Laos and Its Link to the War in Vietnam* (Simon & Schuster, 1995), 155.
6. "Protocol to the Declaration on the Neutrality of Laos. Signed at Geneva, on 23 July 1962," No. 6564, United Nations, https://treaties.un.org/doc/Publication/UNTS/Volume%20456/volume-456-I-6564-English.pdf.
7. "Protocol to the Declaration on the Neutrality of Laos. Signed at Geneva, on 23 July 1962."
8. Christopher Robbins, *The Ravens: The Men Who Flew in America's Secret War in Laos* (Crown Publishers, 1995), 107–8. Robbins cites the July 24, 1962, edition of *Nahn Dan*, the official newspaper of the North Vietnamese Communist Party.
9. Secretary of Defense Robert McNamara to President Johnson, memorandum, December 21, 1963, *FRUS 1961–1963, Volume IV, Vietnam, August–December 1963, ed. Edward C. Keefer (Government Printing Office, 1991), Document 374.*
10. Neil Sheehan, Hedrick Smith, E. W. Kenworthy, and Fox Butterfield, *The Pentagon Papers: The Secret History of the Vietnam War* (Bantam, 1971), 274.
11. Col. Joseph D. Celeski, *Special Air Warfare and the Secret War in Laos: Air Commandos 1964–1975* (Air University Press, 2019), 79.
12. Jan Churchill, *Classified Secret: Controlling Airstrikes in the Clandestine War in Laos* (Sunflower University Press, 2000), 108–10; Celeski, *Special Air Warfare*, 137.
13. Churchill, *Classified Secret, 111*.
14. Churchill, *Classified Secret*, 113.
15. "Charles Ervin Shelton," History of MACV-SOG, https://sogsite.com/charles-ervin-shelton.
16. Seymour Hersh, "How We Ran the Secret Air War in Laos," *New York Times Magazine*, October 29, 1972, 18–19.
17. Hersh, "How We Ran the Secret Air War in Laos."
18. Hersh, "How We Ran the Secret Air War in Laos."
19. Branfman, *Voices*, 25.
20. Branfman, *Voices, 26*.
21. Alfred McCoy is a historian who specialized in Southeast Asia and CIA covert operations. His works in the area include *Laos: War and Revolution* (Harper & Row 1970), cowritten with Nina S. Adams, and *The Politics of Heroin in Southeast Asia: CIA Complicity in the Global Drug Trade* (Harper & Row, 1972).
22. "War-Related Civilian Problems in Indochina," Hearing Before the Subcommittee to Investigate Problems With Refugees and Escapees of the Committee on the Judiciary, April 21, 1971.
23. Branfman, *Voices, 50*.
24. Branfman, *Voices*, 63.

25. Branfman, *Voices*, 80.
26. Branfman, *Voices*, 83.
27. Branfman, *Voices*, 89.
28. Branfman, *Voices*, 90.
29. Branfman, *Voices*, 133.

Chapter Eighteen: Opening a Dark Door

1. Catherine Downes, "Playboy Bunnies Tell the Best Tales," *D Magazine*, September 21, 2018.
2. Paul Heckmann, "Playboy of Dallas," Memories, Inc., Apirl 18, 2019, https://meminc.org/playboy/.
3. Heckmann, "Playboy of Dallas."
4. Heckmann, "Playboy of Dallas."
5. Heckmann, "Playboy of Dallas."
6. Nancy Bishop, "Dallas Playboy Club closes," *Dallas Morning News*, May 1982.
7. Heckmann, "Playboy of Dallas."
8. Paul Heckmann, "Gene Cook, 'Boogie Machine' & Playboy," Memories, Inc., June 2, 2019, https://meminc.org/genecook/.
9. Heckmann, "Gene Cook."

Chapter Nineteen: Blow

1. Jacob Uitti, "Behind the Drug Crazed Song 'Cocaine' by Eric Clapton," American Songwriter, July 17, 2023, https://americansongwriter.com/behind-the-drug-crazed-song-cocaine-by-eric-clapton/.
2. Associated Press, "Eric Clapton rethinks playing 'Cocaine,'" East Bay Times, October 3, 2006, last updated August 17, 2016, https://www.eastbaytimes.com/2006/10/03/eric-clapton-rethinks-playing-cocaine/.
3. "Mind Matters: The Body's Response to Cocaine," National Institute on Drug Abuse, November 1, 2019, https://nida.nih.gov/research-topics/parents-educators/mind-matter-series/cocaine.
4. *Merriam-Webster Dictionary*, "euphoria," accessed April 14, 2026, https://www.merriam-webster.com/dictionary/euphoria.
5. Sigmund Freud, *Cocaine Papers* (Stonehill Publishing, 1974), 47.
6. Tom Foster, "The King of X," *D Magazine*, May 2025.
7. Peter Simek, "How the Starck Club Changed Dallas," *D Magazine*, March 18, 2013.
8. Hannah Evans, "Dallas' '80s singles scene was wild enough, but robbers added danger to bar life with a Mickey Finn spree," *Dallas Morning News*, December 26, 2019.
9. Simek, "How the Starck Club Changed Dallas."
10. Emily Freeman, "After the Party: When cocaine becomes your only friend," *D Magazine*, March 1, 1983.
11. Bob Hayes with Robert Pack, *Run, Bullet, Run: The Rise, Fall, and Recovery of Bob Hayes* (Harper & Row, 1990), 273, 275, 276.
12. Hayes, *Run, Bullet, Run*, 297, 287.

13. Hayes, *Run, Bullet, Run,* 287–88.
14. Jane Gross, "4 Cowboys Named as Cocaine Users," *New York Times,* July 9, 1983.
15. Thomas "Hollywood" Henderson and Peter Knobler, *Out of Control: Confessions of an NFL Casualty* (G.P. Putnam's Sons, 1987), 108–9.
16. Henderson, *Out of Control,* 169.
17. Thomas Hollywood Henderson with Frank Luksa, *In Control: The Rebirth of an NFL Legend* (Thomas Henderson Publishing, 2004), 86.

Chapter Twenty: Lima Site 118A

1. Susan Williams's excellent book *Spies in the Congo: America's Atomic Mission in World War II* (Public Affairs, 2016) addresses Bonner Sr.'s role in securing uranium ore in the Congo for the development of atomic weapons.
2. Douglas G. Bonner III, "A Teenager's Visit to the CIA Base at Nam Yu: Lima Site 118A," September 2020. An abbreviated version of the essay can be found in *Bucknell Magazine* 14, no. 3 (Summer 2021).
3. According to Barry Popik, on his website The Big Apple—an "up-to-date etymological dictionary (over 39,000 entries) investigating the word origins and meanings of American words, names, quotations, and phrases"—the nickname "was probably coined or at least popularized by George Washington Bacon 3rd (1946-1976), who was awarded the CIA's Intelligence Star." According to Popik, other derogatory nicknames have included Cocaine Importing Agency, Certified Idiots of America, Clowns in America, and Crooks in Action. Popik, "Christians In Action (Central Intelligence Agency or CIA nickname)," February 8, 2012, https://barrypopik.com/blog/christians_in_action_central_intelligence_agency_or_cia_nickname.
4. Although there were no Catholic directors in the 1990s, the 2000s saw three—Michael Hayden, Leon Panetta, and John Brennan—while prior to that, "[s]ome of the most influential directors in CIA history have been Catholic-men such as Walter Bedell Smith, John McCone, William Colby and William Casey." Deacon Greg Kandra,"Why the CIA is Called the Catholic Intelligence Agency," Aleteia, May 5, 2016, https://aleteia.org/blogs/aleteia-blog/why-the-cia-is-called-the-catholic-intelligence-agency/.
5. Memorandum for the President from Melvin Laird, Secretary of Defense, subj: US Military Operations in Laos, attached as Tab A to Memorandum for the President from Henry A. Kissinger, subj: Background on U.S. Military Operations in Laos, October 22, 1969, https://www.cia.gov/readingroom/docs/LOC-HAK-510-5-12-6.pdf.
6. Kenneth Michael Absher, "John Kearns and the Cold War in Laos: Recalling a CIA Officer's Sacrifice," *Studies in Intelligence* 46 no. 4 (2002): 46.
7. Fort Benning was originally named after Henry L. Benning, a Confederate brigadier general; the name was changed in 2023 to Fort Moore, after Lieutenant General Hal Moore, a highly decorated veteran of three wars (World War II, Korea, and Vietnam). Moore's medals included the Distinguished Service Cross, the Army Distinguished Service Medal, the Legion of Merit, Bronze Star, Air Medal, and Purple Heart. He commanded the First Battalion, Seventh Cavalry Regiment, at the Battle of Ia Drang during the Vietnam War. That battle was the subject of the book *We Were Soldiers Once . . .*

and Young (Random House, 1992), which Moore coauthored with journalist Joseph L. Galloway. Mel Gibson portrayed Moore in the movie adaptation of the book.

8. "Student Information," U.S. Army, last updated March 18, 2025, https://www.benning.army.mil/infantry/ARTB/Student-Information/.
9. Control of Fort Gulick was turned over to the Republic of Panama in 1984, and it was renamed *Fuerte Espinar. The United States retook control in 1989 but kept the name Fort Espinar. Today it is the location of a luxury hotel, the Hotel Melia. See "A Cannon at a Luxury hotel?," Panama News 12, no. 17 (Sept. 3–16, 2006), https://web.archive.org/web/20070711185844/http://www.thepanamanews.com/pn/v_12/issue_17/travel_01.html.*
10. The character played by Martin Sheen in Francis Ford Coppola's *Apocalypse Now*, Captain Willard, was a MACV-SOG operative when he was sent to find and "terminate" Marlon Brando's crazed Colonel Kurtz.
11. Annie Jacobsen, *Surprise, Kill, Vanish: The Secret History of CIA Paramilitary Armies, Operators, and Assassins* (Little, Brown, 2019), 206–7; Michael E. Haas, *Apollo's Warriors* (DIANE Publishing, 1998), 298.
12. "Madison Alexander Strohlein," History of MACV-SOG, https://sogsite.com/madison-alexander-strohlein/.
13. U.S. Army John F. Kennedy Special Warfare Center and School, *Newcomers' Handbook*, 3, https://www.swcs.mil/Portals/111/NewcomersGuide.pdf.
14. Jacobson, *Surprise, Kill, Vanish*, 207.
15. Kenneth Conboy with James Morrison, *Shadow War: The CIA's Secret War in Laos* (Paladin Press 1995), 237.
16. Joshua Kurlantzick, *A Great Place to Have a War: America in Laos and the Birth of a Military CIA* (Simon & Schuster, 2016), 158.
17. Roger Warner, *Back Fire: The CIA's Secret War in Laos and Its Link to the War in Vietnam* (Simon & Schuster, 1995), 249.
18. Richard Gough, *Tony Poe's CIA War: A Secret War Waged by his Paramilitary Army in Southeast Asia* (Knox Press, 2024), 172.
19. Michael Morrow, "CIA Reported Inside China," *St. Louis Post-Dispatch*, January 17, 1971.
20. "Nam Yu: Lima Site 118A: Where Was It, Why Was it?," The Wanderling, https://the-wanderling.com/nam_yu.html.
21. Warner, *Back Fire*, 53.
22. Alfred W. McCoy, *The Politics of Heroin: CIA Complicity in the Global Drug Trade, revised ed. (Lawrence Hill Books, 2003), 306.*
23. Thomas Fuller, "William Young, 76, Leader In Secret U.S. War in Laos," *New York Times*, April 6, 2011.
24. Richard S. Ehrlich, "CIA Suicide after a life of God and guns," *Free Press*, April 5, 2011.
25. Stanley Karnow, "Defusing Laos: The Fragile Accord," *New Republic*, March 10, 1973.
26. McCoy, *Politics of Heroin*, 342.
27. Michael Morrow, "CIA's Spy Teams Inside Red China," *San Francisco Chronicle*, September 4, 1970; Michael Morrow, "CIA Reported Inside China," *St. Louis-Dispatch*, January 17, 1971; Michael Morrow, "CIA-Backed Laotians Said Entering China,"

Washington Post, January 26, 1971.
28. Morrow, "CIA's Spy Teams Inside Red China"; Morrow, "CIA Reported Inside China"; Morrow, "CIA-Backed Laotians Said Entering China."
29. B. Hugh Tovar, interview by Paul Hillmer, August 15, 2007, Hmong Oral History Project, https://digitalcommons.csp.edu/hmong-studies_hohp/38.
30. Morrow, "CIA Reported Inside China."
31. Tovar, interview.
32. Jerome A. Cohen to Henry Kissinger, January 6, 1971, https://www.cia.gov/readingroom/docs/LOC-HAK-11-6-14-7.pdf.
33. Henry Kissinger to Jerome A. Cohen, February 9, 1971, https://www.cia.gov/readingroom/docs/LOC-HAK-11-6-14-7.pdf.
34. Frank Chapin to Henry Kissinger, memorandum, subj: Professor Jerome Cohen's Letter of Inquiry re U.S. Actions Against Communist China, January 26, 1971, https://www.cia.gov/readingroom/docs/LOC-HAK-11-6-14-7.pdf.
35. Richard Dudman wrote of the capture and captivity in a book entitled *40 Days with the Enemy: The Story of a Journalist Held Captive by Guerrillas in Cambodia* (Liveright, 1971). He wrote that all three of them "had been personally opposed to the Vietnam war for a long time" and that their "biggest problem" during captivity had been "to convince the guerrillas that we were not CIA spies" (179).
36. Michael Morrow, email to Mike Farris, September 18, 2025.
37. Kurlantzick, *A Great Place to Have a War*, 92.
38. Keith Quincy, *Harvesting Pa Chay's Wheat: The Hmong & America's Secret War in Laos* (Eastern Washington University Press, 2000), 281.
39. Kurlantzick, *A Great Place to Have a War*, 157.
40. Kurlantzick, *A Great Place to Have a War*, 198.
41. Morrow, "CIA's Spy Teams Inside Red China."
42. Morrow, "CIA Reported Inside China."
43. Michael Morrow, email to Mike Farris, September 18, 2025.
44. Michael Morrow, email to Mike Farris, September 18, 2025.
45. Kurlantzick, *A Great Place to Have a War*, 157.
46. Kurlantzick, *A Great Place to Have a War*, 199.
47. "Apocalypse Now: The Real Story," TCM, https://www.tcm.com/tcmd/title/47684/the-search-for-kurtz/#film-details. See also, Richard S. Ehrlich, "CIA Operative stood out in 'secret war' in Laos," *Bangkok Post, July 8, 2003;* "Colonel Kurtz," Alchetron, last updated February 16, 2026, https://alchetron.com/Colonel-Kurtz.
48. Team Mighty, "This CIA operative was a real-life 'Col. Kurtz' during the Vietnam War," We Are the Mighty, August 15, 2022, https://www.wearethemighty.com/articles/this-cia-operative-was-a-real-life-col-kurtz-during-the-vietnam-war/
49. Blake Stilwell, "A Green Beret was the inspiration for Colonel Kurtz in 'Apocalypse Now,'" We Are the Mighty, February 28, 2023, https://www.wearethemighty.com/popular/green-beret-inspiration-robert-rheault/.
50. Stilwell, "A Green Beret was the inspiration for Colonel Kurtz."
51. Team Mighty, "This CIA operative was a real-life 'Col. Kurtz' during the Vietnam War."
52. Frank Walker, "Barry Petersen: Man of mystery and Australia's Colonel Kurtz," *Sydney*

Morning Herald, March 6, 2019.
53. Genevieve Carlton, *"15 Stories From the Wild Life of David Hackworth, Who Inspired Two 'Apocalypse Now' Characters,"* Ranker, April 9, 2024, https://www.ranker.com/list/life-of-david-hackworth/genevieve-carlton.
54. Kurlantzick, *A Great Place to Have a War*, 260.

Chapter Twenty-One: Oh, It Was a Scene, Man—Part Deux

1. Tim Allis, "Entertainment Night Moves: Dancing the night away in Dallas," *D Magazine*, December 1, 1982.
2. "Food and Spirits: DINING OUT," *D Magazine*, May 1, 1978.

Chapter Twenty-Two: Adrift

1. *United States of America v. Scott Robin Roston*, 986 F. 2d 1287 (9th Cir. 1993).
2. Onionista, "Onions To Move An Army," National Onion Association, February 25, 2011, https://www.onions-usa.org/onionista/onions-to-move-an-army/.
3. Holley Gilbert, James Mayer, and George Bundy Smith, "Five-alarm blaze hits liner at Swan's Island," *Oregonian, December 6, 1989.*

Chapter Twenty-Three: The Secret City in the Secret War

1. Kenneth Michael Absher, "John Kearns and the Cold War in Laos: Recalling a CIA Officer's Sacrifice," *Studies in Intelligence* 46 no. 4 (2002): 48.
2. Joshua Kurlantzick, *A Great Place to Have a War: America in Laos and the Birth of a Military CIA* (Simon & Schuster, 2016), 80.
3. Kurlantzick, *A Great Place to Have a War*, 93–94.
4. Timothy N. Castle, *At War in the Shadow of Vietnam: U.S. Military Aid to the Royal Lao Government 1955–1975* (Columbia University Press, 1993), 43, 84.
5. Christopher Robbins, *Air America* (G.P. Putnam's Sons, 1979), 116, originally published in Great Britain under the title *The Invisible Air Force: The True Story of the CIA's Secret Airlines* (MacMillan, 1979).
6. Tammy Arbuckle, "Official U.S. Secrecy Persists in Laos," *Washington Star*, February 6, 1972.
7. Arbuckle, "Official U.S. Secrecy Persists in Laos."
8. Craig R. Whitney, "CIA-Aided Laos Base Hit Hard," *New York Times*, January 20, 1972.
9. Kenneth Conboy with James Morrison, *Shadow War: The CIA's Secret War in Laos* (Paladin Press 1995), 237.
10. Absher, "John Kearns and the Cold War in Laos," 48.
11. Ravens is shorthand for the Raven Forward Air Controllers, American fighter pilots who were used as forward air controllers in conjunction with the CIA to help zero in air strikes against the communist forces in Laos.
12. Conboy and Morrison, *Shadow War*, 298.
13. John McBeth, "The CIA's Secret City," *The Nation*, March 16, 2013, https://www.

nationthailand.com/life/30202107.

14. Air America, Inc., Investigation of Aircraft Accident, C-46, XW-PFL NEAR BUOAM LONG (LS-32) LAOS, 02 JUNE 1971, John D. Anthony Papers, History of Aviation Archives, UTD Special Collections and Archives Division.
15. Air America, Investigation of Aircraft Accident.
16. Air America, Investigation of Aircraft Accident.
17. Air America, Investigation of Aircraft Accident.
18. Air America, Investigation of Aircraft Accident.
19. Air America, Investigation of Aircraft Accident.
20. Air America, Investigation of Aircraft Accident.
21. The C-46 was identified in Air America records as XW-PFL.
22. Air America, Investigation of Aircraft Accident.
23. Absher, "John Kearns and the Cold War in Laos," 48.
24. Richard Helms with William Hood, *A Look Over My Shoulder: A Life in the Central Intelligence Agency* (Ballantine Books, 2003), 263. Helms notes in a footnote that "CIA had no objection to disclosing the full names of the fallen. The abbreviated identifications are used at the request of the families involved."

Chapter Twenty-Four: A Time to Heal

1. Matthew Marczi, "Cowboys' Hollywood Henderson Talks Terry Bradshaw, Why He Said Steelers QB Couldn't Spell 'Cat,'" Steelers Depot, October 7, 2024, https://steelers-depot.com/2024/10/cowboys-hollywood-henderson-talks-terry-bradshaw-why-he-said-steelers-qb-couldnt-spell-cat/.
2. Homepage, Sierra Tucson, https://www.sierratucson.com.
3. "9 Celebrities Who Went to Sierra Tucson Rehab," Ranker, January 9, 2024, https://www.ranker.com/list/celebrities-who-went-to-sierra-tucson-rehab/celebrity-lists.
4. Homepage, Prescott House, https://prescotthouse.com.

Chapter Twenty-Five: The Papers: Publish or Perish

1. Robert McNamara, with Brian VanDeMark, *In Retrospect: The Tragedy and Lessons of Vietnam* (Random House, 1995), 280.
2. "It was hardly a secret, however, nor could it have been with thirty-six researchers and analysts ultimately involved." McNamara, *In Retrospect*, 280.
3. Neil Sheehan, "Most Authors Were Given a Promise of Anonymity," *New York Times*, July 18, 1971.
4. McNamara, *In Retrospect*, 281.
5. Leslie Gelb, interview by Brooke Gladstone, "What the Press and 'The Post' Missed," *On the Media* (podcast), WNYC Studios, January 12, 2018, https://www.wnycstudios.org/story/what-post-missed-episode.
6. Gelb interview.
7. Gelb interview.
8. Stanford J. Ungar, *The Papers & The Papers: An Account of the Legal and Political Battle Over the Pentagon Papers* (E.P. Dutton, 1972), 61, 67.

9. Article I, Section 6 of the US Constitution says in part: "The Senators and Representatives . . . shall in all Cases, except Treason, Felony and Breach of the Peace, be privileged from Arrest . . . for any Speech or Debate in either House."
10. Ungar, *The Papers & The Papers,* 127.
11. Nixon tapes, Richard Nixon meeting with Alexander Haig Jr., June 13, 1971.
12. Nixon tapes, Richard Nixon/Henry Kissinger phone conversation, June 13, 1971.
13. Gelb interview.
14. Oval office meeting with Bob Haldeman, June 14, 1971, Nixon Presidential Materials Project, OVAL-519-1, Cassette 747, transcript available at https://nsarchive2.gwu.edu/NSAEBB/NSAEBB48/oval.pdf.
15. Nixon tapes, Richard Nixon/John Mitchell phone conversation, June 14, 1971.
16. *United States v. N.Y. Times Co.,* 328 F. Supp. 324, 330 (S.D.N.Y. 1971).
17. 328 F. Supp. at 331.
18. *New York Times Co. v. United States,* 403 U.S. 713 (1971).
19. *Near v. Minnesota,* 283 U.S. 697 (1931).
20. 403 U.S. 713 (1971).
21. 403 U.S. 713, 717 (1971).
22. Amy Goodman, Daniel Ellsberg, Sen. Mike Gravel, Rev. Robert West, "The Pentagon Papers Then and Now: Unitarian Universalists Confronting Government Secrecy," panel discussion, General Assembly 2007, Unitarian Universalist Association, https://www.uua.org/ga/past/2007/30971.shtml.
23. "How the Pentagon Papers Came to be Published by the Beacon Press: A Remarkable Story Told by Whistleblower Daniel Ellsberg, Dem Presidential Candidate Mike Gravel and Unitarian Leader Robert West," *Democracy Now,* July 2, 2007.
24. *Gravel v. United States,* 408 U.S. 606, 622, 627–29 (1972).
25. 408 U.S. 606.
26. Daniel Ellsberg, "Laos: What is Nixon Up To?" *The New York Review,* March 11, 1971.
27. Ellsberg, "Laos: What is Nixon Up To?"
28. "Secret War, Forgotten War: The U.S. Bombing of Laos," Win Without War, https://winwithoutwar.org/secret-war-forgotten-war-the-u-s-bombing-of-laos/. Win Without War describes itself as "a diverse network of activists and organizations working for a more peaceful, progressive U.S. foreign policy."
29. McNamara, *In Retrospect,* 35.
30. Clark Clifford to President Kennedy, Memorandum on Conference between President Eisenhower and President-elect Kennedy and Their Chief Advisors on January 19, 1961, January 24, 1961, President's Office Files, John F. Kennedy Papers, as cited in McNamara, *In Retrospect,* 35.
31. Secretary of Defense Robert McNamara to President Johnson, memorandum, December 21, 1963, *FRUS 1961–1963, Volume IV, Vietnam, August–December 1963, ed. Edward C. Keefer (Government Printing Office, 1991), Document 374.*
32. Neil Sheehan, Hedrick Smith, E. W. Kenworthy, and Fox Butterfield, *The Pentagon Papers: The Secret History of the Vietnam War* (Bantam, 1971), 274–77
33. Sheehan cites Paper #74 as the source, which was a cablegram from Secretary of State Dean Rusk to the United States Embassy in Laos, dated August 7, 1964.

34. Leonard Unger was the US Ambassador to Laos from July 25, 1962, to December 1, 1964. Sheehan et al., *The Pentagon Papers, 239.*
35. *Sheehan et al., The Pentagon Papers, 234.*
36. *Sheehan et al., The Pentagon Papers, 283.*
37. Markings on the document indicate that it was drafted by Green.
38. FAR is a reference to the French acronym for the *Forces Armées du Royaume*, the official military of the Kingdom of Laos.
39. Sheehan et al., *The Pentagon Papers, 302–6.*
40. *Sheehan et al., The Pentagon Papers, 306.*
41. *Sheehan et al., The Pentagon Papers, 235.*
42. "OPLAN 34A 1964," History of MACV-SOG, https://sogsite.com/oplan-34a-1964.
43. McNamara to Johnson, December 21, 1963.
44. Benjamin Franklin and Benjamin Peirce, *Poor Richard's Almanack for 1735: As Written by Benjamin Franklin [for the years 1733–1741]: the astronomical calculations, annual illustrated ed. (New York, 1849).*
45. Gelb interview.
46. Gelb interview.
47. The full Pentagon Papers were declassified and released to the public on June 13, 2011, on the fortieth anniversary of their initial, unauthorized publication.

Chapter Twenty-Six: Broken

1. Carlos Muchado, "Lineage & Legacy," https://machadomethodcarrollton.com/about/lineage/

Chapter Twenty-Seven: The Death of Lone Star

1. Richard Nixon, "Statement About the Situation in Laos," The American Presidency Project, UC Santa Barbara, https://www.presidency.ucsb.edu/documents/statement-about-the-situation-laos.
2. Central Intelligence Agency, "Clandestine Service," archived on June 12, 2007, retrieved April 28, 2011, https://www.cia.gov/offices-of-clandestine-service/index.html.
3. "The CIA's Clandestine Service," University blogs, Missouri State, https://blogs.missouristate.edu/polsci/files/2015/02/The-CIA-Clandestine-Service-overview.pdf.
4. "The CIA's Clandestine Service."
5. Kenneth Michael Absher, "John Kearns and the Cold War in Laos: Recalling a CIA Officer's Sacrifice," *Studies in Intelligence* 46 no. 4 (2002): 50.
6. Absher, "John Kearns and the Cold War in Laos," 50.
7. Kenneth Conboy with James Morrison, *Shadow War: The CIA's Secret War in Laos* (Paladin Press 1995), 349–51.
8. Christopher Robbins, *Air America* (G.P. Putnam's Sons, 1979), 208.
9. Robbins, *Air America*, 208.
10. Directorate of Plans, "John Peterson (3 July 1945–19 October 1972)," CIA Document No. C06903494.

11. Conboy and Morrison, *Shadow War*, 396.
12. Conboy and Morrison, *Shadow War*, 396.
13. Absher, "John Kearns and the Cold War in Laos," 52.
14. For an interesting study on mortar warfare during Vietnam, see the declassified Rand report prepared by S. H. Miller for the United States Air Force Rand, titled "FAST-VAL: Case Study of North Vietnamese Army Mortar Attack on U.S. Marine Infantry Company and Battalion Command Post Hill 256 near the Ben Hai River," dated November 1971. It describes a "4- to 6-minute 82 mm mortar attack against U.S. Marine Corps units."
15. "Traumatic rupture of the thoracic aorta: A life-threatening emergency and the role of endovascular repair," NIH National Library of Medicine, https://pmc.ncbi.nlm.nih.gov/articles/PMC9958258.
16. Robbins, *Air America*, 211.
17. Joe F. Leeker, *The Aircraft of Air America*, 5th ed. (University of Texas at Dallas Eugene McDermott Library History of Aviation Archives, 2015), https://library.utdallas.edu/special-collections-archives/history-of-aviation-archives/the-aircraft-of-air-america/.

Chapter Twenty-Eight: Uncontrollable

1. *Merriam-Webster Dictionary*, "tardive," accessed April 20, 2026, https://www.merriam-webster.com/medical/tardive.
2. *Merriam-Webster Dictionary*, "dyskinesia," accessed April 20, 2026, https://www.merriam-webster.com/dictionary/dyskinesia.
3. Robert Whitaker, "A Short History of Tardive Dyskinesia: 65 Years of Drug-Induced Brain Damage That Rolls On and On," Mad in America, November 22, 2020, https://www.madinamerica.com/2020/11/tardive-dyskinesia-brain-damage/.
4. INGREZZA, Kinect-Pro, https://ingrezzahcp.com. AUSTEDO XR, www.austedo.com.

Chapter Twenty-Nine: What Really Happened to Lone Star?

1. Oxford Ditionary of Phrase and Fable, "fog of war," accessed May 5, 2026, on Oxford Reference, https://www.oxfordreference.com/display/10.1093/oi/authority.20110803095826962.
2. Carl von Clausewitz, *On War*, ed. and trans. Michael Howard and Peter Paret (Princeton University Press, 1976), 101.
3. McDonald Clarke, "Battle of Bunker Hill," *Poems (New York, 1836).*
4. Sir Lonsdale Augustus Hale, *The Fog of War, by Colonel Lonsdale Hale . . . Tuesday, 24th March, 1896* (London, 1896).
5. "Regret to Advise," CIA Document C06520612, see Appendix B; Recommendation of Honor or Merit Award, CIA Document C06395113, see Appendix C; Report of Honors and Merit Award Board, CIA Document C06395113, see Appendix D.
6. Paul T. Carter, "Thai Forward Air Guides in the Covert War in Lao," *Studies in Intelligence* 64 no. 1 (2020): 34.
7. Chalermchai Thammawetin, AKA Charlie Khachen, AKA Space, email to Mike Farris, January 16, 2026.

8. Charlie Khachen, *The Unknown Warriors: Secret War in Laos,* originally published in Thai.
9. Weera Star, AKA Sparkplug, Facebook Messenger message to Mike Farris, January 15, 2026.
10. Brig. General Soutchay Vongsavahn, *RLG Military Operations and Activities in the Loatian Panahandle, Indochina Monographs (U.S. Army Center of Military History, 1981).*
11. *Vongsavahn, RLG Military Operations, iii.*
12. *Vongsavahn, RLG Military Operations, 84.*
13. Kenneth Conboy with James Morrison, *Shadow War: The CIA's Secret War in Laos* (Paladin Press 1995), 396.
14. Ted Gup, *The Book of Honor: The Secret Lives and Deaths of CIA Operatives* (Anchor Books, 2001), 205.
15. Kenneth Michael Absher, "John Kearns and the Cold War in Laos: Recalling a CIA Officer's Sacrifice," *Studies in Intelligence* 46 no. 4 (2002): 45, 52.
16. John E. Malone, *Top Secret Missions Performed by Elite Commo & Intel Specialists* (Trafford Publishing, 2003), 117.
17. Richard Helms with William Hood, *A Look Over My Shoulder: A Life in the Central Intelligence Agency* (Ballantine Books, 2003), 263.
18. John Prados, *Safe for Democracy: The Secret Wars of the CIA* (Ivan R. Dee, 2006), 356.
19. Paul T. Carter, *CIA Secret Warriors: Thai Forward Air Guides in the US War in Laos: The Untold Story* (Varanya Publishing, 2018).
20. Khachen, *The Unknown Warriors.*
21. Absher, "John Kearns and the Cold War in Laos," 50.
22. Recommendation for Honor or Merit Award, CIA Document C06395113, see Appendix C.
23. Weera Star, AKA Sparkplug, phone interview by Mike Farris, January 15, 2026.
24. Chalermchai Thammawetin, AKA Charlie Khachen, AKA Space, email to Mike Farris, January 19, 2026.
25. Khachen, *The Unknown Warriors,* 134.
26. Khachen, *The Unknown Warriors,* 135.
27. Absher, "John Kearns and the Cold War in Laos," 50.
28. Khachen, *The Unknown Warriors,* 134.
29. Weera Star, AKA Sparkplug, narrative sent to Mike Farris via Facebook Messenger, January 15, 2026.
30. Kachen, *The Unknown Warriors,* 137-138.
31. Chalermchai Thammawetin, AKA Charlie Khachen, AKA Space, email to Mike Farris, February 2, 2026.
32. Vongsavahn, *RLG Military Operations, 84.*
33. *Conboy and Morrison, Shadow War, 396.*
34. *"Regret to Advise," CIA Document C06520612, see Appendix B.*
35. *Recommendation for Honor or Merit Award, CIA Document C06395113,* see Appendix C.
36. *Recommendation for Honor or Merit Award, CIA Document C06395113,* see Appendix C.

37. *"Remarks of the Director of Central Intelligence George J. Tenet at the Annual Memorial Ceremony, June 2, 2000," CIA Document C05543218*, see Appendix A.
38. *Absher, "John Kearns and the Cold War in Laos," 52, 53.*
39. Sparkplug narrative, January 15, 2026.
40. "Regret to Advise," CIA Document C06520612, see Appendix B.
41. Carter, *CIA Secret Warriors*, 264.
42. Absher, "John Kearns and the Cold War in Laos," 52; Carter, *CIA Secret Warriors, 264.*
43. Carter, *CIA Secret Warriors*, 264.
44. Absher, "John Kearns and the Cold War in Laos," 52.
45. Chalermchai Thammawetin, AKA Charlie Khachen, AKA Space, email to Mike Farris, January 16, 2026.
46. Maya Aselstine,"Flashback: Puff the Magic Dragon: Development of the AC-47 Gunship," Air Force Materiel Command, October 20, 2023, https://www.afmc.af.mil/News/Article-Display/Article/3564246/flashback-pull-the-magic-dragon-development-of-the-ac-47-gunship/;

Madeline Hiltz, "A 'Spooky' Aircraft Known as Puff, the Magic Dragon—The Story of the Douglas AC-47," War History Online, August 20, 2021, https://www.warhistoryonline.com/war-articles/spooky-aircraft-puff-the-magic-dragon-douglas-ac-47.html.

47. Weera Star, AKA Sparkplug, phone interview by Mike Farris, January 27, 2026.
48. Chalermchai Thammawetin, AKA Charlie Khachen, AKA Space, email to Mike Farris, February 2, 2026.
49. Sparkplug narrative, January 15, 2026; Chalermchai Thammawetin, AKA Charlie Khachen, AKA Space, email to Mike Farris, January 16, 2026.
50. Sparkplug narrative, January 15, 2026.
51. "Regret to Advise," CIA Document C06520612, see Appendix B.
52. Sparkplug narrative, January 15, 2026.
53. "Thai Funerals: An Overview Guide," Thailand Foundation, https://thailandfoundation.or.th/thai-funeral/; "Buddhist Funeral Rites in Thailand & other South East Asian Countries," Buddhanet, https://buddhanet.net/bfuneral/.
54. Chalermchai Thammawetin, AKA Charlie Khachen, AKA Space, email to Mike Farris, January 19, 2026

Epilogue: Finding Lone Star

1. Memories, Incorporated, https://meminc.org.

Bibliography

Books

Branfman, Fred, editor. *Voices from the Plain of Jars: Life Under an Air War*. 2nd ed. University of Wisconsin Press, 2013.

Carter, Paul T. *CIA Secret Warriors: Thai Forward Air Guides in the US War in Laos: The Untold Story*. Varanya Publishing, 2018.

Castle, Timothy N. *At War in the Shadow of Vietnam: U.S. Military Aid to the Royal Lao Government, 1955–1975*. Columbia University Press, 1993.

Celeski, Col. Joseph D. *Special Air Warfare and the Secret War in Laos: Air Commandos 1964–1975*. Air University Press, 2019.

Churchill, Jan and Harry C. Aderholt. *Classified Secret: Controlling Airstrikes in the Clandestine War in Laos*. Sunflower University Press, 2000.

Clarke, McDonald. "Battle of Bunker Hill." *Poems*. New York, 1836.

Coates, Karen J. *Eternal Harvest: The Legacy of American Bombs in Laos*. ThingsAsian Press, 2013.

Conboy, Ken. *Spies on the Mekong: CIA Clandestine Operations in Laos*. Casemate Publishers, 2021.

Conboy, Kenneth, and Dale Andrade. *Spies & Commandos: How America Lost the Secret War in North Vietnam*. University Press of Kansas, 2000.

Conboy, Kenneth, with James Morrison. *Shadow War: The CIA's Secret War in Laos*. Paladin Press, 1995.

DeForest, Orrin, and David Chanoff. *Slow Burn: The Rise and Bitter Fall of American Intelligence in Vietnam*. Simon & Schuster, 1990.

Dudman, Richard. *Forty Days with the Enemy: The Story of a Journalist Held Captive by Guerrillas in Cambodia*. Liveright, 1971.

Ellsberg, Daniel. *Secrets: A Memoir of Vietnam and the Pentagon Papers*. Viking, 2002.

Ely, John Hart. *War and Responsibility: Constitutional Lessons of Vietnam and Its Aftermath*. Princeton University Press, 1993.

Evuns, Alun. *Brassey's Guide to War Films*. Potomac Books, 2000.

Franklin, Benjamin, and Benjamin Peirce. *Poor Richard's Almanack for 1735: As written by Benjamin Franklin: for the years 1733-41]: the astronomical calculations*. Annual illustrated ed. New York, 1849.

Freud, Sigmund. *Cocaine Papers*. Stonehill Publishing, 1974.

Gamber, Wendy. *The Notorious Mrs. Clem: Murder and Money in the Gilded Age*. Johns Hopkins University Press, 2016

Gough, Richard. *Tony Poe's CIA War: A Secret War Waged by His Paramilitary Army in Southeast Asia*. Knox Press, 2024.

Gould, Jonathan. *Can't Buy Me Love: The Beatles, Britain, and America*. Crown Publishing, 2007.

Gup, Ted. *The Book of Honor: Covert Lives and Classified Deaths at the CIA*. Doubleday, 2000.

Haas, Col. Michael E. *Apollo's Warriors: United States Air Force Special Operations during the Cold War*. University Press, 1997.

Hale, Sir Lonsdale Augustus. *The Fog of War, by Colonel Lonsdale Hale . . . Tuesday, 24th March 1896*. London, 1896.

Hamilton, Mary. "And the Enemy was in us: Vietnam War films and complicating visions of American Masculinity." Master's thesis, University of Texas at Arlington, 2024. https://mavmatrix.uta.edu/history_theses/1/.

Hayes, Bob, with Robert Pack. *Run, Bullet, Run: The Rise, Fall, and Recovery of Bob Hayes*. Harper & Row, 1990.

Helms, Richard, with William Hood. *A Look Over My Shoulder: A Life in the Central Intelligence Agency*. Ballantine Books, 2003.

Henderson, Thomas "Hollywood," with Frank Luksa. *In Control: The Rebirth of an NFL Legend*. Thomas Henderson Publishing, 2004.

Henderson, Thomas "Hollywood," and Peter Knobler. *Out of Control: Confessions of an NFL Casualty*. G.P. Putnam's Sons, 1987.

Hersh, Seymour M. *The Price of Power: Kissinger in the Nixon White House*. Summit Books, 1983.

Jacobsen, Annie. *Surprise, Kill, Vanish: The Secret History of CIA Paramilitary Armies, Operators, and Assassins*. Little, Brown, 2019.

Karnow, Stanley. *Vietnam: A History*. The Viking Press, 1983.

Khachen, Charlie. *The Unknown Warriors: Secret War in Laos*. Originally published in Thai.

Kurlantzick, Joshua. *A Great Place to Have a War: America in Laos and the Birth of a Military CIA*. Simon & Schuster, 2016.

Leeker, Joe F., *The Aircraft of Air America*. 5th ed. University of Texas at Dallas Eugene McDermott Library History of Aviation Archives, 2015. https://library.utdallas.edu/special-collections-archives/history-of-aviation-archives/the-aircraft-of-air-america/.

Malone, John E. *Top Secret Missions Performed by Elite Commo & Intel Specialists*. Trafford Publishing, 2003.

McCoy, Alfred W. *The Politics of Heroin: CIA Complicity in the Global Drug War*. Revised ed. Lawrence Hill Books, 2003.

McCoy, Alfred W., with Cathleen B. Read and Leonard P. Adams II. *The Politics of Heroin in Southeast Asia*. Harper & Row, 1972.

McNamara, Robert S., with Brian VanDeMark. *In Retrospect: The Tragedy and Lessons of Vietnam*. Vintage Books, 1995.

Newman, Rick, and Don Shepperd. *Bury Us Upside Down: The Misty Pilots and the Secret Battle for the Ho Chi Minh Trail.* Ballantine Books, 2006.

Parker, James E. Jr. *Battle for Skyline Ridge: The CIA Secret War in Laos.* Casemate Publishing, 2019.

Parker, James E. Jr. *Cover Ops: The CIA's Secret War in Laos.* St. Martin's Paperbacks, 1995.

Payne, Darwin. *Big D: Triumphs and Troubles of an American Supercity in the 20th Century.* Three Forks Press, 1994.

Pearlman, Jeff. *Football for a Buck: The Crazy Rise and Crazier Demise of the USFL.* Mariner Books, 2018.

Pederson, Rena. *The King of Diamonds: The Search for the Elusive Texas Jewel Thief.* Pegasus Crime, 2024.

Perkins, Steve. *Next Year's Champions: The Story of the Dallas Cowboys.* World Publishing, 1969.

Prados, John. *Safe for Democracy: The Secret Wars of the CIA.* Ivan R. Dee, 2006.

Quincy, Keith. *Harvesting Pa Chay's Wheat: The Hmong & America's Secret War in Laos.* Eastern Washington University Press, 2000.

Robbins, Christopher. *Air America.* G.P. Putnam's Sons, 1979.

Robbins, Christopher. *The Ravens: The Men Who Flew in America's Secret War in Laos.* Crown Publishers, 1995.

Sheehan, Neil. *A Bright Shining Lie: John Paul Vann and America in Vietnam.* Vintage Books, 1989.

Sheehan, Neil, Hedrick Smith, E. W. Kenworthy, and Fox Butterfield. The Pentagon Papers: The Secret History of the Vietnam War. Bantam, 1971.

Shropshire, Mike. *Seasons in Hell: With Billy Martin, Whitey Herzog and the Worst Baseball Team in History: The 1973–1975 Texas Rangers.* Dutton, 1996.

Shultz, Richard H. Jr. *The Secret War Against Hanoi: Kennedy's and Johnson's Use of Spies, Saboteurs, and Covert Warriors in North Vietnam.* HarperCollins, 1999.

Summers, Anthony. *The Arrogance of Power: The Secret World of Richard Nixon.* Viking, 2000.

Swanson, Doug J. *Blood Aces: The Wild Ride of Benny Binion, the Texas Gangster Who Created Vegas Poker.* Viking, 2014.

Ungar, Sanford J. *The Papers & The Papers: An Account of the Legal and Political Battle Over the Pentagon Papers.* E.F. Dutton, 1972.

Von Clausewitz, Carl. *On War.* Edited and translated by Michael Howard and Peter Parent. Princeton University Press, 1976.

Vongsavahn, Brig. General Soutchay. *RLG Military Operations and Activities in the Loatian Panahandle.* Indochina Monographs. U.S. Army Center of Military History, 1981.

Warner, Roger. *Back Fire: The CIA's Secret War in Laos and Its Link to the War in Vietnam.* Simon & Schuster, 1995.

Newspapers, Magazines, and Journals

Absher, Kenneth Michael. "John Kearns and the Cold War in Laos: Recalling a CIA Officer's Sacrifice." *Studies in Intelligence* 46, no. 4 (2002): 45–54.

"Airline Accused of Shipping Heroin." *Rocky Mountain News*, November 5, 1972.

Allis, Tim. "Entertainment Night Moves: Dancing the night away in Dallas." *D Magazine*, December 1, 1982.

Anderson, Jack. "U.S. Is Backbone of Laos Drug Trade." *Washington Post*, September 9, 1972.

Arbuckle, Tammy. "Official U.S. Secrecy Persists in Laos." *Washington Star*, February 6, 1972.

Arbuckle, Tammy. "U.S. Civilians Dying Unheralded in Laos." *Washington Star*, December 27, 1972.

Bishop, Nancy. "Dallas Playboy Club closes," *Dallas Morning News*, May 1982.

Bjornson, Greta. "Meat Loaf: The Many Origin Stories Behind the Late Singer's Name." *People*, January 21, 2022.

Blaskovich, Sarah. "50 Years Later: The wild, nearly unbelievable tales from 'unsavory' Dallas bar J. Alfred's." *Dallas Morning News*, September 9, 2021.

Bonner, Douglas G. III. "A Teenager's Visit to the CIA Base at Nam Yu: Lima Site 118A." *Bucknell Magazine* 14, no. 3 (2021).

Brehm, Brian. "Veterans of once-classified U.S. Army Security Agency finally able to swap stories." *Winchester Star*, November 10, 2023.

Byrnes, Mark. "Dallas, 1963: 'City of Hate'?" *Bloomberg*, November 22, 2013.

"A Cannon at a Luxury hotel?," *Panama News* 12, no. 17 (Sept. 3–16, 2006), https://web.archive.org/web/20070711185844/http://www.thepanamanews.com/pn/v_12/issue_17/travel_01.html.

Carter, Paul T. "Thai Forward Air Guides in the Covert War in Laos." *Studies in Intelligence* 64, no. 1 (2020).

"CIA Airliner Is Missing Over Laos." *Washington Post*, December 29, 1971.

"CIA Dope Tie in Charged." *Oakland Tribune*, February 5, 1972.

"A City That Still Works." *Time*, April 27, 1981.

"Cowboy in Mishap." *New York Times*, October 17, 1984.

Doliger, Cedric. "The Easterlin Hypothesis." *The Frontiers of Environmental History* 29, no. 3 (2004): 205–12.

Downes, Catherine. "Playboy Bunnies Tell the Best Tales." *D Magazine*, September 21, 2018.

Ehrlich, Richard S. "CIA Operative stood out in 'secret war' in Laos." *Bangkok Post*, July 8, 2003.

Ehrlich, Richard S. "CIA Suicide after a life of God and guns." *Free Press*, April 5, 2011.

Ellsberg, Daniel. "Laos: What is Nixon Up To?" *New York Review*, March 11, 1971.

"Eric Clapton rethinks playing 'Cocaine.'" *Alcohol and Drugs History Society*, October 5, 2006.

Evans, Hannah. "Dallas' '80s singles scene was wild enough, but robbers added danger to bar life with a Mickey Finn spree." *Dallas Morning News*, December 26, 2019.

"Food and Spirits: DINING OUT." *D Magazine*, May 1, 1978.

Foster, Tom. "The King of X." *D Magazine*, May 2025.

Freeman, Emily. "After the Party: When cocaine becomes your only friend." *D Magazine*, March 1, 1983.

Fuller, Thomas. "William Young, 76, Leader In Secret U.S. War in Laos." *New York Times*, April 6, 2011.

Galloway, Randy. "Randle Frustration Explodes in Fistic Fury." *The Sporting News*, April 16, 1977.

Gilbert, Holley, James Mayer and George Bundy Smith. "Five-alarm blaze hits liner at Swan's Island." *The Oregonian*, December 6, 1989.

Grathof, Pete. "Sixty years ago, Chiefs franchise won first championship game despite famous coin-flip gaffe." *The Kansas City Star*, December 20, 2022.

Gross, Jane. "4 Cowboys Named as Cocaine Users." *New York Times*, July 9, 1983.

Hersh, Seymour. "How We Ran the Secret Air War in Laos." *New York Times Magazine*, October 29, 1972.

"How the Pentagon Papers Came to be Published by the Beacon Press: A Remarkable Story Told by Whistleblower Daniel Ellsberg, Dem Presidential Candidate Mike Gravel and Unitarian Leader Robert West." *Democracy Now*, July 2, 2007.

James, Caryn. "*Air America* (1990): Review: Film, Gibson as C.I.A. Pilot." *New York Times*, August 10, 1990.

Johnson, Robert "KC". "Did Nixon Commit Treason in 1968? What the New LBJ Tapes Reveal." *History News Network*, January 26, 2009.

Karnow, Stanley. "Defusing Laos: The Fragile Accord." *New Republic*, March 10, 1973.

"Kennedy: Aid Goes to CIA Forces," *Washington Post*, February 7, 1971.

"Laos: The Unseen Presence." *Time*, October 17, 1969.

"Low Moments in Dallas Bar History." *D Magazine*, June 1, 1988.

McBeth, John. "The CIA's Secret City." *The Nation*, March 16, 2013.

Morrow, Michael. "CIA-Backed Laotians Said Entering China." *Washington Post*, January 26, 1971.

Morrow, Michael. "CIA Reported Inside China." *St. Louis Post-Dispatch*, January 17, 1971.

Morrow, Michael. "CIA's Spy Teams Inside Red China." *San Francisco Chronicle*, September 4, 1970.

Nason, Leslie J. "Baby Boomers, Grown Up, Storm Ivy-Covered Walls." *Daily Press*, Newport, Virginia, January 28, 1963.

Naughton, James M. "Deaths of 27 Americans in Laos Disclosed by U.S." *New York Times*, March 9, 1970.

"Nixon Warns of Aid Cut To Drug-Dealer Nations." *Washington Star*, September 18, 1972.

"Oilman Manges sentenced, fined for mail fraud." *Victoria Advocate*, August 26, 1995.

Osborne, Ryan. "How the 7-Eleven Slurpee was invented." WFAA News, July 11, 2024.

"Our Allies, Opium, and the CIA: When the Embarrassed Chuckling Stopped." *National Observer*, September 2, 1972.

Parmley, Helen. "Pakistani cowboy blazes money trail through stores, disco." *Dallas Morning News*, November 8, 1978.

Paterson, Lieutenant Commander Pat, U.S. Navy. "The Truth About Tonkin." *Naval History* 22, no. 1 (February 2008).

Paul, Roland A. "Laos: Anatomy of an American Involvement." *Foreign Affairs* 49, no. 3 (1971).

Peeler, Tom. "They built THIS CITY." *D Magazine*, October 1, 1996.

"Politics and History of Heroin." *California Voice*, September 21, 1972.

Rich, Spencer. "Senators Told CIA Aids Laos." *Washington Post*, May 22, 1971.

Robbins, Christopher. "'*Air America*' doesn't fly right." *New York Times*, August 28, 1990.

Schuller, Tim. "A Prince at the King's Club." *D Magazine*, June 1, 1978.

Scott, Peter Dale. "Air America: Flying the U.S. into Laos." *Ramparts*, February 1970.

Shapira, Ian. "CIA's Memorial Wall for fallen operatives is shaped by a Northern Virginia stone carver." *Washington Post*, May 22, 2014.

Sheehan, Neil. "Most Authors Were Given a Promise of Anonymity." *New York Times*, July 18, 1971.

Sherrod, Blackie. "An Eyewitness to a mugging." *Dallas Morning News*, March 29, 1977.

Shipler, David K. "Slain U.S. Officer Had His Hands Up." *New York Times*, December 16, 1973.

Simek, Peter. "How the Starck Club Changed Dallas." *D Magazine*, March 18, 2013.

Smith, Peter. "A Visit to a Secret American Base in Thailand." *Washington Post*, July 20, 1972

"Smuggling? Yes; collusion: No." *Houston Post*, August 20, 1972.

Sullivan, T.R. "Boys of Arlington: Lenny Randle vs. Frank Lucchesi—Jeff Wilson's Texas Rangers Today." *Rangers Today*, June 27, 2024.

Symington, U.S. Senator Stuart. "Laos: The Furtive War." *World*, August 29, 1972.

"Uncle Sam—drug pusher." Torrington, CT *Register*, July 29, 1972.

Walker, Frank. "Barry Petersen: Man of mystery and Australia's Colonel Kurtz." *Sydney Morning Herald*, March 6, 2019.

Warnock, Kirby. "My Wild Ride Through the '70s Music Scene in Dallas, Thanks to 'Buddy Magazine.'" *D Magazine*, June 10, 2024.

Warnock, Kirby. "Remembering the Lee Park Massacre." *D Magazine*, 1970.

Whitney, Craig R. "CIA-Aided Laos Base Hit Hard." *New York Times*, January 20, 1972.

Court Cases

Dallas Cowboys Cheerleaders, Inc. v. Pussycat Cinema, Ltd., Michael Zaffarano, et al., 467 F. Supp. 366 (S.D.N.Y. 1979).

Dallas Cowboys Cheerleaders, Inc. v. Pussycat Cinema, Ltd., Michael Zaffarano, 604 F.2d 200 (2d Cir. 1979).

Gravel v. United States, 408 U.S. 606, 622, 627-29 (1972).

Near v. Minnesota, 283 U.S. 697 (1931).

New York Times Co. v. United States, 403 U.S. 713 (1971).

United States v. N.Y. Times Co., 328 F. Supp. 324, 330 (S.D.N.Y. 1971).

United States of America v. Scott Robin Roston, 986 F. 2d 1287 (9th Cir. 1993).

Government Documents

Air America, Inc., Investigation of Aircraft Accident, C-46, XW-PFL NEAR BUOAM LONG (LS-32) LAOS, 02 JUNE 1971, John D. Anthony Papers, History of Aviation Archives, UTD Special Collections and Archives Division.

CIA Document No. C06903488, "John W. Kearnes, III (1942–1972)."

CIA Document No. C06903494, "John Peterson (3 July 1945–19 October 1972)."

CIA Document No. C05543218, "Remarks of the Director of Central Intelligence George J. Tenet at the Annual Memorial Ceremony, June 2, 2000."

CIA Document No. C06395??3, "Recommendation for Honor or Merit Award."

CIA Document C06520612, "Regret to Advise."

CIA Document No. C06395113, "Report of Honors and Merit Awards Board."

Foreign Relations of the United States 1952–1954, vol. XVI, The Geneva Conference. Edited by Allen H. Kitchens and Neal H. Petersen Government Printing Office, 1981.

Foreign Relations of the United States 1961–1963, vol. XXIV, Laos Crisis. Edited by Edward C. Keefer and Glenn W. LaFantasie. Government Printing Office, 1994.

Nixon, Richard. "Statement About the Situation in Laos." The American Presidency Project, UC Santa Barbara. https://www.presidency.ucsb.edu/documents/statement-about-the-situation-laos.

Nixon Tapes.

Subcommittee on U.S. Security Agreements and Commitments Abroad of the Committee Foreign Relations United States Senate. https://www.cia.gov/readingroom/docs/CIA-RDP73B00296R000300080001-0.pdf.

Symington, Senator Stuart. "Additional Statements, Laos—Further U.S. Military Operations in this Secret War" to Subcommittee on Criminal Laws and Procedures, July 12, 1971.

"The U.S. Heroin Problem and Southeast Asia Report of a Staff Survey Team of the Committee on Foreign Affairs House of Representatives," December 1972. https://archive.org/details/CIA-RDP74B00415R000100100002-4/page/n1/mode/2up.

Tonkin Gulf Resolution (1964). US National Archives. Updated April 9, 2024. https://archives.gov/milestone-documents/tonkin-gulf-resolution.

United States Constitution.

"War-Related Civilian Problems in Indochina," Hearing Before the Subcommittee to Investigate Problems With Refugees and Escapees of the Committee on the Judiciary, April 21, 1971.

Oral History/Interviews

Chapman, Christian A. Interview by Charles Stuart Kennedy. March 3, 1990. The Association for Diplomatic Studies and Training Foreign Affairs Oral History Project. https://adst.org/OH%20TOCs/Chapman,%20Christian%20A.toc.pdf.

Gelb, Leslie. Interview by Brooke Gladstone. "What the Press and 'The Post' Missed." *On the Media* (podcast), WNYC Studios, January 12, 2018. https://www.wnycstudios.org/story/what-post-missed-episode.

Graham, Bette. "Oral history interview with Bette Graham." University of North Texas. August 3, 1977 and April 2, 1980. https://discover.library.unt.edu/catalog/b2204263.

Leary, Timothy. Interview by *Playboy*. *PLAYBOY* magazine. September 1966.

Minutaglio, Bill. Interview by Ari Shapiro. "Nixon's Manhunt for the High Priest of LSD In 'The Most Dangerous Man in America.'" NPR, January 5, 2018. https://www.npr.org/2018/01/05/575392333/nixons-hunt-for-the-high-priest-of-lsd-in-the-most-dangerous-man-in-america.

Morrow, Michael, emails with Mike Farris.

Star, Weera, AKA Sparkplug, Facebook Messenger messages and phone interviews with Mike Farris.

Thammawetin, Chalermchai, AKA Charlie Kachen, AKA Space, emails with Mike Farris.

Tovar, B. Hugh. Interview by Paul Hillmer. Hmong Oral History Project, August 15, 2007. https://digitalcommons.csp.edu/hmong-studies_hohp/38.

Index

About the Authors

Mike Farris

Mike Farris is the author of nineteen published books, both fiction and nonfiction, including historical true crime. A retired attorney whose practice in Dallas included commercial litigation and entertainment law, he is now an adjunct professor of Political Science at the University of Texas at Arlington.

Paul Heckmann

Paul Heckmann was born in Fort Worth, Texas, but adopted by a couple from Waco. After college at Texas A&I University (now Texas A&M-Kingsville), where he played on two NAIA national championship football teams, he moved to Dallas. There he worked as a model, actor, and club bouncer, then spent the next decade working onboard cruise ships before entering the tech world as an IT Manager.

www.ingramcontent.com/pod-product-compliance
Lightning Source LLC
LaVergne TN
LVHW051038241026
850861LV00032B/202